MY LIFE WAS
THIS BIG

My Life Was
THIS BIG

and Other True Fishing Tales

Lefty Kreh
with Chris Millard

Foreword by Dan Blanton

Introduction by Nick Lyons

SKYHORSE PUBLISHING

Skyhorse Publishing books may be purchased in bulk at special discounts for
sales promotion, corporate gifts, fund-raising, or educational purposes. Special
editions can also be created to specifications. For details, contact the Special Sales
Department, Skyhorse Publishing, 555 Eighth Avenue, Suite 903,
New York, NY 10018 or info@skyhorsepublishing.com.

www.skyhorsepublishing.com

10 9 8 7 6 5 4 3 2 1

Library of Congress Cataloging-in-Publication Data
Kreh, Lefty.
My life was this big : and other true fishing stories / Lefty Kreh with Chris Millard.
p. cm.
ISBN-13: 978–1-60239–359–2
ISBN-10: 1–60239–359–1
1. Fly fishing—Anecdotes. 2. Fishing—Anecdotes. 3. Kreh, Lefty. I. Millard, Chris.
II. Title.
SH456.K754 2008
799.12'4—dc22
2008025265

Printed in the United States of America

To the wonderful people who have shared their lives and their knowledge with me.

I could never thank them enough.

Other Books by Lefty Kreh

Fly Fishing in Salt Water
Advanced Fly Fishing Techniques
Fishing Knots
Practical Fishing Knots and Fishing the Flats with Mark Sosin
Presenting the Fly
The Ultimate Fly Fishing Guide
Saltwater Fly Patterns
Longer Casting
Solving Fly Casting Problems
Lefty's 101 Fly Fishing Tips
L.L. Bean Guide to Outdoor Photography
Casting with Lefty Kreh

CONTENTS

FOREWORD

I FIRST MET LEFTY KREH in 1970. He was writing his book on saltwater fly-fishing and he wanted to include a chapter on West Coast striped bass. I was twenty-seven years old and, along with pals such as Bob Edgley and Lawrence Summers, I had been fly-fishing for striped bass on San Francisco Bay and along the coast since for over a decade. We were all huge fans of Lefty's and had read everything he'd written. Lefty, even at that time—more than thirty-five years ago—was "The Man" when it came to saltwater fly-fishing.

Lefty wanted to experience fly-rodding for San Francisco Bay stripers, so Bob arranged for him to spend a few days fishing with us. Lefty was going to fish two days with Bob and Lawrence and two days with me. I remember being so excited about hosting Lefty that I had trouble sleeping for several nights before his arrival and didn't get a wink the night before we were to fish together. I was like a kid on Christmas Eve.

I knew from the moment I shook Lefty's hand that things were going to go well. He had such charm and charisma. He came off like an old shoe, like one of the boys, and he made you feel as though you were the celebrity, not him. He set me right at ease with one of his bazillion jokes. When he released my hand, he looked down at his own hand and exclaimed, "Where the hell is my ring?" That was followed by an elfin giggle and a hushed snort, just to let you know he was kidding. He still uses that gag a lot when he first meets someone and it always makes them laugh and puts them at ease.

That first handshake was a long time ago, and Lefty and I are more like family now than just close friends. I'm not alone. Lefty has made countless lifelong friends around the world because of the person he is: a mentor, a teacher, a giver, one who shares knowledge rather than exhibits it. I've learned so much from Lefty over the decades I could write a book about it. He's a walking "how to" with volumes of helpful tips that he just can't help sharing. For example, that first day with Lefty on South San Francisco Bay; the wind was howling, pushing my little fourteen-foot Starcraft over the flats much too quickly. Lefty and I couldn't cover the water properly. Lefty sensed my frustration and asked me if there was a hardware store close by. I replied there was, and Lefty insisted we go back to the dock and drive to the hardware store. I had no idea what he was up to. When we got to the store he bought a seventy-five-foot length of nylon rope and a six-foot length of fairly heavy chain. He looked at me and said, "What you need is a drag chain to slow down our drift." That was the first time I'd ever heard of dragging a chain on a length of rope behind a boat to slow it down. It worked like a charm. We caught lots of nice stripers and I've never been without one since.

That was just one of countless useful things I've learned from Lefty over the years. I also learned a lot about life and how to conduct myself as an outdoor professional from Lefty. A few years ago a movie was released that promoted the concept of "paying it forward" or accepting the kindnesses of others with a promise to do the same for someone else down the road. Well, Lefty has been paying it forward for as long as I've known him. In this book he talks about the many people who helped him along with his career, people who made a huge difference in his life.

People like the late Joe Brooks, for example. As you will read in the book, Joe helped Lefty obtain one of the biggest breaks of his career. Lefty has done more than pay that kindness forward. He has helped countless others with their own careers, including me. He's paid it forward innumerable times with eager fans who are new to the sport. He's paid it forward with autograph hounds who crave his signature and with serious anglers who are struggling to crack a new species. I know I wouldn't be where I am today without the kindness and mentoring of Lefty Kreh. For that I am forever grateful.

Lefty is the most successful fishing writer in history. I can think of no other person in this sport who has sold so many books or earned so much respect, love, and admiration. When you look at where he started—fatherless at a young age and living on welfare in the ghetto—his is a classic American success story. In fact, whether you are an angler or not, this book will be an inspiration. Despite the fact that I knew much of his life story, I couldn't put it down. It is a heart-warming, inspirational read about a person who took some bad breaks in life and turned them into something marvelous. It's also a great outdoors and fishing book, loaded with tips and history as seen and experienced by the man known around the world simply as Lefty.

Lefty is an icon at sportsmen's shows, especially fly-fishing shows. When he stands up on the casting platform to share his skills and knowledge, the surrounding aisles become choked with mesmerized anglers who just can't take their eyes off the man—the greatest fly-casting teacher I've ever known. He captivates them with talent and humor and, of course, his commonsense approach to fly casting. Today, at eighty years old, Lefty does it better than anyone else I know. No one is more respected than Lefty and no one in the fly-fishing industry is more loved than Lefty.

A couple of years ago, after Lefty had spent a few days with me and my wife, Cindy asked me if there was anyone who could step into Lefty's shoes when he's gone. No, I said. There are lots of well-known anglers, but none will ever fit into Lefty's old shoes; they're just too big to fill.

Dan Blanton

July 2006

INTRODUCTION
BY NICK LYONS

Lefty Kreh needs no introduction.

No one who has fly fished more than three-and-a-half times does not know and admire him. He is a brilliant teacher of fly casting, an endless fount of invaluable practical information (on all aspects of fishing, from knots to landing an outsized barracuda and not losing two fingers), the author of dozens of helpful books and hundreds of articles, and an ebullient public speaker who can hold audiences of ten to five hundred with his wit, his depth of angling experience, and his inexhaustible store of hilarious stories. I have heard him do so a dozen times.

Fewer people know the man himself. Who is the private Lefty Kreh? What was his humble youth like, his war experience, what were his first jobs, what are his personal views on a host of angling matters and personalities, his evolution to the man he is today?

How fortunate we are that this spry octogenarian has finally shared with us some of the highlights of his full life, offering us a memorable glimpse of the arc of a life "this big." Frank, down to earth, and filled with the anecdotes for which he is so famous, this book reveals the inner man, the special human being who has spent his adult life trying to make angling a more pleasurable experience for the hundreds of thousands of fishermen to whom he has been a great friend.

More news about a great friend is always welcome. And here it is.

Nick Lyons
September 2008

Prologue:
How Big Was It?

In seventy-odd years of fishing, I don't think I can even estimate the number of fish that I've been lucky enough to catch. I've caught them big and small, with luck and skill, in oceans and on streams, in good weather and bad. Of course, when an angler comes home the only thing people really want to know is "How many? How big?" The fact is that true fly fishermen could care less about such stats. Sure there are tales in here of monster fish caught on line that could tow a Mack truck, but great fly-fishing has far more to do with the unique challenges of the sport—casting, tying flies, strategy, and technique—than it has to do with fish tales.

I've caught more than my share of big fish, and while size does matter, for me it's all about the challenge. So, I won't tell you, just yet, about the biggest or the baddest fish I ever caught. We'll get to those later. Instead I'd like to start off by sharing with you the story of the *best* fish I ever caught. It was nearly fifty years ago. It was a 19-pound, 4-ounce jack crevalle. It was a world record for some time, but the size alone is not why I treasure the memory. I have since caught plenty of jacks—several larger than this one—but it was the circumstances under which and the equipment with (or without) which I made the catch that have seared the event into my memory.

It was the late 1960s. I was with Captain Gene Montgomery out of Key West, Florida. Cosgrove Light sits along the Gulf Stream about twenty miles south of Key West. I had a 6-pound test leader and a freshwater reel that had no drag (a Scientific Anglers System 9 reel). It was an outfit that I used for catching little yellow snappers and stuff. The side with the handle had a rim control that you could press like a brake to slow the movement of the reel. It was really designed for fishing freshwater fish. Well, this big jack came up and I figured I'd throw a fly at him. The fly was, of all things, a Deceiver, and he took it. So far so good, but we had an eighteen- or nineteen-foot boat navigating in three-foot seas, so we were really bouncing up and down pretty good. This fish really took off, and I was fighting him for a while without the benefit of a drag. While he was running and while the boat was bouncing, the reel fell off the rod. The spool kept letting out line as the jack kept running, and the handle on the reel, which was spinning furiously, kept banging onto the deck and hopping up in the air. I was running around trying to grab the darn thing. It was like trying to corner a rat. Every time I reached for it the reel would hop up and slide across the deck.

While I was scrambling for the reel, it occurred to me that if I just went ahead and grabbed it I would probably provide too much resistance to the fish's run and I'd almost certainly snap my fragile 6-pound leader. Gene said, "Lefty, when you grab the reel, I'll steer the boat toward the fish to create some slack." He ran us toward the fish and I was able to pick up the spool and get it back on the rod and it was probably another half an hour before I actually landed that fish.

Like I said, I've caught larger jacks in my time—many over 30 pounds—but all on much larger, stronger tackle. Yet under the circumstances—which demanded quick thinking, anticipation, touch, teamwork, and know-how—that's the best fish I ever caught. If I'd done it with a reel with a super drag, that would have been a nice accomplishment.

Doing it with no drag was even more challenging. On top of that, to have the darn reel fall off and still land him, that was really something. That record lasted for years. In fact, I think it lasted until they eliminated the 6-pound test category (A little explanation: In 1965, when we first started it, Saltwater Fly Rodders of America established the world record criteria. We had a 6-, 12-, and 15-pound test tippet you could use to qualify. Well, up until 1981 Mark Sosin and I maintained all the SFRA records. In fact, I tested most of the lines because at the time I had access to a pretty elaborate line tester. The records management got to be too much for us, so in 1981 we turned over the record keeping and line testing to the International Game Fishing Association. Not long after that, the IGFA decided to reclassify the world-record tippets and they eliminated the 6-pound test). I guess technically my jack is still a 6-pound test record, but there's simply no category for it. World record or not, no matter how you slice it, it was the best fish I ever caught.

I started out with this little tidbit for a reason. In many ways, the challenges, rewards, and memories like the one shared above are a reflection of my life. If anyone had been watching Gene and I fish Cosgrove Light that day, few would have bet on our success. The same can be said for a lucky little boy from Frederick, Maryland.

My Life Was
This Big

Chapter 1
The Krehs of Frederick

I was six years old when my father died. As the oldest of my siblings, I accompanied my mother to his funeral and his burial at Mt. Olivet Cemetery in our hometown of Frederick, Maryland. Because my father, Christian Kreh, a bricklayer by trade, had served in the National Guard, "Taps" was bugled out as they lowered his body into the ground. The mix of morbid sounds and images really spooked me. I wouldn't go to another funeral for probably fifty years.

It was 1932, and seeing as the whole country was reeling from the Great Depression, my father's death put an enormous burden on my mother. It fell to her to raise me, my sister, Eileen, who was then four and a half; a brother, Dick, three; and another brother, Ted, who was about six months old. Overnight Mother plunged from near middle-class comfort into the crucible of single motherhood. At the time of Dad's death we lived in a pretty nice house on Wisner Street, but welfare wasn't about to pay the rent on that, so we moved into a cramped six-room house at 617 North Bentz Street, located in what most people would today refer to as "the ghetto." We were one of very few white families in an area populated almost entirely by blacks. What amazes others, and what amazes me when I see what has become of race relations in this country,

1

is that while we surely had racial differences in our little ghetto, we had very little racism. The world around us was undoubtedly racist, but our little piece of it seemed fine. I think the reason for this was that all of us—blacks and whites—had a very important thing in common: none of us had anything. We did have humor. And humor made our world a brighter place.

The black guys I grew up with could find something funny in almost any situation. I remember one time, long after I had left the neighborhood—after my service in World War II—I was a shift supervisor at nearby Fort Detrick. I caught this guy, a black guy, stealing a can of white paint from the government building where I worked. I said, "Sam, what the hell are you doing with that can of paint?"

He said, "It belongs to us."

I said, "What the hell are you talking about?"

He said, "Look, it says 'U-S' right on the can."

I got a kick out of that, and I let it go. A week later he told me he was going to paint his kitchen with it. So a few days passed and I asked him, "Sam, did you ever get that kitchen painted?"

"No," he said. "I took that can home and I was tilting it back and forth to shake it. The lid come off and it all spilled out on the damn floor." He shook his head and said, "You can't trust nothing white."

There are not many places in today's America where both parties would laugh out loud at that line. Two black guys worked for me back then. One of them goofed off all the time and the other one ended up doing a lot of his work. One day the hardworking guy comes to me and starts bitching about the other guy. He said, "He's the laziest nigger I've ever seen." I started to stand up for the accused, but I lost the argument when the harder worker said, "That guy's so lazy he married a pregnant woman."

This is the kind of humor we openly shared. Sixty years before "Can't we all just get along?" we got along just great. As a kid, I ate at the black kids' houses (when they had enough) and they came over and ate at my house (if we had enough). There was an air of innocence to it all. We just accepted each other. They may have had dark skin and we may have had white skin, but none of us really *had* anything.

It's only in looking back that I can really see how little we had. I've fished all over the world: New Guinea, outback Australia, the Amazon; I've fished and foraged with fourth-world natives and lived in their seeming squalor. My friends would say, "My goodness, it's a wonder those people don't revolt." They say that because we Americans tend to look at the poor through the prism of our own materialism. What I learned growing up poor in the ghetto is that you're only unhappy when you know you lack something. When everyone around you is in the same boat, you fit right in. We had so few glimpses of the wealthy world beyond North Bentz Street that we barely knew it existed.

In those days, life on welfare was different than it is today. Back then you didn't get any actual money. Welfare would pay the rent directly. That way the government retained control—I can assure you that back then we weren't buying any television sets with our welfare dollars. My mother cooked on a decrepit stove that held about two gallons of heated water. If it got cold in December, January, and February, the government would have somebody come by and put coal in your cellar for heat and cooking, but you got no money. When we needed a bath, Mother would heat water in buckets and pour it into a washtub on the kitchen floor, where I can assure you we got some memorable scrubbings.

At first, our only heat was the cookstove in the kitchen. Later we were able to get a big round coal-burning stove for the living room. There was no other heat in the house. I remember that the floor in the room in which my brother Ted and I slept was linoleum, and in the winter it would get numbingly cold. We often washed our faces and brushed our teeth with water that was barely above freezing. I was a teenager before the City of Frederick installed a sewer system. It's still debatable which was worse: a trip to the outhouse in the biting cold of February or the same journey in the pungent humidity of August. My mother was a lot of things, and one of them was fearless. Perhaps she had been steeled by trial, but nothing scared her. I remember her returning from the outhouse one night when she saw a stubborn black-and-white cat that simply wouldn't get out of her way. When she challenged the animal, the well-disguised skunk hit her full blast. We were all very alert after that.

For our food, we went to a designated government distribution center. Ours was Winchester Hall, an imposing building in downtown Frederick. It was the center of our existence. As the oldest of the siblings, food detail was my job. Starting at the age of six or so I would take our wagon to Winchester once a week. The folks there would hand out basic food staples—flour, fatback, cornmeal—and I'd wheel them home to my mother. Well, we all know how cruel kids can be. All these food packages had big labels stamped on them. In big block letters they'd say "WELFARE." So, if you were caught by your enemies or, even worse, your friends, coming up the street with a little wagon full of this welfare food, they really got on you. As happens with kids, things occasionally got pretty nasty. Of course, odds were that the next day those same kids were going to make their own trip to the Hall and get the same treatment.

With four children ranging from six years to six months old and virtually no money, my mother simply couldn't afford luxuries, particularly Christmas. Thankfully, there were some kindhearted people in Frederick who went around prior to Christmas and loaded up on toys. A lot of the items were beat up, but these people would repair them, and at Christmas they would have about fifteen or twenty of us kids come in to receive a present. They called it the Empty Stocking Club because they also took mesh stockings and filled them with oranges and hard candy and other treats. It may all sound tragically sad, but trust me, we kids thought it was absolutely fantastic.

Of course, like so many things, the Empty Stocking Club had both its good and bad sides. The good side was the sheer joy of receiving the kinds of treats that kids like us could only dream about. It was truly Christmas for us. The bad thing about it was that the Club naturally wanted to encourage people to donate goods to the program, so they had to publicize their efforts. They would gather up all the welfare kids and take a picture of us with our toys and our candy, and then run the picture on the front page of the *Frederick News and Post*. If you think the grief that came from wheeling home welfare food was bad, just try showing up on the front page of the newspaper as a poor kid. The world really came down on you. I got into more than a few fistfights over those pictures, but when you consider the joy that the Club brought to our family on Christmas Day, it was worth it.

None of us had money, but as kids we really only cared about one thing. Sports was an all-day, year-round obsession in our neighborhood. Between our house and the section where all the black kids lived ran Bentz Street, which had a sixty-foot-wide "grass" median strip in the middle. I use the term loosely because while you could tell that the median was designed to *contain* grass, the surface had long since been trampled down into hardpan dirt. It's on that lot that I got the name "Lefty" from the other kids. I excelled in sports. I could throw well, run fast, and all that good stuff. As you might have guessed, I did everything as a lefty back then. The only thing I did right-handed as a kid was handwriting, and that was because my teacher simply wouldn't let me write left-handed. I guess it was because of the desks we had. We used to sit at these desks that had a chest-high writing surface, but only on the right side; there were no tops for left-handed kids. If you watch a lot of older left-handers write, you'll see that they all curl their arm all the way around in front of them and actually write near their right chest. That's because of the way the desks were made.

Surrounded as it was by fields, farms, ponds, woods, and rivers, Frederick should have been the perfect place for a kid to grow up. Strange as it may sound, I think our upbringing was actually good for us in a lot of ways. People will tell you well that a ghetto kid'll never have a chance. I disagree. I think the ghetto can mold a person for better or for worse. For instance, my brother Ted retired from a fine career with IBM. My sister Eileen and her husband, Paul, owned a store and she held a good position with Sears. My brother Dick followed in the family business and became a respected authority on masonry and has written a number of books on the topic. But ghetto life can also exact a toll. In fact, two of the kids I used to run around with back then died as a direct result of criminal activity. One was killed in prison, the other during a robbery.

The only real difference between them and me was that when I turned twelve years old I was introduced to the Boy Scouts. I used to get in minor troubles as a kid. Nothing major. I never went to jail, but I was habitually doing the kind of things that suggested a little jail time might be in my future. Street stuff. For instance, we didn't like this one neighbor who was perpetually nasty to kids, so we set his garage on fire. Another guy we didn't like had hollyhocks—these big, tall flowering plants—in his yard. He'd done something mean to me, I can't even remember what it was, so I took a corn chopper to the hollyhocks that lined his fence, and proudly yelled "Timber!" as each one fell to the ground. I was only about eleven years old and this guy came out the back door, grabbed a stick, and made it clear that he had every intention of whipping me with it. He chased me at top speed for four blocks, but eventually he just ran out of wind. No way a thirty-five-year-old guy was going to keep up with an eleven-year-old who knew every fence-hole and shortcut in town.

These weren't things you'd be incarcerated for, but they were ornery things that would, if not controlled, ultimately lead to a bad end. Fortunately my uncle, Bill Kreh, had a brother-in-law named Norman Ford who was pretty high up in the Boy Scouts. Norman was more than a scoutmaster, maybe a regional manager or something. Frederick was a small town, so people knew each other. My guess is that because he was sort of in the family, Norman had heard about my problems. My Uncle Bill and Aunt Amy probably asked if Norman could help get their nephew straightened out.

I always loved nature and that sort of thing, so I was a perfect candidate for the Scouts. I was desperate to join, but scouting wasn't free. Unless I could find some way to swing the money, I'd be left out. So Norman and I worked out a deal in which I'd wash dishes after meals and they would let me participate in the camp for free. There were two other guys working KP with me, and when we finished we'd join in the activities with all the other kids.

The first two years they held camp up at Camp Peneil, which is about a mile from Camp David in western Maryland, right near where I lived. I was a natural. First, I knew the terrain like the back of my hand. Second, I knew a lot about fishing for a kid of thirteen years. In fact, that was one of the reasons Norman thought scouting would be good for me. I had already done a lot of fishing. I was catching catfish on the Monocacy River from the time I was just a little boy. I learned to pole a boat when I was eight. I knew what baits to use. For instance, I knew that catfish prowl the banks of a river looking for food, and I also knew that mussels have a strong scent and that catfish have an excellent sense of smell, so I knew that catfish would go for mussels along the riverbank. I knew where to get the mussels and other bait as well. I'm not certain whether this is lore or fact, but I'm told that I received the first angling merit badge ever given. I ended up becoming a Life Scout and I'm pretty confident that I would have attained Eagle Scout if I'd stuck with it long enough.

Scouting was a great escape from my increasingly unhappy home life. My mother was a very bitter woman, one of the unhappiest people I've ever met. I think she felt betrayed by life. She had given birth to four children over a six-year period and suddenly she had no husband. This was on top of the fact that a once-proud woman from a comparatively well-to-do family had been reduced to living on welfare. That shame or frustration ate away at her every day. Sadly, but somewhat understandably, she was angry at the world. Where Mother's bitterness ended and her maternal discipline began was sometimes hard to discern. I recall we had a little peach tree in our backyard. Whenever we got really bad we'd have to go out and pick a limb off that tree and bring it to her. She would use that for a switch. I don't know if it was a surplus of tough mothering or shortage of horticultural care, but that peach tree eventually died.

Unhappy as she was, Mother did eventually remarry. Not surprisingly, Uncle Hen, as we called her second husband, was also a bricklayer. They actually had a child, my half brother Mike. He's a preacher in Marietta, Georgia. He does missionary work all over the world. He's really a neat guy. I visit with him every time I go through Atlanta.

In the first couple of years after our father died, I became the *de facto* leader of my siblings; my two brothers acted as my chief lieutenants. Our fundamental mission was to stay warm and fed. I remember when we found out that you could return soda bottles for two cents. We'd go out and search high and low in an attempt to scrounge up Coca-Cola bottles. I also had a newspaper route, which eventually paid for a bicycle that allowed me to complete the route in far less time. That route almost became more trouble than it was worth. Back then I only had two pair of pants; one was for general use, the other for school. One day I had on my general-use trousers and was in the middle of my route when a German shepherd bolted out of a yard and snapped at my ankle. He barely broke the skin, but he did a helluva number on the pant leg. When I got home my mother was so upset she slapped me.

The next day I got on the bike and slid a baseball bat into the big bag that contained all the day's deliveries. As I approached the scene of the previous day's crime, I kept an eye out for the dog in question. Sure enough, he scrambled beside my right leg and began growling and lunging. I grabbed the bat, clocked him on the head, and down he went. He survived—in fact, he continued to chase just about everybody in town—but he never bothered me again.

As willing as I was to work, I was also determined to get a high school education. Again, money was an obstacle. My mother said, "Look, I don't have enough money for your clothes and for your food. If you can make enough money in the summer to pay for your lunches and your clothes, then you can go to high school." After agreeing to carry my share of the financial load, I started off at the high school five blocks away on Elm Street. I finished my junior and senior years at Frederick High School, thirty-two blocks away. Rarely—and I mean *rarely*—was school ever closed for a snow day. It didn't snow often in that part of the state, but when it did we tramped right through it. There were several times when we walked through six or ten inches of snow and never thought anything of it. If it was time for a haircut, Mother would give us fifteen cents and we would walk twenty-five blocks to Schwearing's Barber Shop on West Patrick Street. If we wanted to go to a distant park or horse around at the river, we walked. I honestly think that all that walking is one of the reasons I feel so healthy today at age eighty-three. That kind of childhood conditioning not only stood me in good stead on countless future fishing expeditions, but it probably saved my life during World War II.

Even though walking was our primary mode of transportation, we lived in the golden age of train travel. There were trains everywhere when I was a kid. They ran through the cities and across the countryside, and it seemed as though I heard them wherever I went. They were a catalyst for imagination. Each winsome whistle suggested new exotic destinations full of fancy people and finery. One of my fondest memories of childhood still springs to life whenever I hear a train's whistle. My mother could listen to the sound of a train whistle and predict when it was going to rain. How she did this I have no idea, but whenever she predicted the rain, it poured. She was uncanny.

CHAPTER 2
A BOY'S LIFE

I HAD TO FIND A way to earn money for high school. In those days any young person who didn't mind a little hard work could usually get a job. My first summer of high school I got a job on a farm in New Midway, Maryland. Twice that summer I mowed a four-acre field with one of the big hand scythes like the old European peasants used. The first time I did it I got so thirsty that I drank six consecutive bottles of Dr Pepper and got so sick that, to this day, if I get near a Dr Pepper the smell sets my stomach to roiling.

Life as a young man was not all hard work and misery. Far from it. I used to shoot a lot of pool, and I got pretty handy at it. In fact, I once holed 129 straight balls. We had some good players. We used to play fifty balls straight—and several times my opponent would break and he'd never get another shot; I'd run the table. After a while I had to give points. I won some money shooting pool, but I was never what you'd call a hustler. Frederick wasn't big enough to attract big-money players, so I don't think I ever even saw a real hustler. It was all local guys. We all knew each other and our abilities too well to be had.

Another thing that helped me a lot in my younger days was the YMCA. I managed to join using money I made from working my jobs and shooting pool. Like the Scouts, the Y had a very good influence on me. That's where I met Charlie Keller, the baseball player. They called him "King Kong Keller." He was one of the greatest New York Yankee hitters ever. A big muscular guy with bushy eyebrows, Charlie was a big deal in those days. He played with the Yankees for eleven seasons (he was with Detroit for two years as well), and retired with several World Series Championships and a career batting average of .286. He had bought a huge horse farm near Frederick and he used to come to the Y and work out in the wintertime. Charlie and I would jog the track together and shoot baskets and stuff like that. He was a really nice guy. Very quiet, but if you look up old baseball players he was something of a legend.

Hunting and fishing were abundant in our area, always within easy walking distance. When I was a kid, everybody had .22s—mostly inexpensive "cat rifles." Unlike today, nobody got stupid with guns because we knew what might happen. We had a single-barrel shotgun at home. A quarter of a mile from my house we hunted rabbits and quail. And the thing was, you could hunt everywhere. In those days farmers would let anybody hunt. Nobody sued a farmer because they fell down a well and busted their leg. We all hunted, and we were pretty good at it, but it was a cost-prohibitive activity. Back then a box of shells cost seventy-five cents. By comparison, all you needed for fishing was a few branches, a hook, and a fresh mussel. When I came back from the army I really got into hunting big-time. I had a few friends—all outdoorsman—and we'd shoot all the time. We did a lot of crow hunting. Every forest had nesting crows in it in May and June. About twenty-five miles north of us, in a place called Taneytown, was one of the biggest crow roosts in the eastern United States. They estimated that a million crows would roost there at night in the wintertime. They came in like spokes on a wheel, from a variety of flyways to this central hub. We would go up there and shoot sometimes 150 or 200 crows in a morning or an evening when they were going out or coming in. I got to be a good shot, good enough that Remington asked if I would put on local shooting demonstrations for them. I used a Model 38 20-gauge Remington, the last machined pump gun that Remington made. I also used a pump rifle, a .22 that was just like a pump gun but was a rifle, and, if I recall, had an hexagonal barrel.

The beauty of working for Remington was that if you agreed to do exhibitions for them, they would give you unlimited ammo for free. They used to send boxes of .22-caliber ammo, wooden boxes about eighteen inches long, a foot wide and a foot high. Each one had something like five thousand shells in it. They would also give us a small cash stipend. Showing off was fun, and I could use a little extra cash, but mostly I was in it for the ammo. I was getting it all for nothing. We were supposed to use it for the demonstrations, but of course we'd sneak in a little rabbit and quail on the side. I hunted passionately up until I was about sixty-five years old. Eventually I found that I just didn't like killing things anymore. A lot of guys I know, guys who are around my age, are the same way. At a certain point in life you just don't want to kill things. That's one of the reasons I still love fishing: You're still immersed in the outdoors, matching wits with nature, but in the end you put stuff back.

I developed an interest in fishing over time, through a series of natural progressions. Uncle Hen, my mother's second husband, kept a homemade boat on the Monocacy River, which ran about four miles outside town. He never locked the boat up; he just tied a chain around a maple tree on the bank (We never locked anything in those days, not even our front doors). Since I knew how to pole a boat from about the time I was seven, I had permission from Uncle Hen to use the boat whenever I wanted. My brothers and I would walk the four miles out to the river to go fishing— even though we didn't have rods or reels or tackle. In the first place, we couldn't afford them. In the second place, we didn't need them. We did what we called "bush bobbing," a type of night fishing where you take three- or four- foot lengths of mason twine, put some kind of hook on the end, bait it, and tie it on the end of a branch overhanging a stream. As the fish grabs the bait, the branch gives and takes and—hopefully—sets the hook. Sometimes, if there were no branches close to water, we'd break off a long flexible limb and stick it deep into the riverbank. For some reason well beyond my recollection, we called these contraptions "jazz poles."

We used to fish a place called Derr's Woods, near Ceresville. In those days there were millions of freshwater mussels and clams in the stream and we knew how to find them. They made great bait, but we quickly learned that if you baited your hooks in the daytime the turtles would eat all the food. After considerable trial and error it occurred to us that turtles didn't eat at night, so we'd go out during the afternoon to pick up mussels and store them in a little backwater place. Just before dark, we'd pry them open like oysters, put them in a bucket, and I'd go up and down the bushes by these streams. After dark, one guy would pole the boat and the other would perch these strings with the bait on them just beneath the surface of the water.

This was really fun. Even as city kids we were immersed in nature. Out here in the limestone areas of the mid-Atlantic we had something called a White Miller—its proper name is *Ephoron leukon*. It's a snow-white fly, a very large fly, which hatches near dark in the last part of July or first week of August. Back when the local rivers were pure, down where the tracks cross the mouth of the Susquehanna, these millers used to hatch out so heavy that they actually halted the trains. When I was a kid, there were so many of them that they occasionally extinguished oil lanterns; there were so many of them attracted to the light that they would clog the vents and the flame would die out. The whole surface of the water would be covered with a sheet of white as if it had snowed on a frozen river. Every fish in the river would be up feeding on these things. You could see catfish with their mouths half out of the water swimming along loading up and then diving like a porpoise and them coming back up. The bass went crazy. Normally you don't catch big bass on little tiny mayflies, you need real groceries, but if you were smart enough or lucky enough to be out there while they were emerging toward the surface you could catch a fish every time you cast.

The whole phenomenon only lasted about two hours, but it was absolutely magical. (Note: There are still tremendous White Miller hatches in the region. My friend Bob Clouser and I were up on the Susquehanna a few years ago and there was a big hatch going on. It got dark and we were still casting and our boat had the requisite white light on the stern. Well, so many White Millers were attracted to the light that when I reached down to get a rod off the deck I couldn't even see it. The hatch was three inches deep on the deck).

As kids we were gone all day long. No cell phones, no worries, no tethers. Sure we lived in the ghetto, but no one ever fretted about what was going to happen to kids in those days. They didn't have to. When we were tired or hungry we'd find our way home. After being gone all day we'd walk four miles home. It was nothing to log ten miles walking on a sunny summer day. We walked all over the mountains gathering berries. I knew where there were some pretty healthy cherry trees and a guy named Earl Starner and I would take a five-gallon can up there, fill it up with these big Bing cherries, and sell them. We knew where all the blueberry patches were, too. We'd get blueberries and sell them (and save a few for ourselves). Sure, the money helped, but you could debate whether we were really in it for the money or the adventure. Take this night fishing, or bush bobbing. As we were setting the bait we'd hear owls hooting in the trees overhead. We didn't have any tents or nothing like that. We had a piece of canvas and if it rained we'd all just sit underneath it, basking in nature and friendship.

In reality, Frederick was far from paradise, but you couldn't have told us that.

Chapter 3
The Fishmonger

As kids, our world changed for good when we found out that Miller's Cash Market at 1 South Bentz Street would actually buy dressed catfish for ten cents a pound. When you consider that the combined cost of a ticket to the movies and a small bag of popcorn was only eleven cents, this was a financial bonanza.

We immediately got to work. We began running the bush bobs twice a night. You'd set them, wait an hour or two, and then you'd go back. Pretty good work if you could get it. As the sun set on nature's amusement park, we would begin to hear throaty American toads calling all along the river. There were thousands of them and they sang their song, "*Wauk, wauk wauk,*" all night. Every gravel bar along the river held thousands of them. Sadly, I haven't heard one in years. There were also small green frogs that we called "sharpies." They made wonderful bait for smallmouth bass. The willow grass beds along the water's edge were chock full of them. As night secured the surrounding terrain, farmers' fields would sparkle with swarms of fireflies. After a couple hours you'd go back and check out the bush bobs. With any luck, you'd see the limbs bobbing up and down and you knew you had money on the line. Hell, this was exciting. Sometimes we caught eight- and ten-pounders. I mean *big* ones.

Then it was off to Miller's. Old Man Miller was a nasty guy, but his money spent just fine. Some guys got a little queasy over fish guts. I didn't mind them at all. Sometimes I'd bring in ten or fifteen pounds of fish in a day. When the fish were biting, I made more money in a few days than a lot of men who worked all week. Through my last three years in high school I was a relative fat cat. But of course, I had bills to pay. I kept enough for my school clothes and lunches, and gave the rest to Mother.

By the time I was fourteen, I had saved enough money to upgrade to real fishing tackle. I bought my first plug-casting rod—a big squared-off metal deal made by American Fork and Hoe Company. I still have it. While the rod was certainly an improvement over bush-bobbing, it did take a little getting used to. This one place I used to go to—we called it Seven Fences because you had to crawl over seven fences to get there—was about four miles away on the Monocacy, below where we did our bush-bobbing. One morning I was off to Seven Fences. It was wet, and farmers in the area had just begun to install electrified fences. Of course, my shoes were wet, and I stepped over a wire fence. Even now, some seventy years later, I can still remember the jolt. I finally managed to step over the fence, but as I walked away, I absentmindedly dipped that metal rod down on the wire for another dose. Either one of those shocks would probably kill me today.

Anyway, the countryside was full of opportunity and adventure for an eager kid. We trapped muskrats and sold muskrat hides. I think we got twenty-five cents a hide. They made fur coats from them and a lot of people liked to eat the meat. We called it "March rabbit." Still, we were far from expert outdoorsmen. We learned from being there. For instance, I was told that if you caught a skunk in a trap and you picked his feet off the ground that he couldn't stink you. I'm here to tell you that's a darn lie. One day I was at Caywood's Springs on the Monocacy River, about three miles from home. I'd just caught my first skunk. So I walked up like I knew better, picked him up by the tail, and he hit me full in the chest with his spray. I must have vomited for twenty-five minutes. I went home and my mother was absolutely furious. She used to hand wash our clothes in a washtub, the kind with the old-fashioned scrubbing board. Somebody told her if you poured tomato juice on the clothes and buried them in the ground for a few weeks the stink would come out. Well, six weeks later we dug them up and they stunk just as bad as the day we buried them. That was my first and last time trapping skunks.

I was learning the ways of the woods and getting by in school. I got Bs and Cs—maybe the odd D—unless it was a class I liked—then I managed to get As. The only class I ever really looked forward to was Problems of Democracy. And the only reason I liked it was the teacher, Miss Delash. I don't remember her first name because we never used it— seemed like back then teachers didn't have first names. Well, she made that class so interesting that I got an A+. I got Cs in English because I hated it. It's hard to reconcile that with the fact that I've made my living in large part by writing for magazines and newspapers and writing books all these years. The very fact that you are reading this book is pretty amazing, considering how much I struggled with English as a child.

So how does a guy who hated English make a career of publishing? They're called editors. I always felt that an editor and a writer are a team. The editor wants it to be the best and you want it to be the best. So, the only time that I ever mess with my editors is when their changes make something materially incorrect. Also, the legendary outdoor writer Joe Brooks, a dear friend and a man we'll talk about at length later on, once told me never to use a big word where a little word would do. I've followed that advice all my life.

While I struggled in the classroom, I was successful in sports. I was the pitcher on the high school baseball team. I was on the basketball team, too. This was back in the days when little guys could still play basketball.

I was a guard, and my deadliest asset was undoubtedly my peripheral vision. This is something that has been helpful in my angling as well. I can see 180 degrees in front of me without any effort. In fact, I can virtually see behind me. When you have that kind of peripheral vision you don't have to look directly at the guy you're passing the ball to. They used to say that Oscar Robertson, who, back in the 1960s and '70s, was one of the standout guards in the NBA, was similarly gifted. He had huge eyes. They used to say that when he slept his eyelids didn't even cover his eyes; that's how big and bulbous they were. Anyway, I could be looking to my left and I could see a guy cutting for the basket to my right and throw the ball to him. I could dribble with either hand and shoot with either hand, which a lot of guys back then couldn't do. During practice our coach used to tell all the guys on the team to keep their eyes on the ball at all times. "Don't watch Lefty," he'd say, "watch the ball." In fact, many years later when I'd become known for fishing, *Sports Illustrated* did a story on left-handers in sports and interviewed me. They said their research had shown that left-handers can generally do a lot more with their right hand than right-handers can do with their left.

There's a funny addendum to that *SI* story. One of the black kids from Frederick was a guy named Ed Posey. Ed and I used to fish carp together using dough balls for bait. Well, Ed was a big sports fan. He loved basketball and football, and he read *Sports Illustrated* religiously. In all the years that we had been fishing together he didn't know that I was an outdoor writer because we never talked about work. Well, *SI* comes out with this profile on me in the dang magazine. A few days later I had a whole bunch of rods and reels and lines to test, and I went down to Point of Rocks on the Potomac. When I got there I saw Ed with his carp rods in the water. So we talked a minute, and I noticed there was a glint of newborn respect in his eyes. He said, "Hey Lefty, I done seen you in *Sports Illustrated*." He said, "What the hell is this fly casting anyway?"

I thought, "Well, I'm gonna impress my buddy." So I got all eight rods out and I cast all of them at once. He's sitting there watching. Then I cast four rods, then I cast two, then I'd switch in midair. Then I did a steeple cast and a skip cast and a curve cast and all these other fancy casts. Ed's sitting there watching—he'd never seen anything like it before. I finally got done with my little show and said, "Well, what do you think?"

He sat silent for a moment and then grunted, "Ain't worth a shit. You ain't caught nothin'." I got the biggest kick out of that.

The follow-up to that story is that I did do a lot of fly-casting demonstrations after the war, in the early and mid-1950s. I used to cast four fly rods at one time. And then I would cast eight. Then I would knock cigarettes out of women's mouths at fifty feet with a fly line. I'll let you in on a little secret: that kind of stuff really isn't as hard as it looks. Anyway, I stopped doing all that hotdogging when I realized that all I was doing was entertaining. Stuff like that never actually helped another person cast better or fish better, so I ultimately stopped doing it and focused on true instruction.

CHAPTER 4
THE WAR

I N J U N E 1942 I GRADUATED from high school. Four days later, I got a
form letter in the mail; like thousands of other kids around the country, I
had been drafted into the U.S. Army. I was to report to Camp Shelby in
Hattiesburg, Mississippi.

I hated the Army. Despised it. It ran counter to my lifelong instinct to
make things better. I am an inveterate tinkerer and self-described inventor.
If I see a hitch in some process or product, I simply have to find a way to
fix it. A visitor to my home will see more Rube Goldbergian gadgets than
he could imagine. From using old beer can cozies for storing fishing line,
to a homemade platform that holds my coffee cup within arm's reach of
my desktop computer, my life is full of necessity's children.

There's no doubt in my mind that my ability to discern flaws and
my passion for addressing them have made me a better fisherman,
outdoorsman, and writer. Years ago, before we had spinning tackle, we
relied on plug casting. The problem there was that the lures we were using,
almost all of which were hollow inside, were not heavy enough to pull the
line off the reel during a cast. The fish had gotten pretty wise to the large
lures we had been using, and we knew they'd bite on smaller lures, but the
smaller lures wouldn't have enough heft to pull the line. So how could we

get added weight into a smaller lure?

I drilled one small hole in the bottom of these hollow lures and another hole in the top. If you held the lure underwater and pumped against that bottom hole you could force water inside it. Then you cast it. If it wasn't heavy enough you could put more water in. Too heavy and you could put your mouth on top and blow some water out the bottom. You could adjust the lure for the exact need of the wind, and your equipment. And because all we were using was water for the added weight, there was no effect on the lure's ability to "swim." Common sense.

I modify almost everything I buy. I had a camera case that used to slide all over the place, so I took old rubber conveyor belt material and fastened it to the bottom of the case. Now it stays still. I don't think that people who make stuff use it. Think about lens caps on cameras. They're black. So are the press-tabs you push in to release them. I take bright colored fingernail polish and paint the tabs so that in low light I can find them quickly. Why they don't make them high-visibility orange at the factory is a mystery to me. I was fishing for crappie and I was using a real bright chartreuse and yellow float about one inch in diameter. I could see that float in just about any light. So I just took two little pieces of teakwood and put a screw in it and bolted it upright on the luggage rack on top of the car, and I can see that thing in a parking lot from 150 yards. I don't even look for my car anymore, I just look for the yellow float.

The Army drove me crazy because it's a paragon of inefficiency. I saw problem after unaddressed problem, but quickly learned that the U.S. Army is not interested in creative solutions or even creative thinkers. We did so many things every day that just didn't make any sense. That whole "hurry up and wait" philosophy chapped me. I know some of this was meant to instill discipline, but it was very impractical. Maybe it's better today, but in those days the military was run very, very inefficiently.

Of course, even I, the great wunderkind, wasn't always as smart as

I thought I was. One day during basic training I was ordered to take some grub up to the forward observation post. Back then the big 155-mm howitzers remained several miles behind the front lines. The eyes and ears for these big guns are the forward observers who have to be positioned in front of the infantry so they can tell the soldiers manning the howitzers when and where to fire. When I arrived with the food at the observation post, three soldiers were lying in the shade manning the telephone and directing the Howies where and when to shoot. These howitzers weighed thirteen tons. If we were told to shoot farther, we cranked the barrel higher. But often if we had to adjust our aim to either side—right or left—we had to actually lift the gun to do so. Beyond that, we had to build and maintain a mound of earth to protect the gun and its operators from enemy fire. This was not easy work. That day, as I saw the observers lounging in the shade and having their meals catered, I pledged that I too would one day be a forward observer. I became one, and only when I got overseas and into actual combat did I realize how tough and dangerous that job truly is.

I was a real Einstein; I had everything figured out. But over time I began to realize that the Army is simply not geared for logic. I remember the Army offered each soldier a special insurance policy, one that paid our survivors in the event that we were killed while in the service. A soldier could choose from two plans, the $5,000 payout and the $10,000 payout. I never knew anyone who bought the costlier option because none of us had the money (we only earned $21 a month back then). Well, I was sitting on my bunk in the barracks when two fellow soldiers started discussing the insurance plan.

"Which policy did you get," asked one.

"I got the $5,000 plan," he replied. "Which one did you get?'

"I got me the $10,000 policy."

Astounded, his friend replied, "You gotta be crazy to spend all that money on that policy b'cuz if you get killed it ain't gonna do you no good."

"Me? Killed?" he asked haughtily. "You think they're going to send a $10,000 soldier to the front lines when they got a $5,000 soldier like you?"

The Army, however, was not without its pluses. As a child and as a Boy Scout I had learned to love the outdoors. And while the uninitiated might see Hattiesburg as the monstrous swamp it sits in, I saw it as a remarkable repository of wildlife. There were still ivory-billed woodpeckers down there. These things were supposed to be extinct. There had been some talk about a pair in Cuba, and just a few months ago *The New York Times* trumpeted the species' revival, but I'm telling you there were ivory-billed woodpeckers back in this swamp in 1942. Beautiful birds. When I'd see one of these stunning and rare beauties I would ask the captain to lend me his field glasses for close-up viewing. All these other guys were going off to the bars and whorehouses in Hattiesburg, and there I was wading into the woods looking for birds. Believe me, they had some doubts about me for a while.

Like everyone else, I was a private when I first went to basic. I was the number-one man on the 8-mm howitzer. To the nascent engineer in me, these weapons were a technological marvel. They were capable of throwing a hundred-pound shell at a church steeple eight miles away. They revolutionized warfare. Just before we were shipped overseas, the army came out with proximity fuses for the 8 mm shell. This meant that we now had the capability to make these things detonate at a designated height from the ground. Instantly, these deadly howitzers became ten times more effective. We could now knock out a German tank from four or five miles away.

Being in the Army in 1942 was very different from being in the Army in 1932. For one thing, the war was on and there was a very good chance you were going to see action. But there's another thing many younger Americans don't realize about World War II; something that's been lost in the hagiography that has enveloped the era: we did not know we were going to win that war. In fact, if Hitler had done a number of things differently, I'm convinced we wouldn't have won it. For example, if Germany had not invaded Russia, but had instead concentrated on getting England and then getting us, Hitler probably would have prevailed. We didn't know we were going to win that war until after we invaded Europe in June of 1944, and even *then* victory hung in the balance at Normandy.

Anyway, I was in Hattiesburg for a little over a year of basic. For the first time in my life, I was around only white guys. The Army didn't allow blacks in the barracks back then. They could run motor pools and maintenance operations and things like that, but they were forbidden from bunking with us. What they did have in Hattiesburg, however, was a Japanese infantry division. Boy, were they impressive. I guess because of the stigma of being Japanese at that particular time in history they worked three times harder than any of us. Whatever the reason, they were unbelievable—not just in training, but when they went into battle they flat ran us into the ground. They just excelled at everything they did.

As much as I hated the army, Camp Shelby did allow some of the fruits of my misspent youth to blossom. Back in Frederick I had gotten pretty good at shooting pool. Eventually, the manager of the YMCA would let me play for free as long as I took care of his tables. So for several years before I joined the Army, I restored the felt on the tables, maintained rails, stuff like that. Well, in the Army, every battery or company has a "day room"—a rec room with Ping-Pong, Coke machines, and card tables. Hattiesburg had all these brand-new pool tables, but since nobody on base knew how to put them together, they just sat there gathering dust. I volunteered to assemble the tables—a move that exempted me from more than one twenty-mile hike. Incidentally, I was in superb physical condition in those days and I couldn't understand the thirty-year-olds when we'd go on the twenty-mile hike. Man, the lead fell out of their rear ends and crushed their ankles. They were so tired. I also felt sorry for many of the big-city boys when they were forced to march or take care of themselves outdoors. We walked so much as kids not only to school and back but also to the rivers and back and on berry hunts that even the longest walks in the army were nothing. Still, I didn't mind missing out on them.

So I fixed up all the pool tables and got some of the guys interested in shooting a little pool. Nothing big, just for fun. Then, a few weeks later, a guy named Willie Hoppe shows up in camp. Hoppe is largely forgotten today, but he is still considered by many to be the greatest all-around billiard player ever. In 1906, at the tender age of eighteen, Hoppe won his first world title by defeating the renowned French champion, Maurice Vignaux, at 18.1 Balkline in a memorable match in Paris. He went on to win the 18.2 Balkline and Cushion Carom titles and, between 1936 and 1952, captured the Three-Cushion title eleven times. In 1940, at 52 years old, Hoppe accomplished what many billiards fans believed impossible: He went through an entire world three-cushion billiards tournament undefeated.

By the time he joined us in Hattiesburg, Willie was in his mid-fifties. His visit was part of a tour of military installations to help out GI morale. He would go around to different company barracks at night and shoot pool or do trick shots to entertain the troops. Well, when Willie got to Hattiesburg he wanted somebody to shoot with him. I knew I couldn't hang with no Willie Hoppe, but I volunteered in a heartbeat, and did I ever learn a lot. For a few weeks I was the billiards version of the Washington Generals, the gag team that gets thumped by the Harlem Globetrotters every night. One of the first things he taught me was point of contact. Have you ever seen the numbers on a pool ball? They're in that little circle. Well, when you're lining up to hit the cue ball, he told me, imagine a circle like that on it. You never want your stick to hit outside that little imaginary circle, no bigger than a nickel, or you'll miscue.

He also told me that you either want to use follow (topspin) or draw (backspin) on most shots and to avoid English (sidespin) on a long shot if you can help it. English makes the ball curve, he said. It may be imperceptible but it's going to curve some. Plus, if you put left-hand English on a ball, it's going to knock the next ball it hits it to the right. That's why your "leave" is so important. The correct leave will allow you to use topspin or backspin while minimizing the need for English.

Willie was in town for several weeks, and we shot pool virtually every night. I was like a vacuum cleaner, just sucking up his knowledge. I came to Hattiesburg thinking I knew a lot about pool, but I learned so darn many things from him. Ever since, I've felt that if you want to learn something, find an expert. If you want to learn to shoot pool don't go to some guy in a mansion that's got a beautiful pool table in his smoking room. Go down to the local pool parlor and learn from some guy who's making his groceries off the game. Either he'll know the game or he ain't gonna eat. That's the guy that you want to learn from.

After our training in Hattiesburg we shipped to New Jersey and then to New York Harbor for a quick layover before setting sail for Europe and the war. I hate New York about as much as I hated the Army, but because it's the publishing capital of the world, I've since had to go a few times in my life. I never developed a taste for the place. For a guy who loves nature and the outdoors, New York, with its asphalt carpet and concrete canyons, is just antithetical.

The layover in New York before shipping out to London was not only my first visit to the Big Apple but also the first time other than my stay at Hattiesburg that I'd ever been outside of Maryland. Somehow, as we bobbed in a transport ship at a pier on Manhattan's west side, I knew there were a lot of guys in my position: homesick, afraid, uncomfortable in the big city. Not to mention seasick. First night on board in New York guys were throwing up all over the place, and we were still tied to the dock!

When we did finally set sail, things just went downhill. I have since learned that October–November is the worst season to sail the North Atlantic. We found ourselves negotiating twelve- to fifteen-foot waves throughout our journey. My bunk was situated far forward, directly beneath the gargantuan anchor that dangled over the bow. Every time the ship would rise and fall that darn anchor would lift up and slam down like a ungodly gong. When it hit that steel hull it sounded like it was going to come right straight through my quarters. I got sick about the third day out and remained so until we got to Great Britain.

It's funny, I have since spent a life on the water: brooks, rivers, sounds, bays, oceans—you name it—and the sea rarely bothered me before that trip or since. I can only think of one other time in my entire life that I even got seasick. I had taken my brother Dick to the Marquesas and then west of the Marquesas along a sand shoal that runs toward the Tortugas. We chummed up mangrove snappers and barracuda and jacks and all kinds of stuff. We started catching some fish and it looked like it was going to be a banner day. No sooner did we start landing bonefish than Dick started to get violently ill. I hate to say it, but rather than comforting Dick and being selfless, I got a little irritated and took him into the Marquesas. Not too long afterward, I got sick myself. All of a sudden I had a whole new perspective on seasickness. From that day on, if anybody in one of my groups ever has trouble with rough seas, I immediately take them to quieter water no matter how great the fishing may be. I have never gotten it as bad as some people, and haven't had it in years, but I've had it bad enough that I know I don't want it again and I don't want anybody else to have to endure it, either. (Note: Over the years I've learned that being seasick often has less to do with the sea than the with the person's placement in the boat. And often it has to do with fumes. You sit all day in the fishing well of a diesel boat, soak up the sun and the rolling water and I guarantee you're at least going to get a little light-headed. Diesel fumes will get people sicker than anything. Also the higher you get up in a boat the more seasick you're going to get. The last thing you want to do is go up in the tower. It may mean fresh air, but the height of a tower just exaggerates the rolling of the boat and makes things worse. Over time, I've found that the one thing that has always helped me and a lot of the people I've fished with was eating some plain old saltine crackers.)

Seasickness aside, my comrades and I eventually found ourselves in London, where we camped out for a couple of weeks. Wow. I thought New York was a shock; this was a whole new world *and* a different language. To a kid from Frederick via Hattiesburg, London verged on the exotic. I remember one of our first nights in port I was dancing with an attractive British gal at a USO function. As the night wore on and the music slowed down she put her head on my shoulder—this was way better than boot camp. However, a moment later in a warm, breathy whisper she told me she was "knocked up." Man, did I drop her fast. A few days later, still shaken by her news, I learned that in Brit-speak "knocked up" simply means tired. Oh, well.

It wasn't long after that hilarious misunderstanding—maybe a few weeks—that they took us across the English Channel and into the fray. The party was over. I was with the 274th field artillery, 69th division (after I had gone stateside it was our division that ultimately met the Russians on the River Elbe). After arriving in continental Europe we traveled across France, into Belgium and head-on into the Battle of the Bulge. My worst experience in the war came on my first day of actual combat. It set a grim tone for my entire tour of duty. We were marching toward the battlefield, and with each step you could see in gory detail the destruction that the Germans had wrought. They knocked the hell out of the place. My initial reaction was shock at the number of dead. I learned a very telling fact about our enemy: In the wintertime they didn't bother burying their dead. As we got closer to the action we saw lots of corpses left behind. They were mixed in with dead horses and dead cows and dead everything else.

In a situation like that you may know that the enemy is about three miles up, but you don't always know specifically where he is. So you're very careful. Everyone is on his own, but you have to follow certain procedures. Yes, you're a fighting unit, but you're really individuals within a fighting unit. And you just keep reminding yourself that you've got a job to do. That first day we were scouting out a ridge that ran about two hundred feet and then went over the other side. It was like a big long hump. One of our lieutenants was running beside me. To this day I don't know what hit him, but whatever it was met him squarely in the chest. The force of the impact knocked his head clean off his shoulders. As his head rolled down the hill in front of me, bullets started whizzing all around.

The Germans had these things called Screaming Mimis, little rocket-type projectiles bound together. The Mimis were filled up with all kinds of shrapnel. They had nuts and bolts and all kinds of stuff in them. When they hit something it was complete devastation. They would shoot these things and you could hear them going "*Shoo-Shoo*" as they blew by you. There would be about eight or ten bound in one shot. They made a hell of a noise. In fact, the noise was so intimidating that I'm convinced it was an intentional part of the design.

Well, the Mimis were whooshing overhead and the bullets were flying, and the lieutenant's head was rolling past my feet and I was terrified. When his head tumbled to a stop I just sat down on the ground and vomited my guts out. I was a sitting duck. I was lucky that I didn't get killed right then and there. That was a stark introduction to the reality of war. After that I was all right. Sort of like taking your first hit in a football game, it conditioned me in a hurry. I would see a lot of gruesome things in wartime Europe, but nothing I saw was worse than that.

On December 16 the Germans started their Ardennes Offensive. Their plan was to use overwhelming force to take control of eastern Belgium and northern Luxembourg. In doing so, they felt they could reach the sea, pin the allied armies against the beach, and force a negotiated peace on the Western front. Thinking that the heavily wooded Ardennes region was an unlikely ground for a German invasion, American brass left that section of our line sparsely manned. The Battle of the Bulge, so named for the "weak" spot in the American line, was one of the bloodiest battles in military history. It lasted five weeks. Over 100,000 Germans were killed, wounded or captured. Nearly 24,000 Americans were captured and 19,000 were killed. The British suffered 1,400 casualties with 200 killed. A total of 800 tanks were destroyed and the Germans lost 1,000 aircraft.

The backdrop for this epic battle was the coldest, snowiest winter in memory—this in a region known for harsh winter weather. The biting cold would have been bad enough. So would the snow. But we would have been able to perform perfectly well under either condition. The crippling part of that five-week battle was the fog. No one could see anything. Neither side's planes could fly, so we were forced into inaction—sitting in these sloppy, frozen trenches, everything covered in snow, doing nothing. We sat still, barely moving, for six days. In the infantry, when you stop for any period of time you immediately dig a narrow trench, a long rectangular slit into which you can climb for protection. If incoming fire breaks out, you're sitting down below ground level. We sat like that for days. That's what really hurt us in the Bulge. We had complete air supremacy because we had just about eliminated all the German airplanes, but we couldn't *exploit* that advantage because our planes couldn't fly in the pea-soup fog.

As we sat in the trenches waiting for the sky to clear, our body heat slowly began to thaw the ground below us. When you finally stood up, this ice cake would freeze on your pants. The one thing I knew from my experience in the cold as a child and from my Boy Scout training was that I had to keep moving. I realized very early on that I had to keep my toes and feet active. I constantly took my shoes off in order to massage my feet. I'd do anything to get them warm and dry. A lot of the city guys had no idea what to do. The fact is we were all freezing to death, and some were just outlasting the others. Sadly, we lost an awful lot of men to the conditions. In fact, in the Battle of the Bulge we lost more people to trench foot than we did to the German's guns. Even with all my precautions I still got slightly frostbitten. Today, more than sixty years later, my toes and fingers still occasionally bother me. When it gets real cold out, they give me a burning sensation. It's almost as though they're reminded of that lost week in the trench.

When the fog finally cleared, so many Allied airplanes took to the sky that it's virtually beyond description. It was like one of those rare scenes in crow, dove, or partridge hunting where there are so many darn birds that they just black out the sun. The drone of the thousands of engines was a sound I'll never forget. Some of them came in real low and dropped supply parachutes with round containers about 18 inches in diameter and maybe 24 inches high. As you can imagine, we hadn't had a hot meal for some time. Well, these containers had hot pancakes floating in real maple syrup. We didn't wash our hands, no forks, no nothing. We reached in and rolled them up like hot dogs and gulped them down like there was no tomorrow. Other containers had dry socks in them, something we probably needed as badly as the food.

Funny, the things you remember. I think it was a place called Mannheim. There was a tank in the village. It had been knocked out by the Germans and there was a dead American soldier in there. One of my sergeants told me to get the soldier's body out of there, get his dog tags, and bury him. Back then, a GI's shoes were pretty uncomfortable. If you were driving a tank you weren't about to go anywhere on foot, so a lot of the tank drivers used to unlace their shoes and leave them open. By the time we got to the body it'd been in there a few days. Rigor mortis had set in and the body was very stiff. When we pulled the body upward, one shoe slipped off and there was over a thousand dollars in $100 bills inside his shoe. We had his dog tags, so we were able to send the money back home. But, if the shoe hadn't fallen off we probably would have just buried him with the money.

Once the sun came out and the fog was gone, our bombers and our artillery could really handle the Germans. They had a lot of tanks there. The trouble for the Germans was that they were running out of gas. We weren't very far from Bastogne. We didn't know about that until later, but one of the reasons they wanted to get to Bastogne was so they could get fuel. The problem for them was that they didn't have the luxury of running all over the landscape with those things. And boy we knocked them hard. We pushed forward. There were some places I bet there were a hundred tanks in an area maybe a couple of square miles, ours and theirs. Their tanks were far superior to ours. They had that 88-mm rifle on board, which was so accurate, it was like shooting a sniper rifle. But our tanks were more mobile and we had more of them. We knocked out a lot of tracks with bazookas, too. It looked like a demolition derby.

We could hear artillery day and night, pounding in the distance. At night, distant artillery looks like heat lightning. It's a noiseless glow that goes up and then you hear the boom. But you know, when you're twenty years old you don't think anything is going to happen to you. You've got a job to do. Plus, everybody there believed in their country. That was the thing about World War II: we had the unconditional support of the American people.

It's inconceivable that we would have had protesters like we do today. Our president was our president, and we were going to stick by him come hell or high water. And when he went to war, we weren't going to question that. Far from it. Back then, when a president committed troops we rallied around him whether we liked the action or not. In fact, as soon as war was declared hundreds of thousands of guys volunteered for the darn thing. They weren't hiding from the draft, they were effectively jumping the line. We were proud of our country and proud to defend it and our allies.

There were plenty of times I feared for my life. We crossed the bridge at Remagen. The original bridge had already fallen in, but there was a floating bridge there, a pontoon bridge, in its place. We got across that and the road went up the German side. We got to a spot where a cliff had slid right down into the river and they had blasted enough of the remaining cliff off to make a road. There were some Germans on the other side of the river, armed with artillery. We had a narrow passageway to get us around this mountain and a handful of Germans was really holding us up. For a while we felt like targets at an arcade. We eventually got around the bend and killed them. It turned out they were all kids, fourteen year-old Hitler Youth.

Actual combat was intermittent. Some days you engaged the enemy and some days you didn't. While I had become a pretty good shot back in Frederick, we didn't do a lot of rifle shooting in Europe. We shot plenty in training, but in battle we were mostly using big automatic guns. We did have our trusty carbines, however, and we used them quite a bit, especially in the woods. You know, sometimes you'd be scouting and you'd actually surprise a group of Germans or they'd surprise you. Sometimes we had to go into these abandoned houses after them. That was not fun. We used grenades a lot in those situations, but so did the Germans. I remember one time inside Germany I was asked to go scout with two guys. It was after dark and the town looked deserted. The wind had blown the darn doors off the building, and bricks and shingles were slipping off of roofs. I was sneaking along with the two other guys, looking for Germans who were believed to be hiding in a cellar. Out of the cellar door came two potato mashers, the German grenades that looked like a rod attached to an oilcan. They actually looked a bit like the old potato mashers my grandmother used to use. Well these mashers hit the street, and we recognized what they were right away. We started running like hell. We avoided the explosion, but as we were running across a field going back to camp, I hit a low electric fence. Fortunately the current wasn't on, but when I hit that fence I must have looked like a trapeze artist. I made about three somersaults in the air and landed flat on my back. I was certain that I'd been shot. I couldn't breathe, and it was dark so I couldn't assess the situation. I thought, "Well, they shot me. It's over." After a while, my breath started coming back and I slowly got up and hustled back to camp. Turns out I'd just had the wind knocked out of me. I was lucky I didn't have to do much patrolling after that. That was something that they usually let older guys do.

While in Europe I started to seriously consider converting to Catholicism. When I was a kid my mother sent all four of us to the Baptist church every Sunday morning. Small towns have a hierarchy where the people with the money sort of look down on the people who don't have money. To put it simply: We were not treated warmly by the Baptist congregation. I always felt that the people there looked down their noses at us, sniffing at us as if we were some sort of street urchins.

I had been enrolled in the Boy Scouts and, of course, in those days the Boy Scouts really stressed morals. So I became interested in religion. After seeing how we'd been treated by our local Baptists, I was in the market for a new church. If the Baptists' God was as nasty as his congregation, I didn't want anything to do with Him. I started investigating a number of faiths. I was thinking seriously about making a change as I joined the Army, and Catholicism appealed to me more than any other.

I was still in my late teens. I was impressionable. During lulls in the fighting I enjoyed visiting Europe's remarkable Catholic churches and cathedrals, and I gained a firsthand appreciation for the masterpieces within them. You see one of these paintings or stained-glass windows in a book and it may look good, but you see one close up, particularly after being shot at for weeks, and they *come to life*. I remember walking up to one of these paintings in a French church. It was a portrait of a man sitting in a church that had black-and-white marble squares on the floor. He was sitting with one leg kind of extended out. And he had those baggy pantaloons with the long stockings. The churches were pretty much deserted, because we were still in combat, so I got up close. I looked at this pair of pants and it looked like somebody had glued the silk of his trousers directly onto the canvas. I took my finger and touched it just to make sure it was paint. The artist had painted the sheen perfectly. I was really impressed by that. I eventually converted to Catholicism upon returning home from the war.

To be honest, I've never thought much about the war since then. Many years later—it was back in the 1980s—I was leading the occasional tour for Frontiers International Travel Agency, the biggest fishing and hunting travel agency in the world. And I took a group of salmon fishermen to the Ponol River in northwestern Russia, just north of Finland. We had a doctor with us on that trip, a very accomplished surgeon from Boston whose nickname was "Red." He and a couple of his surgeon buddies at home had formed a little folk band just for fun. We were all huddled in this great big tent on the river, drinking vodka, and one of the Russians breaks out a guitar. After a few drinks this Russian guy starts singing, "You're in the Army Now," and at least a dozen other folk ditties. The vodka flowed. The women on the trip, local women who cooked our meals, all got up and started doing that Russian-style dancing. Then Red borrowed the guitar. This really wasn't that long after Vietnam, maybe twelve or fifteen years; the Cold War was still very much on, and Red sang this song about why powerful countries can't keep peace. I looked around and thought to myself, *When it comes to just plain folk, everybody wants to get along with everybody else. It's the darn politicians that cause all the trouble.*

Chapter 5
After the War

After we broke Hitler's back at the Bulge, we pretty much knew we were going to win the war in Europe, and the War Department started making plans for releasing servicemen and women from the military. They created a points system. You got so many points if you were married. You got additional points for having children. If you had battle stars you got more points, etc. I was unmarried, no children, and had only five battle stars. My point total was so low that I was immediately shipped to the States for a brief furlough, after which I was to be sent to the Pacific Theater to fight the Japanese.

In May of 1945, they took us from Leipzig to Camp Lucky Strike in France. I was back home in Frederick by mid-August 1945. On August 6, about a week prior to my arrival in Frederick, President Truman had dropped the atomic bomb on Hiroshima. America was awaiting Japan's next move. On August 14, I was in uniform walking down East Patrick Street in Frederick when the sirens in all the firehouses suddenly started whirring. Car horns started honking wildly. People were dancing in the streets, and I kid you not, I must have been kissed by one hundred women. Of course, I wasn't objecting, but it took me a little while to figure out what all the pandemonium was about. Then it dawned on me:

Japan had surrendered. The war was over.

With no need to send me to the Pacific, the Army dispatched me to Fort Chaffee, Arkansas, and gave me my discharge. I was home for good by late September. Many of my comrades in the 69th Division, several of whom had far more points than I, wouldn't get home for several months. Other than surviving, it may have been the only good break I ever got from the Army.

Throughout my time in the service, fishing and hunting were distant memories. Needless to say, with a war on there had been no time to cast a line. The land was so torn up, anyway. I mean, everywhere we went—all across France and Belgium and into Germany, the land was just completely shredded. We never even thought about it. We were all worried about staying alive and getting home. Now that I was home I planned to make up for lost time.

Postwar Frederick was very much like the Frederick I had left behind: simple. It was still a community of unlocked doors and cooperation. Me and a guy named Jack Griffin, who went on to become a well-known basketball coach, used to hitchhike to Washington, D.C., and back (one hundred miles, round trip) to see the basketball games. I remember one time we got a ride from D.C. and only made it about 30 miles, to Rockville. We had to walk all night to cover the remaining 20 miles. I used to hitchhike about 16 miles to see a girl I was dating in Brunswick, too. People would pick you up at nine, ten, eleven o'clock at night and bring you right home. There wasn't always a ride, of course. One night I had to walk all 16 miles *back* from Brunswick. I eventually found a new girl in Frederick.

Hitchhiking was not a big deal back then. It was perfectly safe. My first two cars didn't even have locks on them. Most people never even knew where the key was to their front door. You didn't hear all this stuff about little children being taken by crazy people. And I may be looking at the past through rose-colored glasses, but it seems to me that people didn't rob each other back then, a least not in my neighborhood. In Frederick we had a built-in alarm system. We all had so little and we knew how much everybody else had. If you ever showed up with something that belonged to someone else you were dealt with.

When I got out of the Army they had a thing called the 52/20 Club. For your first fifty-two weeks out of the service they'd pay you $20 a week, which doesn't sound like a lot of money, and it wasn't, but in 1945 you could pretty much get by on it. Well, I did that about four or five weeks and I got bored to tears. If you were a woman chaser it was paradise, but I wasn't and I really started to get bored. Eventually I began to ask around about jobs. There were jobs everywhere—clerk in a grocery store, gas station attendant, other menial stuff like that. I really wasn't interested. I was looking for something that could help me build a career in spite of the fact that all I had was some military service and a high school diploma. I did have one advantage: With so many young men still overseas wrapping up World War II, I had little competition.

Somebody told me that nearby Fort Detrick was planning to switch from military to civilian operations and that I should go look over there. During the war Fort Detrick had been a supersecret biological warfare research and development center. Even with the end of the war, America remained suspicious of our ally, the Soviet Union, so the work at Fort Detrick would continue.

The fort was a massive installation right on the northwest corner of town. In its World War II heyday there were between three and four thousand people working there. I headed over. My Army experience was probably helpful, but it also helped that I had never smoked. I tried cigarettes one time and thought, "If I've gotta blow this stuff out to get a breath of fresh air, I ain't doing it." I never smoked again. That was important because new employees would be manning the building that grew all of the experimental bacteria for all the Army scientists at Fort Detrick. We grew 1,800 gallons of anthrax a week and concentrated it into just a small piece of mud.

The building was under a pump that created a slight vacuum so that fresh air came into the building but no air at all left the building. In fact, all the air that came into the building would eventually be burned. Employees who wanted to smoke had to leave what they called the "hot area" to light up. You had to take the white coveralls off and then you would have to go into a shower. The clothes all had to be autoclaved and then you went outside there and you smoked your cigarette and got redressed and came back in. The government was keenly interested in nonsmokers for these jobs because if you didn't smoke you weren't going to have to spend a few hours a week going in and out, getting dressed and undressed, for cigarette breaks.

I got the job in the pilot plant, starting January 1, 1948. We grew the bacteria that our scientists worked on. The pay was seventy-nine cents an hour. I was the fourteenth person hired, so I had some seniority. This was shift work, meaning I'd work four to twelve one week, twelve to eight the next and then eight to four the next. While the irregular hours kept a lot of people away, it was perfect for me. I was single, I always functioned well on little rest, and the schedule meant that two weeks out of three I could fish and hunt for three hours a day and still go to work. That's when my interest and skills in the outdoors really matured. I had been successful as a young fisherman, but I hadn't ever really been a student of angling. Now I had the time, the inclination, and enough pocket change to become one.

It was in this archetypal postwar utopia that I met my wife. The situation was right out of a Norman Rockwell painting. The Tivoli Theatre in Frederick was one of those classic movie theaters with the ticket office enclosed in a little booth out front. I walked into the theater with two of my buddies to see a film (for the life of me, I can't recall the title). The usher accepted their tickets and let them in, but he said to me, "You can't get in here."

I said, "What are you talking about?

He said, "This is a child's ticket."

I went storming out to the ticket window, but quickly cooled my jets when I saw that the clerk was a great-looking blonde with a fabulous figure. I was barely even interested in girls. Sure, I had just gotten out of the war, but all I really wanted to do back then was make up for all the hunting and fishing I'd missed out on during the war. She said, "What's wrong? You look upset." I stuttered apologetically and explained the mix-up. We started talking, and it must have been a good five minutes before I even asked about the replacement ticket. I didn't have the courage to ask her for a date, so I went into the theater and all through the show all I did was think about her.

It was the last show of the night and as we came out of the theater, the blonde in the booth was getting ready to go home. I scraped up my courage and asked her name.

"Evelyn Mask," she said.

I asked if I could walk her home, and we ended up sitting on her parents' front porch and talking for nearly an hour.

In those days, you didn't get any nookie until you were married—after the ring was on the finger and the paper was signed. Long story short: six months later we were engaged. A year later we were married. I was Catholic and so was she, and nine months from our wedding day our daughter Vicky was born.

I wanted Ev to raise our children. This may sound Neanderthal today, but I did not want her working outside the home. Fortunately, she felt the same way. I think the migration of the mother from the home to the workforce is one of the fundamental problems with our society today. I think kids need a mother's touch all day, not just in the harried few minutes Mom can cram in before meals or bedtime. In the rush of "modern" women trying to validate themselves, they've neglected their kids and their own maternal instincts. And in my opinion, society has paid the price for it.

Since we were relying on my income alone, money was tight. We had a kitchen table, two chairs, some kitchen utensils, and a bed that we bought at a used furniture auction. My in-laws gave us a used Sears and Roebuck radio, and I built an icebox that held a 12 ½-pound block of ice. We never knew we were poor, never felt so, especially when people were so willing to extend credit. When we went shopping salespeople would say, "It's only two dollars a month." Didn't sound like much, so we started buying. Eventually that kind of thing caught up with us. We found ourselves unable to make the payments. We got a bad credit rating, which really unsettled both of us. We'd always seen ourselves as thoroughly upstanding. I told Ev, "We're going to get out of this and it's never going to happen to us again."

In addition to the job at Fort Detrick I began trapping furs. With these other extracurriculars, we eventually worked our way out of our newlywed debt. Since that time, Ev and I have paid cash for virtually everything. Our newspaper bill, for example, is paid a full year in advance. I own one credit card and I only use it for travel emergencies.

During our courtship and for about six months after we were married, Ev and I fished together often. But with Vicky, and our son Larry's arrival soon after, we found fewer and fewer opportunities to fish as a couple. The kids became the focus of our lives. I'm here to tell you that Ev and I have been blessed with two great kids. They've never been arrested, never been in any kind of trouble. To this day we spend a great deal of time with them and thoroughly enjoy them. Both our kids make us feel like we're the two greatest human beings on earth. We're lucky; not many parents have that today.

Of course, neither of the kids was perfect, but where would the fun be in that? I remember back when Larry was about 8 years old I decided we'd have good old-fashioned father-son day of fishing. I took him up to the Potomac River. I anchored the boat and put the bait out. The first thing he did was fall out of the darn boat. Now, he could swim okay, but the fact is that he fell out of the boat. I fished him out and got him back in the boat. I had to build a fire on the riverbank to dry his clothes out and keep him warm. While I'm working on the fire, the kid steps on a brand-new Fenwick rod and busts it. It went on like this all day.

So we got through the afternoon without killing anyone. We got up to the boat dock, put the fishing gear in the car, and started heading home. Little Larry was sitting next to me, underneath my arm as I drove. I said, "Son, you know in a couple more years you're going to be poling this boat and running the motor and doing this and such all by yourself."

His reply wasn't smart-ass, he just wanted to know the ground rules. He said, "Dad, when I'm in charge can *I* cuss *you?*" Classic.

CHAPTER 6
I HAD SUCH FRIENDS

I WAS LUCKY. MY INTEREST in the outdoors was accelerated because someone who knew far more than I did took the time to help me. Truth be told, I was not a particularly good fisherman in the mid- to late 1940s. Yes, I had learned a lot about fish as a kid, but I was still a relative novice at plug casting, and I was virtually unaware that fly-fishing even existed.

During my first few years at Ft. Detrick I hunted and fished more than most people do in a lifetime. The central Maryland of the mid-1940s was an outdoorsman's paradise. I lived five miles from the Blue Ridge Mountains. The Monocacy River, where I fished as child, was just a short walk away, and the Potomac was only a few miles farther. There were farm ponds everywhere and they were loaded with hefty largemouth bass. While trout and bass kept me occupied most of the year, rabbits, quail, squirrels, grouse, and other game kept me busy during the winter hunting season.

In the late 1940s Jason Lucas was the fishing editor of *Sports Afield*, and he was way ahead of his time. He was a plug caster, and in those days the plug-casting reels were very heavy. The only thing that could drag line out of them was a similarly heavy lure. Well, there were small groups of plug casters in the late 40s that were throwing distance casts. They'd made tiny light aluminum reels for their sport, primarily for tournament use. They used them with very small line and threw small lures long distances. Lucas was a pioneer in the use of smaller lures to go after bass. Most of the lures used for bass in those days were 1/2 to 3/4 ounce and some were as long as 4 inches. Lucas wrote that he used 1/4-ounce and 3/8-ounce lures and a lot of the lures he was recommending were not even 2 inches long.

Lucas was really the first one to write about this stuff. He covered other subjects that fascinated me as well; topics such as migration routes in lakes and stratified areas. All this before anybody else. He was constantly breaking news about these plug reels and these light lines (remember, nylon was virtually unknown at the time). I had a sense that this was the future of fishing, at least bass fishing, and I wanted to learn more about it.

The rap on Lucas back then was that just about everybody who ever met him—or claimed to have met him—said he was an ornery, irascible SOB, but he was a real authority on the American and international fishing scenes. He was the first person who wrote about bass migrating away from the shoreline and suspending over structures. He was the first person to advocate fishing deep for largemouth bass as opposed to simply fishing the first ten feet of water. He was really a pioneer in many ways.

Well, in the audacity of my youth I wrote him a letter. Back then Lucas was a mysterious creature. He used to travel the country in an Airstream camper. He'd do his fishing, handwrite his submissions to the magazine, and mail them in. When I told friends that I was going to write Jason Lucas, I might as well have told them I was going to call on the Wizard of Oz. "You'll never get to him," they said. "Even if you do, you'll never hear back." But what did I have to lose?

Lucas did more than write me back. He wrote me a three-page legal-sized treatise telling me in precise detail what models I should buy:

reels, model numbers, where I could get them. It did two things for me. First, it introduced me to tackle that could utilize small lures, which were much more effective on bass at that time. Second, it made me realize that as an outdoor writer, which I would become much later, I needed to communicate with people. Now, when people write to me I take the time to write back. Sure, it eats up a lot of time, but if Lucas took the time to help me, I was going to take the time to help other people.

I went out and bought the tackle that Lucas recommended. This was early in the evolution and these reels were not machined well. In fact, those of us who were using these things had to carry screwdrivers in the boat because every once in a while the line would get behind the spool through a gap in the spool and the sides of the reel. You'd have to take the reel apart, pull the spool out, put the line back on the spool correctly and put the spool back on the reel.

That correspondence was the only communication I had with Lucas until several years later, when he wrote me a letter telling me that he had written a book called *Lucas on Bass*. I bought a copy and still have it. (I also recently bought a second copy that's in much better shape). That book is very hard to find today, but it in my opinion it's a must-read for anyone truly interested in the history of bass-fishing technique. In it, Lucas essentially laid the foundation for modern bass fishing. He's a towering, if a largely unrecognized, figure in the history of fishing.

Of course the late Buck Perry is still remembered by many as the father of modern bass-fishing technique, but he came along several years after Lucas had written about how bass move in lakes, and about fishing different depths. Perry invented the Spoonplug lure and really was the father of "structure fishing," a system that, using his lure, helps find where the fish are.

Perry's theory was that fish move predictably because they follow the contours of the lake bottom. To help figure out where fish—any variety of freshwater fish—would be, he crafted a device that combined elements of lures known as "spoons" and "plugs," which he patented in 1946 as the Spoonplug. He described it as "a shoehorn that's been tromped on by a horse."

Perry designed seven sizes—the largest for deep water, the smallest for shallow water. To map a river or lakebed, he used the smaller ones to tap the bottom, then gradually substituted larger sizes to go to deeper water until he found fish. Mr. Perry could cover a new lake in a few hours. He never accepted the excuse that fish weren't biting, responding, "You've got to go out and make them strike."

The Spoonplug failed to take off in its first decade, but in 1957, Mr. Perry demonstrated its effectiveness in the "fished-out" Lake Marie near Chicago. When he pulled out fish after fish, the *Chicago Tribune* and others published feature stories. As you can see, Perry was more focused on lure and technique whereas Jason Lucas was more focused on tackle and technique.

Lucas was not a bad guy. His reputation as a pill probably stemmed from the fact that he was extremely opinionated, and never afraid to put his opinion in print. I remember when the double-haul technique used in fly-fishing was coming on the scene. Lucas wrote that the technique was nothing but a tournament caster's trick and that it would never find a place in fly-fishing technique. Of course it's one of the most important casting techniques our sport has today. He was wrong on that one, but he was right on many more things.

My correspondence with Jason Lucas turned my fishing around, particularly in terms of fishing with lures. But as far as fly-fishing is concerned, I was about to make an acquaintance that would inexorably change my life.

In 1947, I met Joe Brooks. At the time, Joe was an outdoor writer from Baltimore. Just after World War II he started writing about fishing in the United States and Canada for *Outdoor Life* magazine. Many of the seven million men just home from the war eagerly read everything he wrote and he quickly became the best-known outdoor writer in America, as well as a very popular author and one of the most authoritative all-around figures in the outdoors business.

Luckily for me, Joe would become my friend and mentor. He helped me enormously in my evolution from Fort Detrick bacteria farmer to outdoor writer and teacher. I will never be able to express my appreciation for all he did for me. He was not only a superb outdoorsman and a prolific writer but also an ethical and considerate guy. He instilled in me, at a relatively young age, the tenets by which I've since tried to live my life: love and respect for the outdoors, respect and empathy for your reader, honesty and integrity in whatever you do. Whenever I have been able to help up-and-coming outdoor writers and instructors I always tell them what Joe Brooks taught me more than half a century ago: there are two kinds of outdoor experts—those who display their knowledge and those who share it, and there is a world of difference.

Joe—at 6-feet-plus—was an imposing, athletic figure (few know that he actually passed on an opportunity to pitch in the major leagues). He wasn't haughty at all, but he commanded respect. When I met him he was still writing primarily for the Towson, Maryland–based *County Paper*. It was a local newspaper, but he was beginning to become well known around the country. Joe was a terrific guy. He was a Maryland native and had spent many years in his family's insurance business. Unfortunately, he also had his struggles with the bottle. Eventually his family tossed him out of the business over his drinking. That's when he started writing a column for the *County Paper*. When World War II ended he was working at the paper, and he told his boss, Fen Keyser, "Don't pay me, because if you do I'll just drink it up." So Fen held on to the money for him. While Joe was working for Fen, a woman from Canada who had been hired to promote fishing up there invited Joe on a PR trip. The idea was to get influential fishing writers to see how great the fishing was up there.

I can tell you that in those days there was some truly incredible fishing in Canada. Once you drove north of Montreal, there were only dirt roads. I was up there a few times in the late 1950s. We'd just drive around and rent a boat when we came to a nice stream or lake.

When Joe got to Canada, a girl named Mary showed him around. Eventually they fell in love and got married. And from the day he met Mary until the day he died, Joe never drank another drop. General George Patton used to say that the only way for a real soldier to die is from the last bullet of the last battle of the last war. Well, Joe died the fisherman's equivalent. In 1972 he was in Paradise Valley, Montana, fishing for trout. He passed out on the river and never regained consciousness. What a way to go: in a beautiful place, doing the thing you love most.

One day, after reading a few articles that had appeared about me in other local papers and in *Maryland Conservationist* magazine, Joe called me and said that he'd heard I was the "hottest bass fisherman in the state," and then asked if I might take him fishing. I told him I wasn't so sure about my status in the state, but gladly offered to take him out in my canoe.

I decided that we would fish the Potomac, downstream from Harpers Ferry. On the appointed day, as I brought the canoe down to the riverbank, I noticed Joe was stringing up a bamboo rod with a fly reel. Up to that point in my life the only person I had ever seen use a fly rod in all of central Maryland was Old Sam Gardner. Sam used a short (7-foot) bamboo rod to catch little trout throughout the Blue Ridge. I don't think he ever cast more than about 20 feet. Amazing as Sam was, and as little as I knew about fly-fishing at the time, I was certain it would take far more skill to fly-fish the broad, open waters of the Potomac. I respectfully said, "Joe, I have an extra plug-casting reel if you'd like to use one."

Joe replied quietly, "Thanks, but let me just try this one for a while."

There was a spare, I reassured him, in the event that he decided to use it later on.

We got into the canoe. There was at least a ten- to twelve-mile-an-hour breeze rippling the surface that day. And even though I was plug casting and I had the local knowledge, Joe caught as many fish as I did in the morning. That impressed the hell out of me. It's rare that a decent fisherman will get out-fished on his own turf. The real revelation came after lunch. We were sitting on a limestone ledge that ran out into the river. The rock face sloped upstream. After finishing his lunch, Joe picked up his fly rod and walked to the upstream side of the rock. There were a lot of little dimples in the water, ripples that I thought had been made by minnows (I now know they were caused by fish rising to the surface). Joe stripped off some line and dropped it to the rock at his feet. I looked down and I was amazed at the diameter of his line. You have to remember that in 1947 spinning tackle was just coming into this country. Most of us that fished hard in freshwater used 6- to 10-pound test braided silk line, which was pretty thin. Well, he was using this monster rope-looking fly line and I thought, *Good God*.

Joe tied on a little streamer, which I now know is called a Black Ghost. He began to false cast and I was absolutely entranced. I didn't know then that every September armies of ants try to fly across the Potomac and millions of them fail and fall in the water. This migration is an annual windfall to local bass that just love to eat ants. Well, Joe dropped the Black Ghost fly into the middle of one of those "minnow dimples" and immediately hooked a smallmouth bass. He proceeded to do this over and over and over, about eight times. He caught a fish after about every two casts. It was like picking apples from a tree. I was awestruck by his skill and by this advanced form of fishing. I remember thinking, *I've got to have me some of this*.

The very next day I drove my Model A Ford to Baltimore, no mean feat in those days. Back then it took about two hours, today it's a forty-five-minute hop. I met Joe at Tochterman's Sporting Goods Store (still operated today by third-generation Tony Tochterman) and paid for the tackle that Joe handpicked for me. It included a green 9-weight South Bend fiberglass rod (fiberglass was just coming out on the market as an affordable alternative to bamboo); a Pflueger Medalist fly reel (which I still have); and Cortland GAF fly line. In those days fly lines weren't numbered. Instead, they had letter designations, which were very confusing. The GAF line I bought that day would be equivalent to one of today's No. 9 fly lines.

Joe took me to nearby Herring Run Park and gave me a fly-casting lesson, preaching the old-fashioned 10-to-2 o'clock technique. He left town the next day (I wondered if I was really *that* bad!). He left to start a new job running the MET tournament in Miami, Florida. At the time, the MET (officially known as the Metropolitan South Florida Tournament) was the largest fishing tournament in the world. After Joe left town, Tom McNally, another respected outdoor writer from Baltimore, also chipped in with some lessons. He reinforced the conventional trout casting method—10-to-2 o'clock and back—and I went nuts over it.

I was completely hooked, determined to master this exciting new sport, but almost as soon as I got started with my new tackle and my freshly learned technique, the tinkerer in me took over. I began to look for ways to improve upon on the 10-to-2 technique. For instance, I started fly-fishing the Potomac with longer casts because I learned quickly that the longer I kept the fly in the water the more fish I caught. Gradually I got away from the old 10-to-2 o'clock motion that Joe and Tom had taught me (and which had been the only method taught in this country for the last hundred years or so) and began to experiment with the method I've been teaching for the last fifty years. I learned that while the 10-to-2 method worked well on small streams, it *only* worked on small streams. It offered no versatility. Several years later I wrote a piece on the topic for *Outdoor Life*. In it I suggested a longer back cast. The piece, illustrated by the renowned Nat Smith, was one of the major turning points in my evolution as an outdoor writer. More on all that later.

Around the time I met Joe, I had a growing family with growing expenses and I wasn't exactly breaking the bank at Fort Detrick, so I supplemented my income. I trapped muskrat and mink, and, at about two dollars a hide, I was doing pretty well. I trapped a few foxes, but they were really hard to catch, very sharp animals. I also tied flies for a place called E. K. Tryon, a hardware store up in Philadelphia. There really weren't many fishing shops in those days. So throughout the 1930s, '40s and even '50s, people went to hardware stores for their fishing tackle. Tryon had a big hardware catalog and they sold a lot of hunting equipment and fishing tackle as well. I met one of the Tryon reps as he came through town. When he found out that I tied flies, he told me that they were having a hard time getting flies and so I started tying for them. I had a love-hate relationship with that job. I was tying dozens of beautiful flies—most with inferior neck feathers from India and China—none of which I was going to be able to fish. That was a bitter pill to swallow, but the little money I got for the work softened the blow.

The tackle we used in the years after World War II was pretty primitive by today's standards. Most fisherman used level-wind plug-casting reels, which cost between two and five dollars, a good portion of most guys' weekly pay back then. In addition to being expensive, these reels required an educated thumb; there were no magnetic or centrifugal brakes and backlashes were common. Machine tolerances were nonexistent, so the spools were lined on either side by gaps that devoured fishing line and caused constant jams. We all carried screwdrivers back then for the express purpose of taking apart the reels, untangling the line, and putting everything back together.

It's hard to believe, but the lines themselves were made of braided silk.

Wizened fisherman of the era will never forget the tedium of having to remove the silk line from the reel after each day of fishing in order to dry out the silk (If a wet silk line was left on a reel for several days it would simply rot. This went for silk fly line of the era as well). In fact, many of us used wooden line dryers for that purpose. It was not until monofilament line arrived on the scene in the late 1940s that we could finally do away with this headache. Still, while early monofilament may have been more durable, it was wiry and it tended to backlash badly. Also, because of its stiffness, it did not cast as well as braided silk, but it was cheaper and that pretty much made it our preference.

The few fly fishermen of the time were also using gut leaders. These things were so brittle that they actually had to be presoaked before use. I can remember that all of us back then had these little aluminum boxes with felt padding inside. What we'd do is soak the felt pads in water and then place the coiled gut leaders between the pads to soften them up.

The rods themselves were, more often than not, bamboo. Everybody used them. Today I meet a lot of fisherman who have a bamboo rod passed down by their dad or granddad. Each of them is convinced it's a rare artifact from a bygone era. I don't have the heart to tell all these folks that bamboo rods (whether fly-fishing, saltwater, or plug casting) are extremely common. I'd estimate that 90 percent of the bamboo rods out there today have no meaningful value beyond the sentimental. Of course, how could you put a price on fishing with your granddaddy's rod?

By the late 1940s, however, bamboo was becoming obsolete. Rod makers began to offer metal rods as an alternative. For plug rods I had a preference for the square steel ones produced by American Fork and Hoe Company. One of the best and most expensive rods on the market at that time was made of beryllium copper. Perhaps the worst fly rod ever manufactured was an old steel telescoping model. It was so limber that when fully extended it would sag toward the ground. A cast of more then twenty-five feet was virtually impossible.

It was 1947 or 1948 when the first spinning reels came to the United States. That doesn't mean that that was when spinning reels were invented. Far from it. About twelve years ago in New Zealand I saw a collection of French spinning reels that were manufactured in the late 1800s. It was 1947 or 1948 until these spinning reels were being imported in large quantities to the United States. My first such reel was a French-made Bache Brown. At first I used braided line, and I am here to tell you it was horrible. Soon afterward I switched to the new wiry, stiff Dupont monofilament, which was only slightly better, however it did allow me to cast lighter lures. I can remember magazine articles appearing at the time full of predictions about the demise of the plug-casting reel. So-called experts were convinced that in the future the only kind of fishing we would be doing is spinning. They said that with the new spinning reels backlashes would be a thing of the past, but of course they never mentioned the horrid tangles that awaited spinners, tangles that were often more maddening than plug-reel backlashes. Spinning did ultimately prove itself superior when it came to throwing light lures or small bait up to a distance of about 65 feet. For longer distances, however, and especially with lures weighing a ½-ounce or more, plug casting remained the way to go.

Even fraught with early problems, spinning reels would eventually alter the course of fishing history like no other advancement before or since. By the 1950s, many would-be fishermen had decided that plug casting was simply too difficult to master, so they turned their backs on the sport. When better mass-produced spinning equipment came along, it gave millions of people an easy, inexpensive way to enjoy fishing. Those Zebco closed-face spinning reels did more for the sport of fishing than any other product in my lifetime. Beyond bringing millions of kids and adults into fishing, the spinning reel also laid a good foundation for the future fly fisherman. As spin casters became more proficient, many of them evolved to fly rods.

I vividly remember my old Bache Brown spinner. Unfortunately, I also remember its demise. I had saved up for months in order to afford it and when I got it I was tickled with it. At the time, I was working the four p.m.-to-midnight shift at Fort Detrick. One day I disassembled the reel to clean it only to realize that it was nearly four o'clock and time for work. I placed all the parts in a small paper bag and set it aside. As Ev prepared to put out the garbage that night, she (understandably) assumed that the crumpled brown bag was trash. The reel was lost forever.

Even with technological advances in the sport, fly-fishing was rare in the United States well into the 1950s. At that time I only knew of three places in the entire country where you could actually buy fly-tying materials: Reed Tackle in New Jersey; E. Hille's in Pennsylvania; and Herter's in Wisconsin. The first two were pretty expensive, but their materials were truly first-rate. Herter's was much less expensive and, accordingly, the quality of the materials was spotty. Over time, however, Herter's became a gigantic force in the American fishing industry. I bought some of my earliest fly rods and spinning rod blanks and components from them. They supplied me with genuine junglecock necks for just a few dollars, good English hooks, all sorts of hair and fur materials. The problem with Herter's was that everything was always on back order and you never knew when you'd actually get them. Herter's really blew it. Although they did become the country's leading supplier, they were done in by their own poor service and inconsistent quality. I heard recently that the company is making a comeback. I wish them well.

It wasn't simply reel and lure technology that was blossoming in the postwar years. Rod technology was advancing by leaps and bounds. Word had gotten out that a rod maker in California was coming onto the scene with fiberglass rods. Bob Ditchburn of Gettysburg, Pennsylvania, was one of the country's finest gunsmiths and a wonderful fishing buddy of mine, and he had bought an early Conolon fiberglass rod blank and built a plug-casting rod for ¼- and ⅓-ounce plugs. I picked it up and simply couldn't believe how light it was compared to my square, steel casting rod. I immediately contacted Conolon and bought a rod just like Bob's. When I started fishing with that newfangled fiberglass rod, the guys in Frederick told me, "You just wait 'til it gets cold, Lefty. That 'glass' is gonna snap like you wouldn't believe." It seems quaint now, but they thought of fiberglass like the glass you'd find in a window. This new equipment was very modern and mysterious.

I began to fly-fish Lander, on the Potomac River, and our general area using popping bugs and some of the conventional streamers of the day. In retrospect, these were pretty crude flies, but you have to bear in mind that virtually no one was using fly tackle in those days. I don't think that the smallmouth bass in my area or anywhere in the country had ever seen a popper or a fly. In fact, as crazy as this may sound, back then a lot of people thought fly-fishing wouldn't work for bass. But I was catching a lot of fish. Many times I arrived at the dock with the full limit of ten bass, many of them better than 2 pounds. (Nowadays I catch and release, but back then I actually kept the fish just to prove to doubters that I could actually catch them on fly.) When bystanders would see my haul they would inevitably ask what kind of tackle I was using. When I told them it was fly tackle—and even when I showed them that the only tackle I had in the boat was fly rod, fly reel, fly line, and flies—they refused to believe me. "Come on," one guy said to me, "I know you caught those bass on hellgrammites."

Same thing happened in the Chesapeake Bay. Several of us began to catch striped bass on fly there and when we'd write about it, people would call us liars and say, "You can't catch saltwater fish with a fly rod." The resistance against it was astounding.

It was also around this time, the mid-1950s, that Jim Green revolutionized fishing-rod technology when he invented the sleeve-type ferrule now used virtually all over the world. Prior to Jim's ingenious idea, all rods were made on a mandrel and cut into one or two pieces with male and female ferrules. The pieces were constantly getting stuck together or they'd wear down and come loose, often to the point that they would separate in mid-cast. Jim had a great idea, but didn't know anyone in the manufacturing business. He made an acquaintance of Phil Clock, who at the time was making seven-strand braided fishing wire. Phil immediately saw the value in Jim's sleeve ferrule concept. Jim and Phil flew to Bainbridge Island to meet with Don Green (no relation), who was then building Grizzly brand rods, which at that time were the finest fiberglass rods in the business. Don was a gifted engineer and he was contracted to build the first batch of fiberglass rods using Jim's ferrule design. The new rod line was dubbed Fenwick and for many years they set the standard for all sorts of rods, from fly-fishing to surfcasting to ultralight spinning. Jim eventually moved to Bainbridge to assist in their manufacture. They ended up being an incredibly productive duo. As Don once told me, "I taught Jim how to make fly rods and he taught me how to fly cast." Don built every Fenwick rod for years, and unlike so many thriving business partnerships, the duo remained friends for life. I acted as a spokesperson for Fenwick for decades. Phil once told me that I was most responsible for giving Fenwick a foothold in the Midwestern and Eastern markets.

After Fenwick went through a series of new owners, Don eventually dissociated himself from the company and, in 1980, began his own company, Sage rods. They are widely regarded as the finest fly rods ever made. I remained associated with Fenwick until Don moved on. Once he started Sage, I stayed with him there until 2003. I also began to do some work for Scientific Anglers in the late 1950s and am still associated with the company today.

There's a bittersweet end to what would seem to be one man's fishing industry fairy tale. Jim Green never filed for a patent for his revolutionary ferrule design. Phil, looking out for Jim, ultimately filed for a patent, but died before such a protection was granted. In the end, Jim Green, a man who revolutionized the global fishing scene, got nothing more than a new job in Bainbridge Island for his creation.

CHAPTER 7
BUGS CROSS AND THE INCREDIBLE SHRINKING LURE

As I mentioned, I used to fish at a place on the Potomac called Lander. It's about forty miles north of D.C. There was an old guy named Bugs Cross who had a landing there and we used to rent a boat from him.

A little history: In the middle part of the 1800s, the C&O (Chesapeake and Ohio) Canal ran from Washington to Cumberland, 135 miles, along the Potomac River. It ran from the mountainous terrain of western Maryland to the sea-level locale of Washington, D.C. Primarily, the canal transported coal, but it ferried the basics such as food and clothing along that route, as well.

Bugs Cross was born on one of the canal boats and became a lock operator. When most shipping had been transferred to the railroad, the U.S. government bought and shut down the canal, but grandfathered the lockkeepers, allowing them to live rent-free in their canal-side homes until their deaths.

Bugs lived with his wife at the Lander, Maryland, lock, which used to be a tremendous place to fish for bass, catfish, carp, all that stuff. Bugs had a place about two hundred yards up from the shoreline and another little cabin right on the water that he used for his business. While these places gave him a roof over his head, once the canal shut down he was without income. So Bugs would dip minnows out of the river and sell them as bait, or he'd rent you a boat. I use the term "boat" loosely. I'm not sure the Coast Guard would have been too keen on Bugs's operation. In addition to leasing out boats, he also maintained boats for other people and stored them in the winter.

A note about these old riverboats: it really wasn't until the 1950s that outboards became popular, so up until then everybody poled these riverboats. Back then, most people were building their own boats. They were pretty unique, very simple, reliable, and efficient. They measured about 38 inches wide and anywhere from 14 to 16 feet long. In those days the two sides were made of cypress boards 14 inches wide and 1-inch thick and there was not a knot in them. What you did is you took the cypress boards and put them on sawhorses, tied ropes around the ends, and bent them into their basic boat shape. Then you put the floor in, regular old tongue-and-groove oak. Oak swells up when it gets wet, and if you put the oak slats too closely together, they would split from the force put forth by the swelling. So what we would do is take dimes and put them between the tongue-and-groove slats to make sure we were one dime's width short of final closure. Then when you put the boat in the water and the oak swelled, everything fit perfect. Both ends of these boats came up out of the water. The reason for that is that when you poled them they would not create drag. These were heavy boats, too. That's not a good thing when you are carrying the boat to the shore, but when you're poling, especially when you're poling a long distance, heavier is much better. Sure, aluminum canoes are light, but when you stop poling a light boat it immediately stops moving. For short little hops in a pond, that's good, but if you're going to cover a long distance you'd rather have a heavy boat that is capable of building and sustaining momentum.

By the mid-'50s, I was about thirty and had known Bugs for many years. At that time I was working at Fort Detrick as it transitioned from war to peacetime. One day, after long, heavy rains, a buddy named Kit Nelson and I came across Bugs sitting on a log, crying. His business had been washed away in the flood and now he had no way to make money. It dawned on us that they were tearing down the military barracks at Detrick, so Kit used a little bit of cunning and somehow got us access to materials—lumber, siding, roofing shingles, everything. All things that would've been thrown away. We took it all over to Bugs's place, and built a little house that lasted him a good, many years.

Bugs was a little guy, maybe five-foot-two. I bet he didn't weigh 120 pounds. At the end of the day when he walked from the waterside cabin to the house, he had to cross the lock, which had a bridge with no sides. Well, he used to get to drinking a little, and one night as he was crossing the bridge, he fell off. Three or four days later I went up there to fish and I saw him lying on his bunk. The whole side of his face was green; he'd broken his jaw. I wanted to take him into a doctor, but he wouldn't hear of it, and he suffered for about six weeks with it. Finally it healed itself. He was one tough rascal.

Bugs was a walking, talking repository of the area's history. He would tell us old stories about the glory days of the canal. He actually lived on the canal boat, which was both a home and means of transport. He had all kinds of fascinating stories about surviving floods and things like that, but he was also a keen observer of the river. Of course, he fished it, too, and was an endless source of tips. He'd tell me where to fish and when to fish, and over time I learned a lot about fishing the Potomac from him.

In those days Lander was full of bait. Hellgrammites, crayfish, and minnows were abundant. All that bait used to draw big smallmouth bass. It was not at all unusual for a good angler to catch several 3- or 4-pound smallmouth in a day. In the midst of this natural bait buffet, Bugs once gave me a tiny 3/8-ounce lure. It was only about as big around and as long as your little finger. He'd found it on a log that had been floating down the river. Somebody had apparently hooked the log and lost the lure. Bugs let me borrow it, with the emphasis on borrow, and I couldn't believe how many fish I caught with that thing. I immediately started scouring all the catalogs for a lure whose name and maker I didn't even know. My buddies did the same. We went nuts trying to find one like it. There was no Internet back then so I pored over every magazine, book, and catalog I could find.

Finally, I stumbled onto a Montgomery Ward catalog and found the Holy Grail: the "Miracle Minnow" as it was called, was manufactured by Wright & McGill. At 89 cents apiece, I could barely afford one, but I promptly ordered a dozen in a rainbow assortment of colors. I told my fishing buddies about my discovery and for the next few years we really pillaged. We caught untold numbers of smallmouth bass, three- and four-pounders, all over the Potomac, Susquehanna, and Shenandoah Rivers. Over time, of course, we began to see a decrease in their effectiveness. Amazingly enough, just five years later the Miracle Minnow was far from the Holy Grail, but just another reliable lure. In fact, about twenty years after that realization, I was doing some consulting work for Wright & McGill. They had long since stopped making the Miracle Minnow. In fact, they were shutting down a plant when a guy asked me, "Lefty, is there anything here in the plant you want?"

"Yeah," I said, "I'll take some of them leftover Miracle Minnows." I brought them back home and must have swam them through ninety miles of water and never got a single strike.

After the Miracle Minnow, we went through a series of other must-have lures. The first was the Mepps Spinner. For a short but memorable period of time, whenever you threw a Mepps Spinner in the water everything nearby wanted a bite. Eventually, it too became just another lure in the tackle box. Some old-timers may recall that the next hot lure was the Floppy, a rubbery minnow-like lure from France. That was followed in succession by the Rapala and the Slug-O and the Gizit tube lure. All of these "sure things" saw their heydays come and go. The same thing has happened over time with flies.

For years all we ever needed if we wanted to catch bass on a fly rod was a popping bug. Then the Clouser Minnow was unbelievably productive. In fact, the Clouser Minnow has probably been the most popular fly designed in the last fifteen years. It's still useful in both fresh and salt water and appropriate for virtually any type of fish. It offers size flexibility; that is, it can be effective at 10 inches long or 1 inch long. By adjusting the weight of the eyes you can customize the swimming depth of the fly. I have to date caught eighty-six species of fish on versions of that lure, about a third of which were caught using a combination of either chartreuse and yellow or chartreuse and white on the wing (Not surprising, really. There's an old saying among fishermen: If it ain't chartreuse it ain't no use).

As popular as the Clouser has proven, I've found that in areas where this lure is heavily utilized its appeal to bass is also fading. For years, the best fly pattern for tarpon in the Florida Keys has been the Keys-style tarpon fly, dressed with a few short, splayed wing feathers and a collar. Today's tarpon are increasingly refusing this design and smart anglers are relying on other patterns.

I'm baffled by this phenomenon of obsolescence. Some observers have theorized that fish adapt over time; that they eventually become wise to the lure and begin to avoid it. I don't think so. Take that Miracle Minnow. That thing was virtually off the market for thirty years. How would any of today's fish know to avoid it? I'm no scientist and don't profess to know anything about genetics, but I conclude that the information about these lures is somehow passed from generation to generation. How else would a species of fish that hasn't even seen a certain lure in four or five generations know that it shouldn't be fooling with that lure? It's a mystery of fishing that no one has ever been able to solve.

Chapter 8
The Writing Life

I WAS BECOMING A DECENT fisherman and over time my reputation as an angler began to spread around central Maryland. With more and more frequency, my hauls were finding their way into local newspapers and the odd fishing publication. Back then I fished quite often with Henry Decker, who edited the local paper, *The Frederick News & Post* (the same paper that chronicled our poverty each Christmas). One day in 1951 Henry surprised me by asking if I would be interested in writing an outdoor column for the paper.

I was stunned. As I explained earlier, I had not done very well in English as a student and I never attended college. I told Henry that I was more than a little uncertain about my writing ability. His reply was, "Lefty, you can learn to write well in a year or less, but it takes thousands of hours to become a knowledgeable outdoorsman. I'll help you with the writing. Don't worry about that."

Henry was right. If you look back at all the really great writers of the 1950s and 1960s—the top fishing and fly-fishing writers—they were all outdoorsmen first. You had guys like Charlie Waterman, Joe Brooks, Al McLane, Nelson Bryant. Ted Trueblood was another one. These were all solid outdoor guys *first* who were *then* coaxed into writing. Today most aspiring outdoor writers do it backward. They take journalism courses and then go out and try to learn to hunt and fish. That's an entirely different creature.

It's hard to believe now, but in 1951 there was not a very big market for outdoor writing. At that time in the United States there were only four magazines on fishing and hunting: *Outdoor Life*, *Field & Stream*, *Sports Afield*, and the little-read *Fur-Fish-Game* out of Nebraska. There probably weren't ten outdoor newspaper columnists in the country; New York, Miami, Chicago, Los Angeles, and Pittsburgh were the only ones I was aware of. Anyway, Henry talked me into doing this local column called "Maryland Afield."

From day one, I concentrated on "how-to" and "where-to" journalism. I always favored how-to stuff because it was popular right from the very beginning. In fact, one of my earlier magazine stories was a tip from an old friend of mine named Herman Dailey. He was one of the black kids from the neighborhood. I stopped him on the street one day and said, "Herman, I believe you catch more carp than just about anybody else in town."

He said, "That's right."

I said, "Well, I'd like to write a story about that in my new column. What are you doing? What's your secret?"

Herman looked all around and said in a conspiratorial whisper, "I'm putting strawberry Jell-O in my carp dough."

Carp dough is cornmeal and flour and other stuff mixed together and cooked into a gummy mess. The stickiness is helpful because it keeps the bait on the hook when you cast it out. I couldn't believe ol' Herman. I mean, no one had ever heard of putting Jell-O in carp dough.

About a week later I saw Herman on the corner. He was still catching more carp than anybody else, so I said, "I really would like to write about that strawberry Jell-O."

I eventually sold that story to *Sports Afield* magazine. The fact of the matter is that the strawberry Jell-O trick works like a charm. To this day I use it all the time (refer to page 176 for recipe).

It seemed then (and now) that readers simply couldn't get enough of this kind of information. Clearly there had been an untapped demand because Henry Decker quickly upped me to two newspaper columns a week. Not long after I started with Henry, other papers in Maryland and Virginia contacted me about doing columns for them. By the mid-1950s I was writing several outdoor columns for different papers in Towson (once a week), Rockville (once a week), Frederick (twice a week), and Montgomery County, Maryland (once a week). When Jack Davis, the ex-AP executive, took over the *Winchester (Va.) Star*, he had me do a whole page for him once a week. This was not a syndication deal in which one column ran in all of these different papers. These were original works, every column, every paper, every day.

Although I have since become best known for writing about fishing, back then I had a very broad canvas and a surprisingly diverse audience. These columns covered a broad range of outdoor topics, from hunting and fishing to how orchid seeds migrate in the jet stream; how an outdoorsman, studying the way cockleburs attached to his pants, was inspired to invent Velcro. (The guy—his last name was actually Velcro—patented his idea and couldn't get anybody interested in buying his product. After the patent expired clothing makers all over the world picked it up. He never made a penny.) In another column I'd write about why trees on one side of a hill would have richer fall colors than the same species of tree on the other side (the difference is not in the trees themselves, but in the PH of the soil). I used to write columns about birds—how to identify them, what to feed them—and I'd get letters from little old ladies who planned their whole day around their bird feeding. Here are a few samples:

Bird Houses

With the coming of spring, millions of songbirds will be winging their way back to Maryland to take up housekeeping. Build them a proper birdhouse and place it near your home. You'll be surprised at the endless hours of enjoyment you'll receive by watching the birds raise their young.

Make the house with the idea that it is for a specific bird. Unless the house is made the correct size, you may have some nuisance birds such as the starling or English sparrow residing there.

The most critical factor in birdhouse construction is the size of the entrance hole. One too big or too small will discourage certain desirable birds from nesting there.

(The article went on to describe materials, disease prevention, and placement before we moved on to fishing.)

Fish Are Biting

Despite cold weather, high and muddy rivers, and rain, many local fishermen have been making fine catches. The Potomac and some of the smaller creeks have been the most rewarding spots. The Monocacy hasn't been too kind to anglers.

Catfish and yellow suckers (sometimes called smoothscales) and bluegills are the three types of fish most anglers are hooking. John Fox, local bait dealer, says he is selling many night crawlers and minnows. Some of his customers have reported taking many catfish on minnows.

Fox said he knew of seven smallmouth bass that had been caught since the season opened on January 1. One of these bass weighed more than two pounds. All were taken on minnows or worms.

. . . Ed Fox, an excellent bait fisherman, has been catching yellow suckers from local creeks. This fishing is usually best after a rain. The water washes food into the creeks and the suckers feed greedily. During this time an angler using small worms can often take a stringer of these delicious fish.

Typically these columns ended with a question about fishing rules entitled "It's The Law" or some upcoming event on the outdoor calendar. Typical of these entries were:

It's The Law

QUESTION: Can two or more fishermen have their minnows in the same bucket?

ANSWER: Yes, each man may have thirty-five (35) minnows in the same container

Boat License

Don't forget, the boat license law goes into effect on July 3. If you have an outboard more than seven-and-a-half horsepower, you must secure a license from the Tidewater Fishery Commission, Annapolis. The fee is six dollars for three years.

On top of my writing schedule I was also working at my real job at Ft. Detrick five days a week (In fact, I would keep that job from 1948 until 1964). It was a full plate. Fortunately, in my younger days—up until I was about seventy—I never really needed much sleep. I functioned very well on about five hours a night. That's because back in the days when I was doing shift work I learned the value of power naps. I could snooze for fifteen minutes and wake up fully rested and refreshed. While fishing, I could lie down in the bottom of a canoe and catch a few Zs while a buddy paddled to our spot. That quick little nap would be as helpful to me as a couple hours of sleep for most people. In fact, a few years back a research sleep therapist at Johns Hopkins told me that if you fall asleep for less than twenty minutes you wake up alert and refreshed, but if a person sleeps for more than twenty minutes you actually awake groggy because the longer you sleep the more thoroughly your body shuts down and the harder it is to ratchet the body up. Even today I would say I average about three ten-to-fifteen-minute naps per day.

My journalistic beginnings were as humble as they were busy. My first typewriter—a used, fifteen-dollar Royal—was considered an antique when I bought it. My office was a 4-by-8-foot kitchen pantry that had a 60-watt light bulb dangling from two strands of wire, but I was proud of it. After moving to two columns a week for Henry, he and I quickly realized that the next stage in the development of this column was photography that would complement and illustrate the text. Popular as my column was, the newspaper wasn't going to hire a photographer for my pieces, so I set out to learn photography. Rolfe Castleman, the photographer for the *News & Post*, became my mentor. Although Rolfe was working for a small-circulation paper, he was way ahead of his time. The standard newspaper camera of the day was the Graflex, the big bulky cameras you see in the old movies, the ones with the massive flashbulbs popping off. The more advanced photographers were using 2-1/2-inch twin-lens reflex cameras such as the Rolliflex. This was a model where you looked down through the viewfinder through one lens. The lens below it actually took the picture.

Rolfe was the first newspaperman I knew who used a 35mm camera. Back then critics said the 35mm negative was too small, but while the prints weren't quite as sharp as those taken with bigger cameras, they were more than good enough for newspaper work.

My first camera was a big investment. Ev and I drove our Model A more than an hour to downtown Washington, D.C., where I paid the enormous sum of $29 for a twin-lens reflex camera. That was a lot of money back then, but I only used it for about a year until Rolfe convinced me to upgrade to a 35mm. Eager to improve, I listened to everything Rolfe said, and in no time I was producing photos worthy of publication for my columns.

Having just a basic knowledge of photography gave me a real leg up when it came to chronicling the outdoors. It's hard to believe, but as recently as the 1950s, outdoor magazines would hire a writer to do a story, say, on Mexican sailfishing. Well, the writer would go to Mexico, write his story, send it in, and then the magazine would hire a painter to illustrate the story. With Rolfe's help I had become handy enough with a camera that I could shoot the photographs while I was on location. Because I had access to the *News and Post's* darkroom and developing paper, I could produce ten or twenty professional-quality prints or slides along with my article. I saved the magazine money and time, and the reader got a much more realistic (if less romantic) depiction of the setting and the action.

More important than the money, my devotion to photography gave me a lifelong passion and hobby. Over the years I've come to enjoy photography as much as I do fishing. For several years I taught outdoor and advanced nature photography for the National Wildlife Federation. I also served as L.L. Bean's photo consultant. In fact, of all the books

I've written, I think the two best have been the photo-heavy *Presenting The Fly* and the *L.L. Bean Guide to Outdoor Photography*. I'm still an avid student of photography. In addition to the casting demonstrations I regularly conduct at outdoor shows around the country, I also offer clinics on shooting better pictures. Here are a couple of basics that I've picked up from a lifetime of shooting for magazines and books:

The first rule of good photography is this: Most of what you shoot you ought to just throw away. If a shot was out of focus when it was taken it's *always* going to be out of focus. Just throw the darn thing away.

The difference between real photographers and frustrated photographers is that the pros actually read the owner's manual.

Cameras are like guns. If you can't shoot well with the $200 model, you're not going to shoot any better with the $5,000 model.

Don't take pictures of people with their sunglasses on, they look like raccoons. Unfortunately, squinting doesn't look much better, so I have a trick for you. Before you shoot that picture of your buddy who just caught his first tarpon, have him take his glasses off. Now, instead of having him squint through his moment in history, have him look down and close his eyes. Focus the camera on the top of his head. When you're ready to shoot, tell him to look up. The subject will have about three seconds to smile without squinting before the sun hits the eyes.

I like candid shots to look candid, not posed. To do that, rather than simply ask my subjects to smile, I ask them to talk to me. Sounds crazy, but you'll be amazed at how that little suggestion not only relaxes the subject but also brings personality back into their face and eyes. Same thing goes when having someone pose for a "casting" shot versus catching someone in the act of casting. The latter works much better.

The tripod is your friend. Nobody wants to drag a tripod around all day, but they make you slow down, which helps you consider and compose the shot. This inevitably leads to better photographs.

Finally, frame and focus your photographs so that only the things you want in the photo are in the photo. If the fish is the star of the shot, don't have a lot of background stuff that will detract from it.

As busy as I was with newspaper work, I began to gravitate into magazines as well. The first story I ever sold was a piece for *The Pennsylvania Game News*. The topic was the little-known practice of hunting squirrels from a canoe. At that time (and even today) very few people had heard of it. At dawn squirrels work riverbanks pretty aggressively. So we'd get up early in the morning, get into a canoe on a wide section of river, maybe fifty yards wide, and within a couple of hours two guys could bag a dozen or so squirrels. It was great fun. Not long afterward I did a companion piece on duck hunting from canoes. I put chicken wire on the bow and stern of a canoe and covered the chicken wire with oak branches (oaks keep their leaves in the winter). In addition to camouflaging the canoe, I put seats on the floor of the canoe so my body would be out of sight. When a river gets about four or five feet above usual, ducks simply can't manage the rushing current in the middle of the waterway, so they tend to migrate out to the riverbanks. We would work the banks and get our eight-duck limit almost every time we went out.

About this time, the mid-1950s, I began to realize that most outdoor writers (myself included) had unparalleled knowledge of their own backyards, but had very limited knowledge about hunting and fishing across the country and even less so outside the United States. If a guy was from Ohio he didn't know anything about, say, hunting grouse in South Dakota or where to find striped bass on Cape Cod. The obvious reason was that most writers worked on limited budgets and had never traveled much beyond their home state or region. People traveled more as the 1950s wore on, and I got the bright idea to put together hunting, fishing, and wildlife photography clinics and slide shows all over the country. I figured I could kill a few birds with one stone. While having my travel expenses and a modest fee paid by my hosts at fishing clubs and outdoor groups around the country, I could lecture on wildlife in other areas. In each new area I visited I would inevitably meet and/or fish with the most knowledgeable locals. I learned a lot of what I now know about the outdoors by doing theses slide show trips, and I never could have afforded these eye-opening journeys had they not been underwritten by someone else.

I started promoting these clinics to fishing clubs and outdoors clubs and Chambers of Commerce. As you might suspect, if a guy goes into a fishing club, gets up and lectures on techniques related to their type of fishing, the best two or three guys in the club are undoubtedly going to say, "That sunuvabitch ain't as good as me. I'm gonna show him something." They'd want to drag me out to their favorite spot and show me up. I'd end up staying two or three extra days, and while they were showing me up, I was also creating my own mental atlas of the best fishing locations, types of fish and tackle, and so on, from the best guys in the area.

Using this method, I was ultimately able to fish in each of the fifty United States, Australia, South America, and every province in Canada. For a period of time, I went to Europe every year for a couple of years. Since I was working at Fort Detrick I had to find a way to cram this stuff in on weekends and during my vacation time, which at twenty-six days a year, was pretty generous. Even now, I wonder how the hell I did it. But when you're younger you can do a lot of things you wouldn't even think of doing now.

On the heels of my slide show tour, I began to appear at the odd fishing show around the country. I would do appearances for Fenwick, the first major American maker of fiberglass rods, and for Scientific Anglers, who invented the modern fly line. That's where I started doing the hotshot tricks I talked about earlier, you know, snapping cigarettes out of women's mouths and all.

With all this traveling, it occurred to me that there was a gold mine to be made writing for national magazines. Up until now I had been writing my local newspaper columns for pretty small change, about $5 a week. And whereas the *Pennsylvania Game News* was paying me $85 per article, the big national magazines such as *Sports Afield* were paying their contributors $250 or more for an illustrated story, which to a guy like me in the 1950s was a helluva lot of money.

Back then, trust was a big thing. After doing my slide shows all over the country for fisherman and angling organizations, I had come to know a lot of the magazine editors personally. They knew me, and they knew that I knew what I was doing. They also knew I took the work seriously and that I wouldn't screw with them. One of the problems that editors had back then (and still have today to some degree) is in judging the veracity of the stories they get. I mean people tell fish stories all the time over a beer, why not tell one in a magazine article? I remember *Outdoor Life* once ran a story and photo of this guy who claimed that he'd shot this beautiful mule deer at a specific location out west. Well, the magazine ran the story and the picture of this guy proudly cradling the dead mule deer. Well, some reader out west recognized the landscape and began to dispute whether the writer could have actually killed a mule deer there. Turns out the guy had killed the deer several hundred miles away and faked the pictures. The editor darn near lost his job over that.

Back when I was getting into magazines, if an editor could trust you, that was key. Another key was innovation. Magazines and their readers were (and are) desperate for ideas and techniques that haven't been tried or haven't been written about before. As a tinkerer, that was right up my alley. For instance, in the mid-1950s I did a groundbreaking piece on decoying. I got a bunch of balsa wood decoys from Herter's for two bucks apiece and hung them all around my blind. I carried with me a few pocketfuls of small gravel. I also had one decoy attached to an anchor and a special gizmo I had hooked up that allowed me to lower and raise the decoy's head into and out of the water to make it look like he was feeding. From time to time I'd toss a little gravel out on the water to make ripples in the surface. I had noticed, when flying over duck blinds in the Chesapeake Bay, that the strings tied to decoys were probably as obvious to ducks as they were to me, so I tried using monofilament instead of string. I stood up on a bridge and took one picture of four ducks with string and another picture of four with monofilament and the difference was astounding. I sold the tip and the photo to a magazine for a quick hundred bucks. Of course, all this photography meant that I would need a darkroom, so I enclosed the toilet in the basement and used the sink.

With the trust of the nation's outdoor editors, a knack for innovation and the ability to produce my own photos, I was on my way. In fact, by the early 1960s I had been presented with the opportunity to share my knowledge on the small screen as well. Dave Smith was a superb cameraman who did a lot of work for the State of Maryland's Department of Natural Resources. He did a lot of films that were designed to promote hunting and fishing or conservation across the state. Well, I worked with him on a film to promote bass fishing in the region. It was called *Bugs Over Bass*. It's hard to believe this now, but the common belief back in the late 1950s and early 1960s was that after Labor Day fish didn't bite. The goal of our film was to prove that you could catch bass year-round in Maryland, even through ice. David and I got along so well that he said he thought we ought to try to produce a television show. David would shoot it, I would be the on-air host, and all we would need was some funding.

David connected us to Bailey Goss, a longtime television announcer in Baltimore. He was one of the announcers for the old Baltimore Colts broadcasts. During his football and wrestling telecasts he did live commercials for National Bohemian Beer, a beloved local brand. Bailey helped us land "National Boh" as a sponsor for our show. Among the three of us we were able to round up enough sponsorship to actually produce *Chesapeake Outdoors*. Aside from a few prerecorded pieces of footage, the show was live, no rehearsals, no guarantees. One time we had a snake expert join us. One of his rattlers got loose on the studio floor, and ended up near my feet. We didn't see much in the way of poisonous snakes in Baltimore, so I remember struggling to keep my cool. While continuing to speak into the camera I nervously waited for our guest to bag this poisonous thing. He used a J-shape loop on a long stick to lift up the snake, and I remember wondering why the snake wouldn't just wriggle out of the loop. The trainer told me that snakes have remarkably weak eyesight and that when lifted just a few feet off the ground they lose their bearings and simply hold on for dear life. I wished I had known that before.

The show was about more than just hunting and fishing, we covered the whole outdoors. For instance, we used to have my old friend Bill Moran on the show. Bill and I grew up together as children. He went on to become the foremost knife maker in the United States. He died recently, but he used to get thousands of dollars for one of his pieces. Bill was really into American history. In the studio that day he wore one of those deerskin suits with the fringe on the sleeves. I had always assumed that the fringe was just a meaningless decoration. Not so, as the viewers and I learned from Bill. Each strand of fringe has a purpose. He went on to explain that in the olden days, when the leather got wet the fringes actually provided a capillary action, pulling the moisture out of the garment and allowing it to drip-dry.

After about three years the show had run its course. Bailey died in a car accident, and I was pretty much out of gas. I'd had it with sponsorship headaches. The thing about these shows is that the sponsors know you need them to make the show work. They know that you have to have your contract signed by late summer so that you can start getting your shows produced in time for the winter. Using all that leverage, they will delay and haggle and finagle all the way down to the last possible minute of the last possible day to get what they want out of the producers. On top of that standard frustration, we had a sponsor who had a mistress. I have to admit she was real pretty. She looked like Marilyn Monroe, but she was dumber than a rock. I mean this woman would have picked up a snake to kill a stick. I have no objection to pretty girls, but our problem was that the sponsor would write us a check each year under the conditions that I had to feature his gal on the show once a year. Well, we swallowed our pride and did as we were told for a couple years. We'd take her fishing and she'd hold the rod upside down and we'd have to tell the cameraman to stop filming and put it in her hands correctly. This was real film, too. She must have been great in bed because what that guy put up with was just horrible. Eventually I ran out of patience. After Bailey's death I walked away from the show. I vowed I would never get into the hornets' nest of TV again. Turns out a few years later I had an opportunity to do a prime-time outdoors show sponsored by Exxon, but I would've had to move to Burbank, California, and I wasn't going to move to that part of the world no matter how much they wanted to pay me.

This may not surprise those of you who have seen me, but TV was not my destiny. However, by the early 1960s it was becoming increasingly clear that even if klieg lights were not in my future, outdoor journalism was. My reputation as a knowledgeable observer of the outdoor scene was growing. I was doing more and more writing and gaining more and more notice. That fact was driven home in October 1964, when I had three different bylined articles running simultaneously in each of the big three outdoor magazines.

Chapter 9
Lefty's Deceiver

I STARTED TO BECOME VERY interested in tying my own flies. Like any other fly fisherman, I was always inventing new designs. I never really kept track of the designs or charted my success or failure with them, because, as any flytier knows, 90 percent of what we tie never ends up being worth a damn anyway. However, in the late 1950s—I think around '57 or '58—I stumbled onto one that worked.

Back then the Chesapeake Bay was absolutely loaded with striped bass. The town of Crisfield, Maryland, had a crab-packing plant that was situated right on the river. Each night, as the plant closed down, the workers would toss unprocessed crab parts into the river. Of course, this formed a fantastic chum line. Tom Cofield, then outdoor editor of the *Baltimore News and Post*, was a frequent fly-fishing companion of mine. He and I used to have remarkable outings in Crisfield, but there was one problem: Most of the flies of that era had feather wings that frequently tangled or under-wrapped the hook, thus spoiling the retrieve. It was indescribably frustrating to cast to breaking fish only to find that the fly had fouled. After one such maddening foray I told Tom I was going to design a fly that wouldn't foul on the cast. It would have a fish shape, but could be made in a variety of lengths. It would also swim well underwater but when lifted for the back cast, it would be sleek and offer little resistance. This was the genesis of the lure that has since become known around the world as the Lefty's Deceiver.

The first ones I tied were pretty simple. They were a wing of four to eight saddles tied at the back and a simple bucktail or calftail color at the front. The original Deceiver was all white (still one of the best colors for this model). It was actually three or four years before I added other colors, the first of which was a red collar. A Deceiver can be any combination of colors that suits the angler, but over the years I have had the most success with a lower portion of the wing in yellow or white and a collar of the same color or chartreuse. The top of the wing is also chartreuse. In recent years, I have had great success in deeper water by making a cone head on the Deceiver. In very clear water I use synthetic materials such as Unique hair, and I draw more strikes than I do with more opaque feathers and hair.

Lefty's Deceiver is now used around the world in salt water (although it is a popular freshwater pattern as well). Without being boastful, I think it's accurate to say that the Deceiver and the old Clouser Minnow are two of the most imitated saltwater flies in the sport. Many flytiers have added a feather or two or an epoxy head or big eyes to the Deceiver and named it after themselves. I am often asked if this bothers me. Not in the least. As long as people enjoy the pattern and have success with it, what do I care? In reality, there are almost no new fly patterns to tie. The Lefty's Deceiver is really only a concept and there are probably two thousand people who have put a different feather on it or a different eyeball or something, but basically these are Lefty's Deceivers. In fact, there is a guy who wrote a book called *700 Salt Water Flies*. He has about twenty-five different kinds of Deceivers in there. He's got Charlie's Deceiver and Jim's Deceiver and Pete's Deceiver. They're all Deceivers.

A lot of people who develop flies really get ticked off when people steal them. As long as someone is using the fly and having fun with it, I'm happy. What I do object to, however, is when big companies like Orvis take your fly pattern and drop your name (they call theirs "The Deceiver") and they sell thousands of them and don't share any of that revenue with the designer. It happens all the time. There are some companies like Unqua that will pay you a royalty on your fly, but the biggest retailers are not doing that. In fact, you might be surprised to know that the only fly that was ever patented was the Teeny Nymph. Its claim to fame was that it was the only fly ever made entirely out of one feather. Of course, that patent has long since expired. You can copyright a fly, but you can't *patent* it because almost all flies are compilations of several other techniques used on existing flies.

In my entire career I have only seen a few truly innovative fly designs. One was the Dahlberg Diver. It was designed by Larry Dahlberg, and it had a spun deer hair head on the front that was trimmed to a cone with a collar on it. A long pull on the line would cause the fly to dive and wiggle under the water and if you stopped pulling, the buoyant deer hair would pop the fly back up to the surface. You could use it as a popping bug on the surface or as a streamer or as a combination of the two, depending on how you stripped the line. Larry's design is marketed by dozens of people who have simply changed the name, but Larry can't do anything about it. It's unfair, but life is unfair. Imitation is the sincerest form of flattery.

I remember there was a guy named Bob Nauheim from California who about twenty or thirty years ago developed what is now the standard bonefish fly. It was a fly where the hook was tied point up so that it wouldn't catch on the bottom. He put a little bead-chain eye on the front end and a little wing. The bead-chain eye would make it drop quickly to the bottom, where bonefish feed. Bob called his fly Nasty Charlie. There's a cute story behind the name. Charlie Smith was a guide in the Bahamas. And on the day Bob first used the new fly he happened to be fishing with Charlie, who saw how well Bob fished with it. Charlie said to Bob, "That sure is a nasty fly." Bob named it the Nasty Charlie. About a year later Orvis found out about this fly, started copying it, and renamed it the Crazy Charlie and has since sold so many thousands of these things that the original name is completely forgotten. Very few people know that a Crazy Charlie was originally named a Nasty Charlie.

Well, the Lefty's Deceiver worked exactly as I had envisioned it. Word began to spread among the few fly fishermen who were then working salt water. It was not fouling lines and it was attracting lots of bass. Ultimately, I wrote an article about the design for *Maryland Conservationist Magazine*.

I have long believed that with the exception of permit and bonefish, you only need three fly patterns (in a range of sizes and color combinations, of course) in order to be sufficiently equipped to fly-fish salt water anywhere in the world. Those three flies are the Popping Bug, Lefty's Deceiver, and the Clouser Minnow.

Most flies are very specific in how they're tied. The Clouser and the Deceiver are more overall design concepts rather than specific, detailed designs. How to attach the feathers and other details are up to the individual angler. So, when we have baitfish that are very thin, such as the sand eel in the northeastern United States, or a more football-shaped pilchard or menhaden, the Lefty's Deceiver gives us the leeway to imitate either one of them.

If you were going to imitate a sand eel, the Deceiver would be tied with two or three thin feathers and with a very thin collar to present a very thin profile. If you wanted the fly to emulate the menhaden, then you would tie it much bulkier so it would resemble that football shape of menhaden. In addition, suppose you were fishing in very shallow water or you wanted to catch fish that were near the surface. You might tie it much fuller, put extra saddle feathers on the back, and extra buck tail on the front, which will make it more buoyant. Then, if you want to fish deeper, along the rocks for striper or on the reef or something, before you start tying the fly you wrap lead wire on the shaft of the fly or use weights called coneheads. The weight on the shaft of the fly makes the fly sink horizontally. The conehead makes the fly dive because all the weight is at the front end. In Key West they love to chum for blackfin tuna and kingfish. The chum sinks very slowly. A lot of times they'll throw dead minnows out. So there you would need a fly that would be fairly well dressed so it would float just like the food or chum.

Last year up in Cape Cod we were fishing 9- or 10-inch sand eels for striper. We didn't have 10-inch feathers, so we put on some synthetic hair at the back and some feathers on either side to give a little bulk to it. Now you end up with something that's 9 or 10 inches long.

Take the jungles of Brazil, for example, where they have very large Peacock Bass. These get up to 22 pounds on fly. If you know you're fishing for average peacocks, between, say, 3 and 10 pounds, you'd use a Deceiver with feathers and a little bit of that synthetic hair so that the total fly would be about 4 or 5 inches. But now if you want to go for the larger fish, use the same 2/0-size hook, but extend the synthetic hair so that the fly is now about 10 inches long with the feathers along the side.

The beauty of the Deceiver is its flexibility. Its adaptability allows you to fish all kinds of fish on one basic premise: big fish want groceries, not samples. And it's true: Lefty's Deceiver allows you to serve them what they want. I remember the first time I caught a sailfish. I was in Costa Rica. We were using a teaser, which allows the sailfish to taste some bait and then you jerk it out of his mouth and you do this over and over 'til he's close to the boat and so ticked off he'll eat anything. You throw a fly slightly across and behind him and it helps hook him in the mouth. Anyway, back in Costa Rica this guy teased this 7-foot sailfish up to the boat. When the fish was 20 feet away from the boat I looked at this little 6-inch Deceiver that was on my line and I yelled up to the captain, "Do you think that that monster is going to eat this little fly?" The captain's response was classic: "Don't elephants eat peanuts?"

Great answer, but the fact is that elephants eat peanuts for treats, not for their primary diet. The point is that a big fish will eat small bait (tarpon are a great example), but given the choice between hors d'oeuvres and entrees, they'll take the meal anytime.

Fish with huge mouths, however, do not need large hooks. They suck in all the water surrounding the fly or the lure and, aside from tarpon and billfish, almost all fish have soft mouths. Even for peacock bass I only use a 2/0 hook, which is not a real large hook. The fly itself is synthetics and some feathers and some bucktail, which weighs very little. So with a 9-weight line (not a very heavy line) you can cast it. However, the heavier and more air resistant the line is, or the more water it soaks up, the heavier the line you need. A lot of flies are made with rabbit fur. One of the reasons I don't use rabbit flies, although they're very effective, is that when you pull them out of the water they retain a lot of that water's weight during flight. You need to have heavier lines and work harder.

My greatest thrill is that the Lefty's Deceiver has given millions of hours of fishing success to thousands and thousands of anglers. I can live without the credit or the royalties. I got all the credit I needed in 1991 when the United States Postal Service honored the fly by putting it on a 29-cent postage stamp. On the stamp it doesn't just say "Deceiver," it says, "Lefty's Deceiver."

CHAPTER 10
THE BEST CAST I EVER MADE

AT THE BEGINNING OF THIS book I wrote about the greatest catch (other than my wife, Ev) of my life. Given the amount of fishing I've done in my life and the countless number of casts I've made to fish all over the world, it might seem hard to pick the best cast I've ever made. But it's really not. My greatest cast stands out from all the others quite easily. What's interesting is that there was nothing remarkable about the fish, or my tackle, or anything else. Still that one cast stands out against all the others in my career.

As anyone knows, it's not hard to add line on a cast. In other words, if you were fishing to a target forty feet away and suddenly you see another fish at sixty feet, you can make a fast back cast, a fast, short forward cast, and shoot another twenty feet of line. That's pretty doable for just about any decent caster. What is really difficult is to shorten a cast—to go from, say, a forty-foot target to a twenty-foot target on the spur of the moment.

Back in the 1960s when I was still living in Florida and running the MET, my son, Larry, was poling me in the Keys near Sawyer Key, in the backcountry behind Sugarloaf Key. I remember it like it was yesterday. It was a spring high tide and we had been catching a lot of baby tarpon—

ten- to twelve-pounders—as they swam around the mangrove roots looking for minnows. We came around this little island and there was an indentation on the coast, and as we made the corner I had about forty-five or fifty feet of line out on the water. With the tide high, we had water under the mangroves. Suddenly, about thirty feet away, I saw four or five of these baby tarpon—ranging from 10 to 20 pounds—come out from under the mangroves. I had to make my cast immediately because they were going to see us. So I made my back cast, and while it was going back I was frantically tucking line in. I made the forward cast, still stripping in line. In mid-cast I actually reduced the length of the cast from about 40 feet to about 25 feet. God help me, I dropped the fly right in front of the tarpon and he took it. I was stunned.

Larry didn't even realize what had just happened. I had to explain to him that that was the best cast I ever made. That's one of the great aspects of fishing. The greatest moments this sport provides are not necessarily world-record catches in exotic locations. Here was a forgettable fish in a very accessible destination, but the circumstances carved it into my memory bank. The fish was only 35 feet away, and only weighed about 15 pounds, but of all the casts I'd made before and all the casts I've made in the roughly forty years since, that was the absolute best. Incidentally, lest you get the idea that life with Lefty was one brilliant fishing success after another, on that same trip Larry and I went to the Content Keys, which back then were some of the most remote of the Florida Keys. We were heading up there and by the time we got to the Barracuda Keys the tide was really going out fast. We had a little 12-foot Boston Whaler. I made a misjudgment and tried to get into the Gulf going over this light sand flat. We ran out of water and I grounded the boat.

CHAPTER 11
THE MET

B Y THE MID-1960S, MY friend Joe Brooks had been doing freelance outdoor writing all over the world for years. As early as 1952 he did a TV show on tiger fishing in Africa. He'd been to Chile and Bermuda and a list of exotic places as long as your arm. Joe was up there with Al McLane and Ted Trueblood in the very top tier of fishing writers, particularly fly-fishing writers.

Joe was the manager of the MET from 1947 into the mid-1950s. This was the premier fishing tournament in the United States, if not the world. The MET had some corporate support and corporate sponsorship, but it was run by a board of directors that was comprised of some outstanding businessmen in south Florida. The event had two main purposes. The first was to support the angling industry in the region and the second was to convince people to move to Florida. The MET was created in 1929, a time when there weren't a helluva lot of people living down there. In fact, as late as 1964 there wasn't another tournament in all of South Florida, including the Keys. This was *the* event, the only event. It ran sixteen weeks and boasted 250,000 contestants. Because of its sheer size and because of the role angling played in the area's social scene (like golf in other towns) the MET was also one of the biggest social happenings on the South Florida calendar.

When Joe left the position he handed the job to George Robey, an outdoor editor from Ohio. George died of a heart attack in the office about nine years later. Even for all the MET's significance, when Joe called me in 1964 after George died and asked how I'd like to run the MET, I was baffled. I asked, "What the hell is the MET?"

Joe said, "Lefty, it's like being the mayor of all South Florida fishing."

I didn't need to hear another word, but there would be a few hurdles to negotiate before I could start shopping for sunglasses. First was the fact that only a few weeks earlier I had decided to leave my job (after eighteen years) at Fort Detrick. I had become irreversibly tired of working for the federal government and wanted out. I had accepted a position, effective January 1, 1965, as the head of parks and recreation in a newly developed community called Columbia, Maryland. However, deep down I knew that once I briefed the developer, Jim Rouse, on this new opportunity in Florida, he would understand. And he did.

The second hurdle was my family. We had two kids, fourteen and twelve, and we had lived in small-town Maryland virtually all our lives. Sure, I had done some traveling, but Ev had not traveled much at all. The idea of such a dramatic change produced some trepidation, but the picture that Joe had painted of the sporting life in Florida was very compelling. I had experienced fishing in the region and knew it was supreme. I would also be making more money, not much more, but enough to make it interesting.

Ev, God bless her, jumped on board and headed with me to Florida. She was a small-town gal with a small circle of close friends, and she didn't know anybody south of the Carolinas. On top of that, I was going to be gone an awful lot (one of the requirements of the job was that you travel throughout the whole of south Florida). We were still paying for everything with cash, and when you need to find a home and furniture and schools and all, you can burn a lot of green.

When I first arrived in Miami, it was clear to me that the people down there had figured that since I was from Maryland, I couldn't possibly know anything about fishing. I'll be honest with you, they were some of the most puffed-up, egotistical anglers you ever saw in your life. In fact, shortly after my arrival, Joe Brooks told me, "If you can get along with these high-class light tackle jokers down here you can handle anything."

The fact was, however, that I had not done a whole lot of billfishing, which was the most popular type of fishing among Floridians at the time. What little knowledge I did have, however, had come from a pretty remarkable source.

CHAPTER 12
CUBA, CASTRO, HEMINGWAY, AND THE BIGGEST BASS I EVER SAW

In late 1959, about five years before I was offered the MET job, Joe Brooks was the fishing writer for *Outdoor Life*. He had a huge readership and a lot of influence. A few weeks after the Cuban Revolution, he called me and said that somebody in the freshly installed Castro regime had contacted him saying that the new Cuban government wanted to promote sportfishing in Cuba. Joe said he had been asked by Castro's people to head up a group of American outdoor writers to see the fishing firsthand. He said, "How would you like to go to Cuba?"

I said, "For what?"

He said, "For fishing."

Joe had fished in Cuba many times, and he'd told me all kinds of stories about how rich the Cuban waters were. Besides, it was winter in Maryland. It didn't take me very long to say yes.

Joe also invited Howard Gillelan, who was also on the editorial staff of *Outdoor Life*. The other guy in our group was a newspaper writer who died a year or so later and whose name I simply can't recall. Anyway, we were flown to Cuba, and an emissary of Castro's met us at the airport. The event we were to attend was the 14th Annual Hemingway White Marlin Tournament. Yes, that Hemingway. As you probably know, Ernest

Hemingway was revered down there. To Hemingway, Cuba represented the ultimate refuge. In 1932, he'd set out with pal Joe Russell for what was planned as a two-day fishing trip. They stayed for four months, and Hemingway made the island his home.

Hemingway was supportive of the Castro regime, and in the weeks and years during and after the revolution—when virtually every last wealthy American had packed up and left—Hemingway was outspoken in his support of the reforms that Castro planned to initiate in the wake of the Batista regime. He made Cuba his primary residence for the remainder of his life. His love of the country, its people, its natural resources, and its way of life and his support of Fidel Castro, made Hemingway one of the early linchpins of Castro's PR war against the United States. To this day, Hemingway's home, Finca Vigia, in San Francisco de Paula, and his boat, the famed *Pilar*, are maintained as museum pieces by the Cuban government.

We went down to Cuba for eighteen days. Hemingway himself was there for the 14th Annual White Marlin Tournament, and unlike us journalists, both Ernest and Fidel were competing in the event. It was a three-day tournament, mostly trolled bait, and because the floor of Havana Bay drops to ocean depths almost immediately, the city's skyline remained within sight for most of our trip. The first day I rode on Castro's boat and for the next two days I tagged along with Hemingway. Castro was very personable and very approachable. However, there was one rule—we were not to talk politics. Any other topic was fair game, but early on it was made clear that we were there to take in, talk about, and promote sportfishing.

Well, no matter what you wanted to talk about, if you were interested in chatting with Castro, you'd better have some basic understanding of Spanish, which I did not. Howard, on the other hand knew a little *español* and managed more than a few discussions. Any conversations I had were pretty much stop and go. I did have several pictures taken with him—in fact, I visited his office and took some great shots there, but they were all on printed on Ektachrome and faded so badly that they became worthless. I threw them away a couple years back.

We stayed at the Hotel Nacional, and since this was immediately after the revolution we were the only guests in the entire hotel. That is not an exaggeration. There was not another soul in the building. Although the American group did not compete in the white marlin tournament, we did fish elsewhere. I remember we traveled from Havana southeast by railroad to fish the famed Treasure Lake. The railroad runs across the swampland of the Zapata Peninsula, which looks exactly like the Everglades. I'll never forget that as we rode this narrow-gauge railroad (used for transporting sugarcane) the wheels of the train cars were actually running through water. If you looked back behind the train, the tracks would actually rise up out of the water after the engine passed by and if you looked ahead they would be sinking down under the coming weight of the train.

At that time Treasure Lake was regarded as the greatest largemouth lake in the world. It really wasn't a lake *per se*, but a series of lakes and lagoons and swamps connected by a network of waterways. The bass were absolutely huge. I know this is going to sound like a fish story, but it's 100 percent true. As part of their effort to promote fishing, the Cuban government was just starting to build some tin-roofed lodges (liberal use of the word) on some of the dry land in the Zapata. We found a partially constructed hut that had some mosquito netting on it, and we decided to settle there for lunch one day. Well, as we got closer to the hut, we could see that the laborers who had been building it had been eating some of the local fish on their lunch breaks. The discarded heads of the departed fish were scattered around the work site. As we walked up to the lodge, Howard, Joe, and I spotted a monumental head of a departed largemouth bass.

It stopped us dead in our tracks. A few years after this trip I would go on to run the MET Tournament, the largest fishing tournament in the world, and I have sized up a lot of grouper and snapper in my day, but the head of this bass was beyond anything that I have ever seen in my life. That fish alone was in my estimation way over the world record, which was then something on the order of 22¼ pounds. I would say this fish was no less than a 26- or 27-pounder. It looked like a big grouper. You could have put a soccer ball in this thing's mouth. I have never since seen anything close to it. Of course, none of the people down there really knew or cared about world records, and besides, *so many* of the fish there were huge. So, here you had these workmen, routinely and unknowingly landing world-record bass, only to fry them up over a campfire on their lunch break.

After we finished our lunch one of the guys who was escorting us asked if I would show the group how to catch fish on a fly rod. I walked over to the water's edge and thought, Man, I hope I can do this on command, but I quickly realized that there were so many darn fish there that Grandma Moses could have handled it. I made a couple casts and caught a few 6- and 7-pounders just like that (of course, I acted like it was normal).

This was a lost world (in fact, I caught my first big bonefish on this trip, too). You'd be fishing for bass with a big popping bug or something and a big tarpon or snook would bolt out of the water. On smaller rods we caught buckets and buckets of a local fish, a *villajaca*, which was the Cuban version of a bluegill.

We got back on the train and went farther south-southeast to the Bay of Pigs, which is where the railroad ended. There we got in boats and caught a bunch of thirty- and forty-pound tarpon. We saw some real big ones, but didn't catch any. Wherever we went, people were very friendly. In fact, I believe that in those early days of his reign, Castro was positively disposed to the United States. Batista had milked all the country's money so when Castro took power, it was a very poor nation. I think we made a mistake in cutting him off. Why we did it, who knows? A lot of the people I know who have followed it closely feel that Che Guevara was the problem, but I don't think he was truly reflective of Castro's point of view. Many of the locals will tell you that the real reason we cut Cuba off was because many American politicians and their supporters had money in the gambling and prostitution trades in Cuba. When Castro nationalized everything, those Americans lost all their money and reacted in anger. I don't know about all that, but I do know the Latin mind-set: When they love you they love you and when they hate you they hate you. In the forty-six years since Castro's takeover, we ended up with the latter. Conversely, the Russians and the Communists saw an opportunity to build a bridge to a nation just 90 miles off our coast and moved in.

After observing from Castro's boat on the first day, we switched over to Hemingway's, the renowned *Pilar*. It wasn't a very big boat, maybe thirty-five or forty feet long. It made sense; if you want to catch sailfish, you need to be able to chase them. Maneuverability is key. Billfish boats need to be able to back down fast and go ahead fast, and they have to make turns quickly. The *Pilar* was an authentic fishing vessel; it wasn't designed for cocktail cruises. It was constructed in a Brooklyn, New York, shipyard specifically for sportfishing and had a pretty wide beam for its size. She had a 100-horsepower inboard diesel-powered engine with twin screws, double rudders, and a decent amount of bunkroom below deck. She had a flying bridge, too. By the standards of the era it was a very good boat.

As we boarded the vessel, which shared its name with a shrine in Zaragoza, Spain, and was also Ernest's second wife's nickname, Ernest introduced us to his mate, Gregorio Fuentes. He told us matter-of-factly, "He is the best billfisherman in the world." Gregorio was more than Hemingway's aide de camp. He was also the inspiration for Santiago, the indefatigable fisherman of *The Old Man and the Sea*.

I was still living in Maryland at the time, and I had never been billfishing. My introductory course would be taught aboard the *Pilar* with Hemingway and Fuentes by my side. I spent half the time on the boat picking Gregorio's brain. He showed me how to make strip bait, bait that you cut out of the side of a fish. Small tuna and dolphin are great for this. You cut the meat almost in the shape of a fish, then sew a hook back into the rear part.

You can take a dead bonita and a piece of monofilament and tie a loop at both ends. Then you take a needle with the eye widened so you can slip one of the loops through the eye. You run that needle through the fish's eyes, across, and out the other side, which pulls one of the loops through. Then you disengage the monofilament from the needle and bring the two loops around so they're even together. All you have to do next is flip the hook through the loops and throw the thing overboard. That loop aligns everything evenly so that the fish swims just like a bonita. Ingenious.

Gregorio showed me all kinds of stuff. While the other guys were peppering Ernest with questions about Havana's legendary nightlife, I glommed onto Gregorio, who showed me how to debone a mullet by running a hollow tool up by the spine and removing it. That makes a mullet's body floppy and flexible. Then he showed me how to take an egg sinker—that's an egg-shaped sinker with a hole through the center—and wire it in front of the mouth and nose so the fish sinks. After that, you rig a hook into the body, and, when you troll, it looks just like a live mullet swimming through the water.

I did spend quite a bit of time over the next few days with Hemingway, as well. The thing I remember most was his physique. He had a barrel chest and very powerful legs. With thin, bony ankles and bulging, muscular calves, they appeared to be the legs of an athlete. Despite his intimidating appearance, he was very soft-spoken. I would say we got along well.

I was devoted almost entirely to fishing and conversations about fishing. I got the feeling that if I'd tried to get him to talk extensively about journalism he might have thrown me overboard. However, between my compatriots' eager questions about Cuban nightlife and Ernest's authoritative recommendations, I did ask him one question about writing. I was beginning to spread my journalistic wings with articles in newspapers and magazines, but I was just doing it on the fly. Here I was, fishing alongside a man who might very well have been the most successful living author in the world. I figured I might be able to learn a few things.

I asked him, "Ernest, what makes good writing?"

Without hesitating, he said, "It can't be edited." I found that fascinating. He figured that once you've added something or taken something away, you've diminished the author's original vision and intent.

I thought that was a very powerful comment.

"Ernest, I think I have a story that'll prove your point," I said. "A pretty good example of some writing that couldn't be improved upon by editing." Then I told him the story.

Back in the old days, if you were heading from Baltimore up to Pennsylvania or northern West Virginia, you pretty much had to drive through my hometown of Frederick, Maryland. By the mid-1950s, though, people were tired of getting caught up on Frederick's main drag and they built a bypass around town. They brought all these laborers up from Baltimore and Washington and these guys would work all week, then go home for the weekend. Well, when I had a little free time, I'd go down to the shacks where these guys ate lunch and listen to their stories. I was down there one day with a guy who had not been home for three straight weekends. He opened his old metal lunchbox, sipped at his coffee, and took a few bites of his sandwich. Then, he opened a letter from his wife. The guy made three passes with his eyes over the text of the letter, then looked up and said, "My God, I'ma goin' home this weekent."

One of the other guys asked him, "Well, what did the letter say?"

"It say, 'Honey, there's going to be some screwin' goin' on at this house this weekend. If you ain't here, you're gonna miss it.'"

Hemingway cracked up. When he finally finished laughing, he said "You can't edit that."

Beyond that, most of our conversations revolved around fishing. You could tell he really loved it. I liked Hemingway. The stories are true: He was a very, very good fisherman.

In the end, Fidel Castro won the tournament. I know what you're thinking—the whole thing was rigged for the pleasure of the dictator. But the fact is, you couldn't rig this event. It wasn't a catch-and-release tournament; you had to bring every fish in for measurement. As it turned out, Castro had caught more white marlin than anyone else.

With the tournament over and my introduction to world-class billfishing complete, I headed back to Maryland. Hemingway himself would soon leave Cuba for good. I only saw him one other time. I was visiting Sun Valley, Idaho, and he had a home in nearby Ketchum. I bumped into him on a downtown street in Sun Valley. We got to talking about Gregorio and the *Pilar* and our three days of fishing, and Ernest got all pumped up. We talked for a little while, wished each other well, and that was it.

Somehow I was not shocked when, a year or so later, I heard that he had killed himself. I knew that he had been in failing health. His memory had deteriorated and he could no longer write. He used a double-barreled shotgun to end his misery. Of course, you never know what you might do until you're actually in such a situation, but if confronted with a long-term illness for which there was little comfort and no cure, I think it would be practical to kill yourself. At eighty years old, I have seen too many people go bankrupt to keep themselves or their spouse alive. I wouldn't do that to Ev. Actually, I admired Ernest for doing what he did; I thought it took courage.

Two footnotes to the whole Hemingway experience. I went back to Cuba as recently as 2003. I fished the *Archipelago de los Jardines de la Reina*, Gardens of the Queen, a 100-mile stretch of narrow mangrove islands that parallel the southern shore of Cuba and run about fifty miles offshore. I am happy to report that the fishing there is still magnificent, like the Florida Keys in the 1950s and 1960s.

Second, I was never really a fan of Hemingway's writing. The guy I really enjoyed reading back then was Robert Ruark. For a number of years he wrote a magazine column and he also wrote a number of books. Among them were *The Old Man and the Boy, Robert Ruark's Africa*, and *A Hunter's Wanderings in Africa*. I'm not an eloquent writer—I'm a guy from Frederick with a high school education—but Ruark was something. I remember he once referred to a boat coming up a river as a "rust-scabbed ship." In another book he was talking about how he and another guy were arguing at a bar while "our martinis sweated on the mahogany." Ruark was a raging alcoholic who eventually drowned in a bathtub, but he made things come alive for me. For what it's worth, my other favorite writer was Charlie Waterman, a good friend who died only recently.

CHAPTER 13
MY EXCELLENT ADVENTURES WITH TED

In 1964 I took over management of the MET. I was responsible for all the operations and answered to a board of directors. In addition to some of Miami's leading businessmen, the board included some of the top anglers in the region. Because the tournament did so much for Florida's economy and because its members tended to be socially respected, it was a pretty prestigious board on which to sit. It was a remarkably colorful group of guys as well. For instance, Lee Cuddy was a director. Lee was a former carnival man who had gone on to corner the American market for cork fishing-rod handles. Back then, any decent fishing rod had a cork handle. He was also a legendary fly fisherman, one of the real pioneers. We also had a guy named Homer Rhodes, a former game warden who lived on a houseboat in the Everglades. He had been a federal warden and the legend surrounding Homer was that he once killed a guy in a fight.

I'll never forget my first MET Tournament board meeting. It was held over at the Miami Beach Rod and Reel Club. Formed in 1929, the MBRRC is the second oldest fishing club in the United States. I rode there and back with Ed Corlett, our distinguished vice president. Ed was a very smooth, cultured guy who ran one of the top law firms in the South. Well, he and Cuddy—who had as much grit as Ed did polish—got into a discussion about some membership rule. They got to going back and forth, things got heated, and finally, at the end of the argument, Cuddy got up and yelled, "Aw, the hell with the MET. I quit. I'm resigning!" And he stormed out the door.

Well, a few minutes later the meeting adjourned. I walked out of the boardroom, crushed. My first meeting at my new job had ended in total rancor. Then I looked up and what did I see? Corlett having a drink with Lee. Corlett being my ride, I waited for him and on the ride home said, "What a shame. Can you believe Lee just quit the MET?"

Ed said, "What're you talking about?"

I said, "It's right here in the minutes of the meeting, he resigned."

Ed laughed. "Get that out of the minutes," he said. "Lee quits at every damn meeting."

And he did. I was there for seven years and Lee quit virtually every time we met.

Well, I learned a valuable life lesson that day. Later on I asked Ed, "How could you argue so vociferously with Cuddy and then go buy him a drink?" I've never forgotten Ed's answer.

"I wasn't arguing with Lee Cuddy," Ed said smoothly. "I was arguing with his idea."

Ed explained to me that as long as you can separate the idea from the person it's easy to keep your cool, and people who keep their cool in an argument are more likely to prevail. Pretty good stuff. I've tried to keep it in mind ever since.

Both my skill at disarming doubters and my new mastery of argumentation came in very handy in my new life with the MET. Experienced in salt water or not, I was now living in Florida and it was time for me to take all that I had learned, both as a kid on the Monocacy and as a young man who'd fished abroad, and put it to work. I got off to a good start when, in my first week running the MET, I went out off Key

West with a very sharp captain named Lefty Regan and caught a world-record blackfin tuna on fly. I think it weighed 19 pounds or so. Most importantly, it was the first blackfin ever caught on fly. Vic Dunaway, who was then the fishing writer for the *Miami Herald* (which sponsored the MET Tournament) made a big deal of it in the paper, writing how the new MET Tournament manager had arrived only a few days ago and already made quite a mark and on and on. Even though it was a just a PR piece, the story bought me a sliver of credibility with the Florida crowd. Still they had their doubts as to whether anybody from north of the Broward County line could really know anything about fishing.

A few days later, partly as a result of the newspaper article, one of the local clubs invited me over for a casting demonstration. What they really wanted to see was how *bad* I was. When I was invited to this little gathering in Florida, I knew it wasn't because they wanted to make my acquaintance. They wanted to test me. I was essentially on trial in front of the club's hotshot light-tackle guys. But I had a trick up my sleeve. Years earlier, when I first started doing casting demonstrations, I had to earn acceptance. It was always arms-folded cynicism until I showed them something startling. Well, precisely for situations such as this I had taught myself to cast about sixty or seventy feet of fly line with my bare hands. No rod, no reel.

So, they had their little meeting and then we went out in this alley where there were some streetlights. They were all standing—arms folded—just waiting for me to flop. So I pulled off about 60 feet of fly line and walked back and picked up the end of the line. Very casually (although with my heart pounding) I said, "You know it's the fly line that actually does the casting." Barehanded, I cast sixty feet of line on the forward cast. Everyone lining the alley took a huge step forward to see how far the line would go. I knew I had them. I think it's safe to say that not one of them could have thrown a line that far *with* a rod. From that moment on I had no trouble with them. They started coming over to my house to get fly-casting lessons. Yes, I had long ago made a conscious decision not to showboat, but I rationalized the performance by telling myself I wasn't showing off so much as I was trying to make my point. I made it. I never had another problem with acceptance, and many of those club members became lifelong friends.

Then there was a bristly local named Ted Williams. Ted, who died in 2002, was and is an authentic American sports icon. In a nineteen-year career with the Boston Red Sox, Ted had a lifetime batting average of .344. In 1941 he was the last man ever to bat over .400 for a season. His mark of .406 still stands today as the gold standard for batting. He led the American League in batting six times; in slugging percentage nine times; in total bases six times; runs scored six times; walks eight times. He was Most Valuable Player in the American League twice, played in eighteen All-Star games, and was named Major League Baseball's "Player of the Decade" for the 1950s. In sum, "Teddy Ballgame," as his fans dubbed him, may very well have been the greatest baseball player of all time. He was also an avid angler, a good friend, and a royal pain in the ass.

After he retired from baseball, Ted maintained a home in New England, but he pretty much retired to Islamorada in the Florida Keys. I may have been the only guy in America who didn't know that. I had followed all sports and played them obsessively as a kid, but once I got older and had kids and was busy working and hunting and fishing, I sort of lost my appetite for professional sports. I sort of figured, why pay someone else to play a sport when I can fork over a few bucks for a fishing license and play myself? If I'm gonna pay, I'm gonna play.

I knew that Ted Williams was a baseball player, but that's where my knowledge of him and the sport ended. One day around 1966 or 1967 I was working in the MET Tournament offices when one of the girls said, "Lefty, someone's on the phone."

I picked up the phone and a voice on the other end said, "This is Ted Williams." By the imperious tone in his voice you'd have thought this was the Creator Himself calling. I didn't even recognize the name.

"So," I said.

Well, that took him back a bit. He regrouped and said, "I hear you're the best goddamn fly fisherman around here."

"Well, I don't know if that's true."

"Well," he said, "that's what I've heard, and I'd like to fish with you."

Just then it occurred to me who this was, and that I might be able to sell a few magazine articles if I hooked up with this guy. I still didn't know much about him. In fact, at the time I probably couldn't have picked Ted Williams out of a police lineup, but I knew a good story when I saw one.

I said, "Okay, I'll fish with you."

"Be here tomorrow at seven o'clock," he said.

"I can't be there at no seven o'clock, Williams. I got a job to do."

"When can you be here?" he snapped.

"Well," I said, "I think I can make it down there on Saturday."

"Meet me at the Islamorada Yacht Basin," he growled, and was about to hang up.

I really didn't mean to piss him off, but I held him on the line. "Wait a minute," I said. "I don't even know what the hell you look like. How will I find you?" I'm pretty sure he'd never heard that before.

He said, "Well, you know Jack Brothers, right?" Jack was a well-known guide in Florida Keys fishing circles.

I said, "Yeah, I know Jack."

"Well," Williams said, "I'll be with Jack." Click.

Saturday finally rolled around and I headed down to Islamorda. I saw Jack and said hello, then Williams came out. He was real brusque, almost rude. I was struck by how tall and skinny he was. As we shook hands he said, "Let's shoot some line."

I'd been around fishing for thirty years and had never heard that expression, but Ted just walked to the end of the dock and started casting; back and forth, and back and forth, and back and forth. Finally he lets the fly line go and throws the whole line. Now, I just met this guy thirty seconds ago. He turns to me and says, "What the hell do you think of that?"

Like I said earlier, I try never to embarrass anyone through fly casting. It's unproductive, unprofessional, and it's just not nice. But thirty seconds into my relationship with this competitive, combative Ted Williams, I knew I had another exception on my hands.

I assessed his casting, which was chock full of wasted movement. "It's okay," I said, "as long as you don't get sick."

He narrowed his eyes and said, "What the hell are you talking about?"

I said, "You sure do have to move around a lot to get your line out."

Then I walked to the end of the dock. Picked the line up, made one back cast, one forward cast, and threw the same amount of line that Williams had thrown out, with about one-tenth the effort.

His jaw dropped. In that instant his attitude changed 180 degrees, and from that day until the day he died he could not have been a better friend to me. I stayed at his place a number of times, both in Florida and Massachusetts. I remember one time I mentioned to him that I was slated to do a fishing show in Worcester, Massachusetts. He came over after the show and we went out to dinner together. With Ted, I always preferred eating out to eating his food. He cooked the most awful meals. I like real plain, unseasoned food, probably a carryover from my childhood days on the welfare diet. In fact, I was once at an elegant fishing banquet attended by President Jimmy Carter. They had a real fancy menu, but I snuck into the kitchen to scrape up a peanut butter sandwich. Anyway, Ted loved to make all kinds of French dishes with wine and gooey sauces and all. I'd scrape the sauce off and eat whatever uncontaminated bits I could find. One time—in fact, it was the last time I ever fished with him—we were together for three days using his home as our base. Throughout the trip I'd only been eating the few sauce-free morsels I could find on my plate. The last night he said, "I'm not going to waste any more time cooking for you. I'm just gonna take you out for dinner." He took me to Kentucky Fried Chicken and we bought a bucket of chicken and two Cokes. It was the best meal I'd had all week.

As friendly as we became, Ted never lost his opinionated nature or his volatile temper. We would get into a discussion over how to fight big fish or how best to cast a certain fly and he would get all riled up. He'd put his fist up in front of your nose and through gritted teeth say, "Goddamn you, Lefty, don't you understand what I'm trying to tell you." I'd just keep thinking about Ed Corlett . . . don't get emotionally involved.

Ted was a darn good fisherman. I knew plenty of men in Islamorada who were better than he was (sometimes fame grants a man more credit than he really deserves), but what I admired about him was his attention to detail. We'd get in these big discussions and he'd threaten to beat the hell out of me and I'd keep my voice down. Eventually, if he realized that I was right, he'd immediately drop the point he was clinging to and focus on learning my technique.

I used to say, "Williams, you're like a goddamn mental vacuum cleaner." As soon as you won him over he was as eager to pursue your thesis as you could ever imagine. That's where Ted differed from most of the really opinionated people I've dealt with. Most of them go their own way even after you've proved your point. Not Ted. He was a tough, tough fighter, but he was smart enough to know when to quit. He was smart enough to learn.

Ted was two people. I don't think even he knew which Ted was going to show up on a given day or at a given instant. He could be the nicest guy in the world and then BANG, like that, he could turn into a real son of a bitch. One time Ted and I and a couple other guys were down there at the Green Turtle Inn having dinner. This was a real nice restaurant in Islamorada. He was giving this little twenty-five-year-old waitress constant grief, to the point that she was over in the corner of the room crying. I said to him, "Williams, do you know how to properly excavate an Egyptian tomb?"

"No," he growled.

"Do you know how to speak Greek?

"No."

I asked him a few more questions he didn't know the answers to, until he says, "What're you driving at, Lefty?"

I said, "Just because you can knock a baseball over a fence you think you can treat people like dirt. You've been so nasty to that little girl over there that she's gone over to the corner to cry."

Boom. The other Ted kicked in. He went from bad mood to good mood in the blink of an eye. He got up, went over to the girl and put his arm around her and consoled her. You would have thought he was her father. To top it all off, he gave her a $100 tip.

Another time we were sitting around after dinner at his home, another one of those sauced-up Williams recipes. Ted had written a fishing book called *The Big Three*. It was about Atlantic salmon, bonefish, and tarpon. As any author knows, you spend a fortune giving new books away to friends and family and people you meet along the way. Hell, I have friends who'll gladly buy me a fifty-dollar dinner, but they don't want to go out and buy my twenty-five dollar book. Well, after dinner he gives me a copy of the book. I knew the money was coming out of his pocket, so I said, "Ted, let me pay you for the book."

He pulled the book out of my hand and said, "Fuck you," then stormed up to bed. The next morning I came downstairs, where Ted was already cooking breakfast. The book was sitting next to my plate, and I decided to not say another word about it and just take it with me.

Anyway, getting to know Ted was just one facet of this wonderful new life in Florida that Ev and I had begun. So much was happening in the fishing world at the time and South Florida was the epicenter of the revolution. If you look back on the major advances, innovations, and improvements in light tackle and fly-fishing, most of them occurred in the 1960s and '70s and vast majority of *those* occurred in south Florida.

CHAPTER 14
AND THEN GOD CREATED FLORIDA

I WAS IN THE PERFECT place at the perfect time. Beyond the job and the supercharged atmosphere, the fishing in Florida was just fantastic. The area was so rich in sea life (and other animals) and had been so lightly fished that it was truly an angler's fantasyland.

Take the Marquesas Keys. They're a small group of islands about twenty-five miles west of Key West. I took my son Larry down there in 1965. He was about fifteen. We had a 12 ½-foot Boston Whaler with an outboard motor (that wasn't all that great). We packed plenty of food and plenty of water and headed over. The Marquesas are shaped roughly like a wedding ring with small breaks in the band. You could enter the center of the ring through an eastern channel. And if you came in quietly, just at dawn, you could look across the surface of the water and see so many dorsal fins sticking up from sleeping permit and tarpon that it looked like a maze of picket fences. Well, here we were fishing and our motor gives out. You can't pole your way out of there—it's too deep. We were about twenty-five miles from Key West and we were stuck. We were there about two and half days until an old Cuban lobsterman came across us and towed us back to Key West. That's how remote the whole area was back in those days. To show you how much has changed, I was there two years ago and there were fourteen guides working the same area.

The point is that the fishing down there in those days was unbelievably good. Fishing in and around Florida in the 1960s was the equivalent of fishing Cuba today. I've been lucky enough to fish Cuba's famed Garden of the Queens twice. Just like Florida in the 1960s, you can get up in a bonefish flat and pole all day long without seeing another human being.

Florida was incredible. I thought I had died and gone to heaven. I was getting paid to do what I loved to do. Plus, I had four months off in the summer. The tournament ran eight months and I had the summer off. I was free to travel all summer doing seminars and clinics. That kind of stuff helped a lot. I was able to promote the tournament, but I was also able to study fishing and hunting all over the country and the world, while continuing to build up my contacts in the editorial world. The few guides that were then working Florida knew that whoever was running the MET Tournament got lots of inquiries from people planning fishing trips. They always wanted to know where to fish and what guide to use. Since the guides knew that I was a *de facto* clearinghouse for customers, they used to take me out fishing. They quickly learned that I never divulged their best fishing spots. Once that trust was established they started taking me to their supersecret best places. In five years' time I knew many good, great, and miraculous spots throughout south Florida. I earned a master's degree in fishing.

It's hard to describe the excitement that was bubbling through Florida fishing circles at that time. Florida was still a frontier and the amount of data we were learning about saltwater fly-fishing was overwhelming. In fact, it all forced me to write a book. I wrote *Fly Fishing in Salt Water* back in the early 1970s. The book is now in its third edition. The main reason I wrote that book was not to make money (I confess, I did all my other books for money). I did that book because I was getting so many questions while running the MET. Guys would call or write and say, "We want to come down to Florida for bonefish, what kind of tackle should we use?" "Where should we go?" Well, I made out forms that we could give to these guys. We asked: Are you going freshwater or salt water? Are you going to fly, spin, plug, or bait? Northern Florida or southern Florida? What time of year?

All their questions and all of our research into the answers formed the foundation of that book. I got so many questions and, as I said, at the time so much new equipment was being developed. For example, the first bonefish flies back then were being tied on 1/0 hooks. Well, one year there was a guy who was catching way more big bonefish than anybody in the tournament. One of my jobs was to check out a guy's flies and leaders prior to certifying a record. Then we figured it out; while everybody else was still using 1/0 hooks, this guy was hauling in copious amounts of bonefish using little size-4 hooks and tying them upside down.

That's just one small example. There was so much innovation and new information coming into the sport through Florida. For instance, during my stay in the Sunshine State, I set twelve world records on fly. Now, I know that sounds spectacular, but let me explain. I was doing some paid promotional work for Scientific Anglers, promoting their fly line. One day the president of the company came down to Miami and I took him out to fish a wreck that very few people knew about. I caught a monster barracuda—30-something pounds. We took a few pictures of it and put it back. That night at dinner, the guy from Scientific Anglers casually asked me, "Lefty, what's the world record for Barracuda on fly?"

I told him 18 pounds.

"Well," he said, "how much was that one you caught today?"

I said, "About thirty pounds."

He sat there quietly for a minute and then looked me right in the eye.

"You ain't too damn smart, are you?"

"What do you mean?" I asked.

He said, "I'm paying you to promote fly-fishing and you're throwing world records back in the water?"

I figured I'd better shape up. So over the next few years I racked up all those world records. That fact is that I didn't actually break many records back then because many of them were open. That is, we had a new category for, say, tarpon on a fly line and no one had yet entered a record. Filling those holes was an easy way to get your name in the record books or promote a fly line. After those early twelve records, I thought, the heck with it. I never bothered entering another world record, although I've caught a bunch since then.

In the 1960s and 1970s the science of fishing made enormous leaps in terms of technology, design, strategy, and technique. Virtually all of those advances occurred in Florida. Whether it was tackle materials, tackle design, fish-catching techniques, or the development of new knots, it all took place in Florida in that period of time. Sure, advances were made before and since in many other parts of the world, but more was learned in those years in Florida than at any time in history. It was fishing's version of the Renaissance.

Back in the early 1960s there were three-dozen guides in the Florida Keys. Now there are over one thousand. There were no skiff guides in Key West. There were probably fewer than half a dozen of them south of Marathon, Florida. The place was an undiscovered, unexploited fishing paradise. Very few people lived there and just about all the people who did live there or visited there went there for one reason: fishing. Whether you were a janitor or a bank president, you were there because you were a fisherman. For a long time, fishing down in those parts was a free-for-all. There were no rules governing fishing. You just went. There was no categorizing or distinguishing between light tackle and heavy tackle. There were no measuring standards for establishing records. Eventually, a number of fishing clubs sprouted up around the region. Some of these were blue-collar affairs and others were very socially discriminating. The Miami Beach Rod and Reel Club was significant far beyond its social cachet, because the rules it established—rules for offshore fishing and what they called "light tackle" as well—would eventually be adopted by most of the clubs that followed. In fact, when the MET Tournament was organized, the tournament adopted the rules of the MBRRC. Then when the Salt Water Fly Rodders was created, most of *their* rules derived in turn from the MET Tournament.

The point is that by the 1960s we had a relatively common set of rules uniting Florida's fishermen. With more people coming to Florida as visitors, snowbirds, or full-time residents, more clubs formed and these clubs would have spin divisions, fly divisions, plug-casting divisions, a light general division that was for 20-pound tackle, and a general division in which you could use anything. All this uniformity heated up competition for records. They were now trying to beat one another, as opposed to fishing aimlessly, as they had in years past. Suddenly the fishermen of Florida were striving to improve their tackle, their techniques, and their strategies. This led to innumerable advancements from which the sport is still benefiting today.

For example, it was in Florida in the 1960s that Dr. Web Robinson, his wife Helen, and their captain, the able Lefty Regan, developed a technique by which they teased billfish to the back of the boat with bait. As I mentioned earlier, they let the fish grab the bait three or four times and each time they'd pull it out of his mouth. They kept tempting the billfish toward the boat and when they got close enough and angry enough—sail extended, lit up like a neon sign—they'd pull the bait away and throw a fly or a lure out there (Web used a fly), and it worked like a charm. Web perfected that technique, which is now used universally. Other fisherman began to take what Web had learned with billfish and transfer it to fishing other species.

Consider the jewfish. Flamingo is on the north side of Florida Bay across from the Florida Keys. Near the markers off Flamingo, there used to be *monster* jewfish. I'm talking about fish weighing 200, 300, 400 pounds in water that's only about ten feet deep. Locals figured if Web could tease billfish in the manner described above, maybe we could tease jewfish using the same technique. They found out first they couldn't do anything if the tide was running fast, because the jewfish would just lay down on the bottom. But during slack tides the jewfish (and the cobia, too) would rise up and suspend themselves near the marker. Of course it's against the law to stand on a marker, but that never bothered these guys. They'd get on the marker and get a live Jack Crevalle, which are tougher than a bad mother-in-law. They'd hook it in the back and suspend it so that the Jack was swimming on the surface. During slack tides you could see the jewfish and the cobia waiting right there, and man, you'd put that two-pound Jack right in front of their nose and it was like rolling a wine bottle through a jail cell. They were all over that thing. As soon as they lunged for it, we'd jerk it away. We'd do this three or four times and then throw the fly in there. That's all she wrote. I remember a guy named Norm Jansik, who caught two jewfish that way in one day. He caught the first one and tethered it up to the marker with rope. Then he landed the second one. These were enormous fish, each weighing between 250 and 300 pounds. He couldn't possibly put them in his boat. So he towed 500 pounds worth of jewfish back to the dock behind his fourteen-foot aluminum boat.

In the evolution of the technique that quickly followed, guys realized that what you really wanted to do was hook the fish just as the tide started to run. You had a companion who manned the skiff. As soon as you hooked the fish, your captain immediately positioned the boat between the fish and the marker. Then you put the motor in neutral and gunned the hell out of it. All that noise and commotion would run the fish away from the marker. That way he couldn't use the marker to cut your line. Now you have him out a ways and the bottom out there is dead flat. If it's 10 feet deep where you are, it's going to be 10 feet deep 600 yards away. They found that the jewfish could smell the markers. And as long as you could keep these huge fish away from the down-current side of the marker, you could wear the fish out.

That's one example of the evolution of technique and strategy that was spawned in Florida at the time, but huge leaps in equipment and technology were happening simultaneously. The drag that's used in all modern plug reels had its origins in these Florida fishing clubs. There were no drags on plug reels in those days. There was a crude version of a drag called a "cub handle" that allowed you to screw a metal plate down, but it was not very good. Essentially, if a fish ran off with your line, the handles on your reel spun like crazy and the line would burn the hell out of your fingers. Well, Norm Jansick and Gordon Young and some other guys got to work on the problem. Gordon was a machinist at Eastern Airlines. He used to take the gears out of the plug reels, machine a depression in them, and then put washers in there with a little Teflon grease on them and voilà, the small-reel drag was born (they already had drags on great big reels, but not on the casting reels). A guy named Lou Childery, one of the sharpest guys I ever met, had a company called Childery Fishing Tackle Company over in Foley, Alabama. Lou heard about these drags and came down and took the drag that Norm and Gordon had fashioned and he sold the idea to the Japanese manufacturer, Shimano. Shimano was the first company to mass-manufacture these reels, but the concept and the technology were developed within these fertile-minded south Florida fishing clubs.

The same things happened with boat technology. People don't realize, but as late as the early 1960s there were no mass-produced flats boats. People were using small boats until Bob Hewes and I worked together to design the first Hewes Bonefish Boat. The outboard motors prior to that time were designed poorly; the lower portion of the engine would catch on sea grass and cause the engine to cavitate. Eventually engines were designed with curved bottoms that actually let the grass slip off. All of this remarkable progress came from the pressure of competition.

During this time I also learned a lot about the proper and timely weighing of catches. As you know, most tournament fish are weighed with the head down. The original reason for this was that people used to fudge the weight by stuffing the fish with things like window-sash weights and things. Anyway, it was during all this weighing of fishes that I learned some interesting things about how a fish's scales can affect the retention of body weight after a catch. This should be interesting to tournament anglers.

The MET tournament covered much of Florida, but I was based in Miami. In those days, if someone caught a contending fish on the west coast the only road that traversed the state was the Tamiami Trail. If they caught the fish on Monday afternoon I probably couldn't get there much before Tuesday afternoon to weigh it. People would complain bitterly that when they weighed it on Monday it weighed so much more than when I weighed it on Tuesday. One day I was called over to the Homestead area to weigh a tarpon that was leading the plug division. I forget the exact weight, but the fish was in the 80-pound range. I weighed it. Afterward I asked some friends at Don's Bait and Tackle, a local fishing hangout, if I could store the fish in their cooler for a few days. I told them I'd like to come back and reweigh it. Well, when I came back a day or so later it had lost something like 10 percent of its body weight. I thought, wow, maybe all these complainers were on to something.

I dug in. I started doing a lot of these kinds of experiments. I went to the Dry Tortugas with Captain Jainey Maxwell, one of the few guys who would sail there in the 1960s. I caught a 102-pound amberjack on

130-pound tackle. We put it in the fish box in the transom of the boat. The box didn't have any ice in it, but it was shaded. First I weighed it on a cotton scale, which is very accurate. It weighed 102 pounds. Then I weighed it again twenty-four hours later on the same scale and the fish had lost less than a pound of its weight. So I began to check more and more species in this fashion. What I found is that any fish with large scales—bonefish, large- or smallmouth bass, grouper, snapper, tarpon— can lose significant amounts of weight after they die. But fish with smaller scales—amberjack, cobia, shark, freshwater trout—they lose very little weight after they die. What happens is that the scales act almost like shingles on a roof and allow body weight to evaporate out. The bigger the scales, the faster the evaporation. The smaller the scales, the slower the evaporation. If you have a fish with large scales and you want a true weight, it's best to keep the fish wet.

Even knot-tying evolved at that time. Up until the 1960s virtually any knot tied in a fishing line compromised the line; that is, the area where the knot was located became weaker than the rest of the line. With virtually all knots—doesn't matter if it's a knot in the 2-inch stern line of the Queen Mary or a knot in your monofilament—the strength of the line is compromised the moment a knot is tied. An 8-pound test line with a knot in it is actually less than eight pounds of test.

I know a couple hundred knots and I only know about two or three knots that leave the line at or near its original strength. Now, combine that fact with another little-known fact: No knot breaks until it slips. I wrote a book with Mark Sosin called *Practical Fishing Knots*. In researching that book I went to DuPont's laboratories and they showed me some super-slow-motion film of knots breaking. To prepare me for how slow the film would be, they shared a clip of an ordinary housefly leaving a tabletop. The film camera started rolling at the sound of impact when a flyswatter landed next to the fly. From the time the swatter hit until the moment the fly's feet left the tabletop took *seven* minutes. That way they could study every minute movement. What they showed me in these knot tests was an incredible eye-opener, even for an experienced fisherman and knot tier.

With the vast majority of knots, once a sufficient amount of tension is applied, the knot will slip. That slippage causes friction, which in turn creates heat. The heat from that friction eventually shears the line. So, if you could create a knot that never slips, the line would always remain intact. In fact, a well-designed knot that's tied loosely will snap sooner than a poorly designed knot that's tied tightly because the loose knot will invariably slip. This was a level of counterproductivity that simply couldn't stand.

The Bimini Twist, originally called the Twenty Times Around Knot, employed these same principles. When you make a Bimini twist you fold the line back, slip your hand inside, and wrap the line around your hand twenty times. Anyway, the significance of the Bimini Twist is that it won't slip. I use them a lot on my light spinning tackle fishing on rivers around Baltimore. When you hook bass and a lot of other fish, they'll try to grub it out on the river bottom. A Bimini gives you far more strength to keep that bass off the bottom.

They'll make Bimini Twists up to one hundred turns and, in effect, it becomes a giant shock absorber, spreading the shock over all those loops. That way you can use lighter line and still benefit from the shock absorber.

On top of all these technical and strategic developments came personal commitment. Standardization of rules encouraged competition. Competition, in turn, fueled personal commitment. One year for the MET Tournament Norm Jansick decided he was going to focus on catching the biggest shark on fly. Norm was not a wealthy guy, but he sure was determined and he was completely devoted to fishing. There's a place called Sandy Key Basin in Florida Bay that used to have hundreds of blacktip sharks. The only problem was that the floor of the basin was an absolute mess. There were hundreds of old fish traps, dead trees, and boat hulls on the bottom, each one of which presented a shark with the opportunity to cut a leader. Norm used a bucket with a glass bottom, and he and his fishing buddy, Bill Cunningham, poled every inch of the basin and charted every single underwater object. When Norm would hook a shark, Bill would gun the motor and get between the shark and the structure and run the shark off it. Lo and behold, Norm won the shark-on-fly division that year. The extent of innovation back then was remarkable and inspiring.

It was in this same era, the mid-1960s, when the long-running TV series *The American Sportsman* was born. The first show featured Joe Brooks and renowned late sportscaster Curt Gowdy fishing for brook trout in Argentina. The show would run for three decades and win Curt no fewer than a half dozen well-deserved Emmys.

I had a small behind-the-scenes role in some of the series' episodes. Although ABC Sports aired the show, the network didn't produce all of the episodes. Curt independently created and produced many episodes. He was the host and would produce a handful of shows a year and sell them to ABC. ABC paid a flat rate for each show, meaning that the more cost efficient Curt could be, the more money he could make.

Well, very often Curt would want to do shows on tarpon fishing or on bonefishing in south Florida. Running the MET Tournament, I knew south Florida's guides, hotels, restaurants, and so on. So Curt would call me and pay me to put together the details of the trip. I would arrange for the complimentary lodging for the crew, I'd get the boats and the guides and all. Then they'd all come down and shoot the show. During filming I would either run the camera boat or the gofer boat. I was involved in a bunch of those shows, probably a half dozen of them, but really as a background person. Still, I got to know Curt quite well and we became good friends. Back then Curt was having a condominium built on Virginia Key, and he had ordered one of those Hewes bonefish boats I had helped design. His boat wasn't ready yet and he had two young teenagers who he wanted to take fishing. I used to leave my boat at his dock so they could go out and fish.

Curt was a real nice guy. I was sorry to read about his passing in early 2006. Before big football games in Florida, like the Super Bowl or the Orange Bowl, he used to come to my office at the MET to get ready for the telecast. He'd try to memorize the names and numbers and positions of the guys on the two teams. Now, some of these big football players have names that look like eye charts, so it was not an easy job. Curt would sit in my office and go over the names and numbers aloud, like "Mjaczerowski, Outside Linebacker, sixty-three."

Then he would have me say a jersey number like, "Number seventy-eight."

He'd say, "Oswaltzki, Left Tackle." He would have every name and number and position in his head by the time kickoff came around.

Three years ago, Curt and Roland Martin and I were inducted on the same night into the International Game Fish Association Hall of Fame. It was a treat to share the table with my old friend and a true outdoorsman.

We lived in Florida—I did more than live there, I immersed myself in it—from 1964 to 1973. All but the final eight months of that period were in the offices of the *Miami Herald*, running the MET. As you now know, the MET was a mecca for serious industry people, particularly magazine editors and that helped me sell more magazine stories. Along with Vic Dunaway I had also worked on the start-up of *Florida Sportsman* magazine, which is by far the most successful outdoor magazine in the country, maybe in the world.

It all happened while we were at the *Herald*. Vic was the outdoor editor, doing three columns a week. There was a guy named Carl Wickstrom who published a magazine called *Aloft*, which was the in-flight magazine for the old National Airlines. *Aloft* was published monthly and since Carl's staff only needed about two weeks to put together each issue of the magazine, he was itchy to launch another publication. So he went to Vic and said he'd like to start a hunting, fishing, and outdoor magazine. Vic was, and probably still is, the most well-known and popular outdoor writer in Florida. He has a great sense of humor and is one of the best humor writers I've ever read. He still does a regular column in the magazine every month. Anyway, he was doing three big newspaper columns a week and Carl was trying to get this magazine going and Vic became the magazine's founding editor while keeping his day job. Vic felt that it was just too much for him to be doing both. He asked Carl if I could come on board as associate editor. Carl agreed to giving me the job and to our one condition: That we have total control over the editorial content of the magazine. Once we agreed on that, Vic and I went out and rounded up our contributors.

I think one of the keys to that magazine's incredible success is a decision we made early on. We decided not go out and look for journalists *per se*. We went out to find hunters and fishermen and campers who knew how to hunt, fish, and camp. If they had lousy pictures, well, I could help out with that. If their writing was weak, Vic, who had an English degree, could edit it for them. The original name of the magazine was *Florida and Tropic Sportsman*. In fact, I still have a copy of the inaugural issue. One of the interesting (and telling) facts about the magazine was that about a third of our early subscribers were not even residents of Florida. I am proud of that magazine not only because it has been successful, but also because it has gone on to produce just about all of the major outdoor writers to come out of Florida in the last twenty years or so.

Chapter 15
Heading North

Between running the MET, doing magazine articles, founding the magazine, and writing books, I was doing better and better financially, but there was one problem. I was on a contractual deal with the *Miami Herald* to run the tournament, so I wasn't receiving employee health benefits or retirement. With two young kids and a wife to think of, I decided that I needed a job where I'd get these other perks. Red Marston had been the outdoor editor over at the *St. Petersburg Times* for many years and he was retiring.

Through my work at the MET and on the magazine, I had become fairly well known around the state. The *Times* offered me a full-time, full benefits package to succeed Red. The package also boasted a nice pay raise, so I took it, and for the next several months I worked with some of the nicest people I have ever worked with in my life. They just treated me great. But shortly after I arrived in St. Pete, *The Baltimore Sun* started calling to see if I'd be willing to move back to Maryland and serve as outdoor editor for that paper. I really didn't want to go back to Maryland; I had come to love Florida. Ev and the kids had long since settled in, but the *Sun* was very persistent, calling on and off for about eight weeks. So eventually I went up to Baltimore for the interview.

The way I saw it, I was so happy in Florida that I had nothing to lose. In fact, I really saw the interview as me interviewing them. I actually brought a sheet of paper with me that had twenty-two questions on it. I was going to make sure that if I did move I wasn't going to be unhappy. For instance, I wanted to know whether they planned to pen me up in an office or let me do things my way: outdoors. My predecessor was required to spend two days a week in the office writing about other sports, but I made it clear that I thought outdoor writers should be outdoors. I told them I would come in one morning a week to do an outdoors forecast, but other than that I'd be my own boss, go where I want, stay as long as I want, and so on. I also told them that I wanted the freedom to write outside of the paper, whether that meant contributing to national magazines or pursuing book opportunities. See, the *St. Petersburg Times* did not want me to write for anyone else with the exception of *Florida Sportsman*. They really wanted to own you. Turns out the *Sun* had a different approach. When I told them I was interested in writing for national magazines and writing books and whatnot, they were all for it. They virtually offered me carte blanche, and while they were at it they pretty much doubled my salary. The fact that the managing editor back then, a highly respected guy named Paul Banker, was a fisherman didn't hurt one bit, either.

I took the job. I did have a few inevitable run-ins with the sports editor, a guy who knew absolutely nothing about hunting and fishing. Unfortunately, that's happening all over the United States right now. Sports editors are taking someone from a football or baseball beat and assigning them to cover the outdoors. I believe that in outdoor writing, firsthand experience is everything. If you're not a serious outdoorsperson you have no business writing for an outdoors page. When I retired from *The Baltimore Sun* they gave the column to a guy who couldn't get along with the other guys in the sports department. His passion was not fishing or hunting or hiking or camping or ecology. It was sailing. In the four short years he was there, the paper's outdoor readership dried up. He liked being outdoors, of course, but he didn't know anything about "the outdoors." He didn't know that you can tell a deer track in the woods by looking at the leaves. When a deer steps on a leaf the leaf turns over and the underside of the leaf is not sun-bleached like the upper side. So if you want to track a deer just follow the path of dark leaves and you'll see exactly where the deer walked.

Early on I said to Paul Banker that an outdoor writer belongs outdoors, not in a gym covering high school basketball. In fact, I've argued my whole career that the sports section was entirely the wrong place to put an outdoor column. Here's why: Sports departments spend 99 percent of their space describing athletic feats that 99 percent of the readership couldn't do (and possibly wouldn't even want to do) if their life depended on it. People may like to *read* about a guy bowling over a linebacker en route to the end zone, but they have no interest in trying to *do* it. Contrast that to an outdoor page. An outdoor page is not a news page, but a service page. Instead of reading about the doings of elite, overpaid athletes, you're reading about what your neighbor or your uncle, your brother, or yourself will be catching tomorrow or later this week. Outdoor readers want to know how to improve, where to go to, how to make it more fun. They want to learn about better tackle, new streams, new techniques, better tents and boats. Readers of outdoor columns want the kind of information they can use. I've never heard of a guy who read about a lineman making a shoestring tackle and then went out and sacked some guy in the street. Unfortunately, that argument never got very far, and today most outdoor columns are still featured in the sports section.

Even after I took the job I had some clashes with this sports editor. He felt that I should have a plan and be able to know precisely what I was going to be writing about two months from now. That may work for the team-sports guy who covers scheduled games, but not for an outdoors guy who has to respond to the whims of nature. Well, he got on my case about it. Since I was now making decent money on the side, I could afford to go to the mat with him. I told the boss, Banker, that either we abide by the initial understanding or I leave. I couldn't do my job the way the sports editor wanted me to do it. As it turns out, the *Sun* had been syndicating my column. Newspapers all over the United States had been picking up my work. Readers loved it. I had a lot of old ladies writing letters to the editor and saying how much they loved my column. Banker came down on my side and I never looked back.

I liked the newspaper life. At least I did in the beginning. The problem was that my *Sun* column appeared on Tuesdays, Fridays, and Sundays, which meant that three days out of seven I had to write a column. I had a firm principle by which I operated in those days: I would not write about something or someplace unless I had actually used it or been there myself. That was great for my readers, but it was tough on me. I had to do something on Day One and write about it on Day Two. I would do something on Day Three and write about it on Day Four. Do something on Day Four and write about it on Day Five. I really only had one day a week off. If I was going on a trip of some kind, say I was going to Belize to fish for five or six days, I had to write three columns ahead of time and submit them so the paper would have something to run when I was on the road. Because I did do a lot of trips, I was often writing six, seven, eight columns a week. I'd go out on Monday and maybe go crappie fishing on the Eastern Shore. Come back on Tuesday, print the photographs, write the column, and turn it in to the paper. Wednesday maybe I would go to Western Maryland and call foxes and write that column on Thursday.

Over time that got a little easier because when you've fished in as many places and with as many kinds of different tackle and for as many kinds of fish as I have you create a built-in library of things you can write about. I could probably sit down right now and right three columns this afternoon without doing any research. Now, if a story idea requires research, I just won't do the column. I might have to look up a fact here or there, but mostly what I write these days comes straight from my head. People ask me how can I write a book in just a few months, but the fact is that it's easy when all you're doing is pulling it from your own mental library. If I had to research these books, they'd take years.

As noted above, I didn't just do hunting and fishing for the *Sun*. I did a lot of nature stuff. I wrote about how to tell the difference between prey and predator. Predators, such as coyotes, have eyes that look straight ahead, while prey, such as rabbits and deer, have eyes that are more toward the side of their head so that they can see what's coming from in front of, beside, and behind them. I remember writing about the often-overlooked relationship between flowers and fishing. There's a plant called the trout lily that thrives all through the mid-Atlantic region of the United States. You'll find it anywhere from Pennsylvania all the way down to North Carolina. It's a beautiful little yellow-spotted lily that stands about 6 inches high. When that flower is blooming there is a mayfly that comes out at the same time called the Quill Gordon. And when the Pink Lady Slippers bloom there is another mayfly that comes out at that time. Well, if you were informed enough to look for these flowers and you found them in bloom, you would know precisely what kinds of flies the local fish are dining on.

Along those lines there's a bush that's actually called a shadbush. And there's a well-known tree called a dogwood. If you're ever interested in catching hickory shad, they arrive when the shadbush and the dogwood bloom. If anglers had the time to spend in the wild all day and study this stuff, they wouldn't need fly-fishing books or newspaper columns, because everything in nature reveals itself over time. That was my job: to take the time to see nature revealed and to pass along what I learned to people who couldn't be there.

Take mayflies. They are a remarkable aspect of the outdoor world and they offer amazing insight into the fish's ecosystem. Mayflies are upright-winged flies. They live in the bottom of the stream for several years as nymphs. In springtime they work their way up to the surface. Eventually they push open their exoskeleton, get out, float along the surface of the water for a while, and then fly into the trees, where they morph into another color. Then they come back that day or the next day, lay their eggs, and die. Well, I once wrote a column about this, that people occasionally remember to this day. You can roughly tell, I wrote, what color mayflies are hatching according to the season. In winter, any mayfly that hatches is black. That's because they're trying to absorb as much heat as they can. Along about the middle of May, depending on your location, you have gray flies. Then sometime between early and mid-May you have dark brown flies, which are called a Henderson's hatch. Then toward the end of May you have a dark cream or yellow fly called the Sulphur. Then in June you have a bright yellow fly called the Light Cahill. Then the cycle goes back the other way and the hatching flies get darker through the winter.

Most people never notice this stuff. I only learned it myself by trying to be observant and then asking questions. I'd ask biologists why one bug was colored like this and why another bug was colored like that. The biologists know this stuff like we know the alphabet. Filling that knowledge gap between them and local fisherman was both my passion and my profession.

Eventually I learned that there are three basic kinds of flies. How do you tell them apart? There's the mayfly, which when it's sitting still has its wings upright and flush against one another. Then there's the caddis fly, which has wings like a pup tent. Then there's the stone fly, whose wings lay flat on its back. And they fly differently. Mayflies fly in a pretty steady pattern. The caddis flies dart back and forth, while stone flies fly with their bodies almost in a vertical position and they're very poor flyers.

I wrote a lot about tides and I think that information was very useful. People tend to oversimplify tides—for example, there's a high tide at noon and then a low tide at six. Well, it's a little more complicated than that. There's usually a high tide that lasts about six hours and then there's a low tide that lasts about six hours and then another high and another low, all keyed to the phases of the moon. What most people don't know is that every other week there are tides that come in both unusually high and unusually low. They're called spring tides because they "spring" up and down. The weeks in between are called neap tides. Neap tides don't go up very far and they don't go down very far. How do you plan around this? Well, it comes back to the moon. When the moon, the sun, and the Earth are all in line there is tremendous gravitational pull and you get high tides. When the sun is at right angles to the moon, they are pulling against each other and you don't get very high tides. So anytime you have a quarter moon week, there's not much in the way of tides. If you have a full moon or no moon, you get spring tide. Most people get lost in all the minutiae about gravitational pull of the moon and all. I tell people simply to look up at the moon. If you see a quarter moon you know the tide just went out and if you can't see the moon or if it's bright you know you're going to get a big tide.

That's great, the reader would be saying to himself, but why is fishing the tides important? Well, in shallow water when you have neap tides, you can't get up on the flats to fish because there just isn't enough water either for your boat or for the fish. If you're fishing for bonefish or permit or tarpon or things like that, they like to feed in the shallow water. But if the neap tide has done away with the shallow flats, you're not going to find any fish there.

The main reason why tide is so important is that saltwater baitfish do not have a home. I've never seen this written before, but it's true. If you go to a local freshwater stream that's got sculpins and minnows and crawfish in it, those creatures have "home" pools where they live. After a big rain, when the water level comes up, these creatures get under a rock or behind a bank or under a cutback or behind a log, because they have a desire to stay in their home pool. Now, you go to Chesapeake Bay and in a basin there you might find crabs floating around, or you've got alewives or menhaden or some kind of baitfish. Unlike the minnows in the stream, the saltwater creatures are nomadic. They don't "belong" anywhere, so when the tide goes out, these saltwater creatures don't resist. First off, there's always the risk that the basin they're in might go dry, so they're not looking to stick around. Second, from the standpoint of expending energy it's not economical for them to fight that tide because they don't "belong" there. If you realize that the creatures fish prey on are at the mercy of the current, you soon realize that wherever currents converge you are going to find a lot of fish.

Consider Florida Bay on the mainland side of the Everglades. During high tide the baitfish come in to feed around the mangroves. When the tide gets back inside those roots, the fish can't get out. The force of the tide keeps them in the shallows near the mangrove roots. What you try to do is fish those areas when the tide starts to fall. That's because as the tide is falling the baitfish know there are big game fish out in the deeper water who want to eat them, so they'll stay in that shallow water as long as they can. In that last few hours of the falling tide they have to come out. When? They'll come out as late as they possibly can. Where? Out of the drainage ditches. So where these drainage ditches meet the main body of water is where the game fish are going to be waiting for these baitfish. That's where you want to be.

So, how do you know which drainage ditches are the hot ones? Easy: Birds. Any time you have a falling tide, and a drainage ditch, just look for scavenger birds such as egrets and gulls. Wherever they're pecking around, you know you have a hot spot. The signs are all there for you.

Joe Brooks told me when I first got into writing, "Lefty, you learn all you can about the birds, flowers, trees, everything in nature because all those things will tell you how you can fish better or hunt better." Of course I was interested in it anyway. To me this stuff is fascinating, but hearing Joe Brooks tell me that made me feel I was going in the right direction and that's how I approached my columns.

I wrote a memorable column about the mythology surrounding water temperature. You hear people say or you read in the bass magazines that a certain temperature is "a bass's comfort zone." That's bull dingy. Imagine you were locked in a meat cooler. Over time your body temperature would drop and your body would have to work harder to try to maintain the old 98.6. Fish aren't that way. Not until the water is freezing or near freezing (and I've caught a lot of smallmouth bass at 34 or 35 degrees) or more importantly, if the water gets really hot, do fish get stressed.

Most cold-water species, such as trout, will die in 75-degree water. But fish don't get uncomfortable unless they are in the very top or very bottom of their range. We used to float down the Potomac River looking for natural spring holes because the ambient water temperature on a hot summer day might be 82 degrees in the river, but around the spring it might be 70 degrees.

Temperature drives the metabolic engine of a fish. The colder a fish gets, the more food he needs in order to run the engine. When people see all these smallmouths eating around a spring hole they mistakenly say that the cooler water is the fishes' comfort zone. It's got nothing to do with comfort. It's because their metabolic engine is running faster. A fish in 85-degree water is going to slow down. He doesn't need much food, but the fish in the cooler water has to fuel his heightened metabolism. These are the kinds of things I loved to write about.

Once I got around the sports editor, it was nice to be home. The Baltimore-D.C. area is also one of the best fishing regions of the country because you've got the Chesapeake Bay and the Delaware Bay that are each within hours, even minutes, of most *Baltimore Sun* readers. You've got the Potomac River, the Susquehanna, the Juniata River, the Shenandoah, all with bass and stuff in them, and you've got the trout streams of the Blue Ridge Mountains an hour's drive away. You have an enormous amount and variety of fishing in the Baltimore area as well as really good hunting.

I knew all the rivers and all the backcountry. I felt very comfortable and informed there. I had spent twenty-something years just roaming every back road. In fact, most of the roads were still dirt when I first started in the outdoors of Maryland. I knew the entire area very well. If someone told me about a certain pond in Delaware I knew just how to get there.

That local knowledge was now backed up by the eight years of "schooling" I had in Florida, not to mention all the traveling I was doing for slide shows and all. The *Sun's* syndication arm had my column appearing in newspapers in Idaho and San Francisco and Houston and Bangor. I was also writing for magazines. For my magazine work I simply wrote the piece on typewriter paper and mailed it to the editor at the magazine. Then in the 1970s, shortly after I came back up to Baltimore, I bought my first IBM computer and a dot matrix printer that must have weighed fifty pounds. I paid $7,000 and was one of the first outdoor writers in the country to have a computer. Then the newspaper started getting computers.

It was very confusing to switch from a typewriter to a computer, but I realized early on that it was a lot easier to write on a computer. First of all you can insert something or change something. Back in the old days, when you finished writing your story and thought of something else to add or found an error, you had to pretty much start over.

At the newspaper we used copy paper that came in triplicate, with a piece of white paper, a piece of yellow paper, and a piece of light green.

They were all attached, and when you typed on the white paper, it copied through like carbon paper onto the other two. I wrote all my columns on typewriters, double-spaced to leave room for editors' comments. I had a desk at the paper that I only used on Thursday mornings. I would go in at six a.m., ahead of the traffic, and I'd call contacts all around the region to get the fishing forecasts: Harpers Ferry, West Virginia; Newark, Delaware; all over Maryland and the Chesapeake area. Sure it kept me busy on Thursday mornings, but this information was totally useless. Think about it. I was calling on a Thursday to see where they caught fish on Sunday, Monday, Tuesday, and Wednesday and I would use the info to tell people where to fish on the coming Friday and Saturday and Sunday. This was not a service to our readers. In fact, it was a disservice. If you have a bunch of tuna coming by the mouth of the Chesapeake Bay today, hell, they might be in Maine in four or five days. Over the sports editor's objections I actually put a disclaimer at the end of each forecast that said, "This information was gathered over the last five days. If you are interested in fishing a certain location, I suggest you contact authorities there for more up-to-date information." It told anybody with a brain that this information wasn't worth a darn anyway. The sports editor complained. He said, "Lefty, I don't like this disclaimer in there."

I said, "Why not?"

He said, "It tells people this information isn't any good."

I said, "It ain't any good. We shouldn't even do it."

I didn't like going over my editor's head, but I told Paul Banker that these forecasts were full of terrible information and, being a fisherman, he knew it. "Let's drop the forecast," I told him, "and give the readers something worthwhile."

Banker said, "I think you're right." So we dropped the forecast for two weeks and we got so much mail from readers who missed their forecasts that we simply had to go back to running it.

Rather quickly my *Sun* beat grew to include not only fishing, hunting, and wildlife but also conservation. And it was in this area that I saw an enormous change. Over the last thirty or forty years there have been incredible changes in the outdoors potential of the state of Maryland. Most of those changes have been for the worse and most of them have been caused by development, or, more accurately, overdevelopment. When we left for Florida in 1964, Frederick was a city of about 15,000 or 16,000 people. Today there are about 80,000 people living in or around the city. It's the second-largest city in Maryland after Baltimore. Paul Crum grew up with me in Frederick County and we used to fish with minnows for bass. On a Friday afternoon after work we would go out and seine minnows out of these small streams, a lot of them as wide as eight to ten feet and at the most hip or waist deep. We'd put the minnows in a minnow bucket and put them under a bridge that had water rushing beneath it to keep the minnows healthy. Next morning on the way to fish we would just pick up the bucket and go. Today, most of those streams are gone. In many places there isn't even a visual clue or reminder that there once was a stream there. Streams that were there, that once upon a time were nice and healthy, were now barely down to a trickle. Another thing is that the farming areas in the western shore of Maryland have pretty much vanished. Most of the land has been taken up by development, which has severely impacted the fishing. The Potomac River, which used to be an exceptional bass river, has seen a precipitous decline in its vibrancy. We used to catch 20, 30, 40 smallmouth bass a day and some of them would reach 3 or 4 pounds. Today, those fish simply don't exist. In fact, I floated over a mile of the Potomac last year, through three or four feet of crystal-clear water. All we saw was one largemouth bass, three carp, and one sucker. Back in the 1950s we would have seen hundreds of fish. There used to be huge amounts of minnows in and around the Potomac's grass beds. Now you can go by fifty grass beds and not see a single minnow.

Here on the Potomac River near Harper's Ferry, West Virginia.
This was my first fly rod outfit—a South Bend Glass rod and a
Pflueger Medalist reel.

1967—fishing the Content Keys—back then a remote place with very few anglers—with my son and favorite fishing companion, Larry.

The Florida Keys—Bob Hewes gaffs a shark for me.

A nice pike that weighed more than 20 pounds. I caught this on fly at North Seal River Lodge in northern Manitoba, Canada, one of my favorite places to fish.

A nice carp—one of the strongest and most challenging freshwater fish out there. This was caught on the west branch of the Susquehanna with guide Mike O'Brien.

Returning to camp on the Alta River, 100 miles north of the
Arctic Circle. Many fishermen regard the Alta River as the
greatest in the world for Atlantic salmon—the fish in the
boat exceeded 25 pounds.

Fishing for largemouth bass in the Everglades with two friends, Jose Wjebe and Flip Pallot, both exceptional fishermen.

An Atlantic salmon caught on the legendary Spey River in Scotland.

A largemouth bass taken on a popping bug (Lefty's Bug), that I'd spent years designing. In various sizes it will catch panfish, bass, and saltwater species.

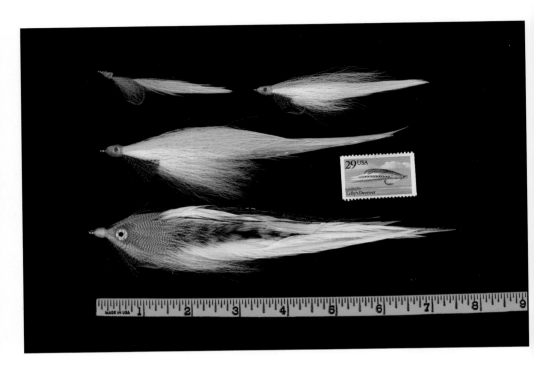

My Deceiver flies, which can be tied in varying color combinations and sizes. It's now one of the world's most popular flies. Also, you'll see the 'Lefty's Deceiver' U.S. postage stamp.

That may be due in part to over-fishing, but that's not the real problem.

Something is wrong with our water systems. It's not just happening in the Potomac; these declines in fish populations are occurring everywhere. Development is not the only problem. One of the biggest problems confronting fishery management today is the well-intentioned but ill-informed biologist. These kids, fresh out of college, come to an area and start making assessments with all the science in the world, but without any historical context. They don't have any historical background on the river they're working and they don't listen to or believe local fishermen who have had intimate knowledge of these waters for decades. For example, while I was at the *Baltimore Sun* back in the 1970s, two really nice, well-educated young men were assigned to work as fishery biologists in my area. I asked them, "What are you going to do about the Potomac?"

They said, "What do you mean?"

I said, "Well, it's in pretty bad shape."

"Comparatively speaking," they said, "we think it's in fabulous condition."

I said, "Where are you from!?"

Turns out they were from Massachusetts, where it was not unusual for a stream to be so saturated with oils and other pollutants that several streams have actually caught fire. When they came down here and saw the crystal-clear waters of the Potomac, they thought everything was in great shape. They had no idea how much the river had declined in just the years since I'd been in Florida. They had no historical context. It's not their fault, but we have people managing fisheries now who never lived in the regions they're studying. Without any historical context, any clean river looks great, but if you've lived in a region for a long time and you've seen the fish population decline, you have a far better understanding, not to mention a sense of urgency.

Our biologists are telling us that the Potomac is in great shape, but the fishermen, many of whom are my friends and many of whom have knowledge of the Potomac dating back to the 1930s and 1940s, are increasingly leaving the Potomac and taking their bass fishing up to the Susquehanna because they can't catch any bass in the Potomac.

The other factor in the demise of the Potomac, and one that can't be discounted, is the migration of city dwellers into suburban and rural areas. The first thing these people do when they move to the country is post "No Trespassing, No Hunting, No Fishing" signs. As all those people move out of cities like Baltimore and Washington D.C., they are buying up more and more land that will never be hunted or fished. Some of them take the wildlife seriously. In terms of promoting birdlife, say, quail, the landowners can do a lot of things like cut down trees to allow shrub cover to grow. But no matter what you do, that piece of land will only support a limited number of quail. You may move the population up by a small percentage, but there are only so many of any type of animal that can live per acre. That takes time and work, and of course, if that land is eventually hunted, it doesn't take long to harvest the population.

Fishing offers far more flexibility. Streams can be stocked. We can introduce species. We have more opportunities in fishing to furnish more recreation. Wildlife managers have a much tougher time. In the 1950s pollution was rampant throughout the industrial Northeast and mid-Atlantic states. Developers were casually dumping anything they wanted into our rivers and streams. In fact, it was in the 1950s that I got my first lesson in how destructive careless developers can be. Not far from our home was a small village called Middletown. A stream called Middle Creek ran nearby. It meandered through the countryside for about fifteen miles before it joined the Potomac in Lander, one of my favorite and most productive fishing spots. Old-timers will remember that we used to fish for rough-scale suckers just below where the two arteries fused. Directly below the mouth of Middle Creek was a long stretch of 7-to-8-foot deep water where the suckers would come to spawn each April. Well, in the 1950s a developer had decided to build some homes in Middletown, not far from the creek. During construction there was a severe rainstorm in which so much mud slid off the construction site and into the water that for a distance of about fifteen miles, all of the creek's great fishing holes had virtually been filled in. In some places there was so much earth in the brook that gravel "sandbars" emerged from the water. Our beloved Middle Creek had been reduced to a silt-filled brook. Seeing that much destruction in less than twenty-four hours of rain was an eye-opener. I became more proactive. Around that same time I wrote about how foolish it was for local farmers to cut down trees alongside streams in an effort to gain back arable land. What would happen is the farmer would cut down the trees, and sure, he'd be able to farm that land for a year or two, until a heavy rain came. Then all that gained farmland—land that had once been anchored in place by tree roots—would get washed away by swollen waters. In the long run, these farmers were destroying their property.

I worked at the *Sun* from 1974 to 1993. In all those years I rarely found myself stuck for a column idea. Every once in a while I'd sit down and say, "What will I write about today?" In those cases, I'd usually focus on common foul-ups, resolving the small things that have the potential for making or breaking your day on the water.

For instance, I'd do a story on shoes. Everybody wears shoes. Then I'd sit back and ask myself what kinds of problems shoes can present to an outdoorsman. Well, take the average guy who hikes or hunts. Most of those shoes have a wide sole that sticks out and catches brush. What I used to do when I bought a new pair of hunting or hiking boots was go to a shoemaker and have him grind off the side of the sole until it was flush with the last. That way I caught far less brush as I walked through the woods.

So when I didn't have a specific fishing tip or location or techniques to share, I'd focus on the small nuisances of the sport. These were often the most widely read columns because everybody who used the outdoors—hunters, hikers, fly fishermen, plug casters, spin casters, walkers—had these little headaches.

I did bits about how to improve your ability to see fish. If you don't wear a hat and you're trying to see fish in the water on a sunny day, good luck. There's so much glare bouncing off the water that you usually can't see them. It gets even harder to see them if you're wearing a hat with a white or light-colored under-brim. What happens is that the light reflected off the water reflects again off the white under-brim and bounces into your eyes. But if you have a dark under-brim, the light is absorbed by the darkness and you'll see much better. Of course a lot of people have light-colored hats that they like to wear in summer. Don't throw them away. Just apply some dark shoe polish to the under-brim (please give the shoe polish a little time to dry before donning the cap).

Most people just accept these little problems instead of doing something about it. For a writer, those everyday frustrations are an endless supply of ideas. For instance, I have a holster for my scissors so they're in the same place all the time. Most people are content to look around for stuff. If I need my glue stick, it's got a little holder, too. My pens are all stored in the same place. My Scotch tape dispenser used to slide all over the place, especially if I was trying to operate it with one hand. So I built a little box to put it in so it never moves.

The crown jewel in my jerry-rigged life is the mailbox. Our mailbox is forty feet from our front door. The mailman comes every day sometime between 9:30 and 3:30. Ev and I are getting older and for a long time we used to just walk out the door every so often to see if the mail had arrived. Well, in the cold of winter a fruitless walk to the mailbox can be pretty frustrating. I was at Wal-Mart one day and I saw these orange hard-rubber balls. I bought one, drilled a hole through it, and then put some parachute cord through it and tied a knot on either side of the ball so the ball would stay in the middle of cord line. Then I screwed one end of the cord to the bottom of the mailbox and made a knot in the other end, opened the mailbox, and jammed the knot in it. Well, when the mailman comes and opens the box, the ball hangs down and I know the mailman came. Not only do Ev and I now save time checking the mailbox but also all the neighbors now look for our orange ball to see if the mailman has come.

I'm going to do an article one day on how tropical shirts should be designed. First, all the buttons should be large. Most of the people who design these things are in their thirties, and they don't know that as we all get older most of us get arthritis. Bigger buttons are easier to handle. You ought to have a spare button on the tail so that if you lose a button you can replace it. This one's a no-brainer for those of you who've ever gone fishing on a high-speed boat: collars ought to be buttoned down. When you're running fast in a boat, loose collars will slap you in the face all the way out and all the way home. Another one: Standard-length shirttails are fine for standard activities like sitting in an office or going to church, but fishing shirts should have extra-long tails so that as you're moving around in a day of fishing they won't constantly become untucked. Plus, the fabric should be resistant to the ultraviolet rays of the sun. Some companies put little tabs on the upper arm so that you can roll up your sleeves and attach them there. Those things are a mess. All they do is catch on things. And with apologies to DuPont, stay away from CoolMax fabric. It itches. At least it itches me.

While my little tips (ultimately collected in a book entitled *Lefty's 101 Fly Fishing Tips)* were helping anglers fish smarter, there was a steady increase in the number of fly fishermen coming into the sport. When I started fly-fishing in the late 1940s I only knew of three fly fishermen in all of Maryland. Now I would estimate that we have at least five thousand or ten thousand avid fly fisherman in the State of Maryland alone.

Ultimately the newspaper business was just too time consuming for me. In the end, with all the books, magazines, trips, teaching, and consulting I was doing I just didn't have time for the job anymore. I was writing three columns a week for them and I was on the staffs of four or five magazines and I was doing books and seminars and clinics and demonstrations for companies. In fact, when I quit the newspaper I got up the next morning and realized that I could get up in the morning and I didn't have to write a column and two days later write another column and so on, it was a huge relief. I told Ev it was like getting out of jail.

Eighteen years. I went to work at the *Sun* January 1, 1973 and retired in January 1992. They didn't want me to go, which felt nice, but I just had too many things on my plate. But they were wonderful to me. They really were.

CHAPTER 16

CASTING AND THE FOUR PRINCIPLES OF FLY-FISHING

As GRATIFYING AND ENJOYABLE AS my newspaper years were, my greatest impact on the outdoor world came through magazine writing. I was inshore editor for twenty years for a magazine called *Fishing World*, which is now defunct. For several years I was the associate fishing editor of *Outdoor Life*. I am still on the staff of *Saltwater Sportsman* and I am still on *Florida Sportsman's* staff. I wrote for several publications outside the country. I was an editor-at-large with the *Federation of Fly Fishing* magazine.

I never wrote for *Sports Illustrated* or *LIFE* magazines. I call that pretty writing. I don't mean that in a derogatory way, but I only have a high school education. I never understood it when people would tell me that some guy was a great writer. I have a friend named Judith Schnell who is a publisher of fly-fishing books for Stackpole Books. She sent me a book that was written by a guy who people had been saying for years was an unbelievable writer. He'd written several books that people raved about and that had sold very well. She asked me if I would read his latest manuscript. I read three chapters and I got so bored that I called Judith and said, "I have to send it back. I like the guy, but this stuff is boring to me." They take a cute little story and they go on for pages and pages before getting to the punch line. I'd rather they just get to the punch line and move on. I told her that if she wanted to send me technical manuals or something else to look at, I'd do it, but due to my own ignorance I just

147

can't appreciate what everybody else says is "great writing."

The fact is that I've found very few so-called great writers that I actually enjoy reading. Robert Ruark is certainly one. Charlie Waterman is one. Some of Nick Lyons's stuff is great. I don't know enough to know why a great writer is great. I can't discern or appreciate world-class syntax. I guess I've always been more of doer than a reader.

As I mentioned earlier, my first real lesson in fly-fishing came in 1947 from Joe Brooks at Herring Run Park. He taught me the standard method, the same one he'd been taught and which had been taught for centuries. In the standard method the angler basically brings the rod from about ten o'clock back to about two o'clock and then back to ten o'clock. After trying that technique for a while I began to realize that it was not the best, most efficient way to cast a fly line. It just doesn't work. In fact, as early as 1947 when Joe Brooks first began teaching me about fly casting, I began to question the technique and tinker with new ideas. I started experimenting by fly casting for smallmouth bass on the Potomac and the Susquehanna Rivers. There, I learned that the longer you can swim the fly through the water, the better the fishing. So I began to search for a method that would give me longer casts without sacrificing accuracy.

Another big influence at this critical time in my development was Al McLane. He was writing a fishing column for *Field & Stream*, and his piece on double hauling caught my attention. I was so enthralled by what he wrote that I can remember actually laying the magazine at my feet and trying to imitate the sketches. That's how I learned the fundamentals of double hauling. Again, though, once I had some comfort with Al's technique I began to modify it.

Through trial and error I gradually learned to take the rod way back behind me and make longer back casts and longer forward casts. I also abandoned the high-hand vertical style of the standard method and adopted a much lower position, a more horizontal profile for my arm. As I began to refine my technique I found that I was not only making longer, more accurate casts with tighter loops, but I was doing it with far less effort that the old 10-to-2 method had demanded.

Over the course of the next several decades—through my stint in Florida, my return to Maryland, and even to this day—I've continued to refine my thinking on the cast. I paid close attention all those years to other fly casters' successes and struggles. I picked up little gimmicks, tricks, and other insight from veteran anglers I'd run into around the country. I began to share my new method, which I call a composite method because it really is borrowed from a variety of techniques.

In March 1965, I wrote an article detailing my new technique for *Outdoor Life*. Many people view that article as a landmark in the evolution of the fly cast. To this day, however, many critics see it as outright heresy, an affront to the traditions of the sport. And therein lies one of the great blessings and burdens of the sport: Tradition.

Fly-fishing has been around for hundreds of years. The first written reference to fly-fishing is in Ælian's *Natural History*. Written in approximately 200 A.D., the book depicts fly-fishing with 6-foot rods as it was then practiced on the rivers of what we now know as Italy. Over the next several centuries the sport slowly evolved. Europeans and the British fished with small wet flies on narrow streams. The rods, usually 12 feet in length, were generally made of wood. The line consisted of a braid of very fine hairs from the tail of a horse. Given the small streams, the likely abundance of fish, the length of the rods and the dynamics of the horsehair lines, most of the casts made in the early days of fly-fishing were very short. As a result, the technique that developed at the time called for a motion from about ten o'clock to about two o'clock. At two o'clock the motion came to a sudden stop that flipped the line behind the angler, who then made a powerful move back down to ten o'clock to complete the cast.

Today we use graphite rods, synthetic line, and heavier flies and generally want to make longer casts. In short, the sport has changed radically over the last few hundred years, so why are we still teaching the old 10-to-2 technique? That's where the obstinacy of tradition comes in. Over the years, millions of new fly fishermen have been taught the 10-to-2. Many of those new anglers have gone on to become instructors. Understandably, they are very reluctant to pass on a method other than the one they themselves were taught. Most of them are trout fishermen, who only need to toss little flies very short distances, anyway. Since the 10-to-2 method works fairly well for short, simple casts, they don't really have a rationale for changing. The Fly Fishing Federation has a casting instructor's program that basically teaches the 10-to-2, rod up vertically, back and forth. Again, most of the people who teach and learn this technique are trout fishermen who are fishing small streams with small flies and casting very short distances. The real schism occurs when a fisherman decides he wants to cast across larger bodies of water, or through a strong wind or to fish that are farther away. In such situations far too many anglers stick with the 10-to-2 method, and for their adherence to tradition they end up with a heap of frustration and a pile of fly line at their feet. I can't think of a better way to stunt the growth of the sport we all love than to keep our practitioners from excelling.

Think about Jack Nicklaus and Tiger Woods. They are the two greatest golfers in the history of the game. If you examine their golf swings you'll find that they are completely different. Most notable is the fact that Jack has the club in a very upright position on the backswing and Tiger has the club far closer to horizontal. Neither of these positions is very important; what's important is the moment of truth, the point of impact. Nobody accuses Tiger of perverting his sport just because he swings differently from Nicklaus. Both he *and* Jack swing in a more radically different manner than Bobby Jones, but they are also playing with far better equipment, technology, and the strength of knowledge gained from nearly a century of swing research. Far from being an anti-tradition heretic, Woods is seen and welcomed as the next step in the evolution of a great game.

That hasn't happened in fly-fishing. Our sport is paralyzed by tradition. Don't get me wrong—tradition can be a very good thing. Our sport itself is a tradition. But when tradition gets in the way of innovation or improvement it can stifle. I *know* that the techniques I have espoused over the last fifty years make fly-fishing easier and more fun for the vast majority of people. If it weren't for the burden of misguided traditionalists we could be welcoming more and more people into our sport to stay rather than watching them come and then go in droves.

People, by and large, are not good casters. It's obvious to me that if we could get newcomers to cast more effectively they would catch more fish, have more fun, and fish more often. In fact, I believe the reason more people don't fly-fish—the same thing that holds retailers and tackle makers from selling more equipment—is reliance on the outdated, outmoded clock method. We could be watching our industry grow as it sold more equipment and booked more trips, but as things stand now, tradition's unhealthy grip is constricting us. Traditionalists often try to drown out, even ridicule, fresh thinking. They've been after me since the *Outdoor Life* piece in 1965.

The headline of my blasphemous article read, "NEW WAY TO FLY CAST." The deck or secondary headline said, "Fly casting isn't tough. With my method, you'll cast farther, improve control, double the rod power with less effort." Still sounds pretty good to me. I went on to explain the basics of the fly cast as I saw them forty years ago and as I still see them through the prism of forty subsequent years of experience. The piece, heavily illustrated with the superb drawings of Ned Smith, covered the basic casting technique I was introducing and then applied that technique to an assortment of roll casts. Here are a few excerpts (written for the right-handed angler).

From the beginning, fly-casting mechanics have remained essentially the same: Stop the rod somewhere between 12 and 1 o'clock on the back cast, wait for the line tug before making the forward cast, and so on. A careful analysis of the conventional way reveals a lack of imagination and an inefficient method of delivering the fly to the fish. . . . The accepted method of fly-casting limits the angler's ability to deliver the fly over a long distance and hinders his control of the line while it's in the air. Most instructors insist that little or no use be made of the arm during the act of casting. God gave us more than thirty inches of arm. Why not use it?

Many fisherman claim there is no advantage in being able to cast one hundred feet or more. But there is considerable advantage in having the skill to cast that far. Most casting is done at less than seventy feet. But if you and your partner, who, let's say, doesn't know how to throw the long line, are fishing at fifty feet and his distance limit is fifty feet, you are having fun and he is working. . . .

The composite method of fly casting is a start-to-finish procedure. It begins with the line on the water in front of you and ends when the line has been cast and returns to the surface. . . . Here is the method: Place about twenty feet of line on the water in front of you. Lower the rod tip until it is within a foot of the surface. Take in all slack with the left hand. Raise the rod tip quickly, but not with a jerk, to about 1 o'clock in a rapid motion. You have not yet made the back cast. You've simply smoothly lifted all the fly line from the water. At this point, only the leader will remain on the surface. This is important. In the conventional cast, water friction clinging to the long length of line lying on the surface steals a tremendous amount of power from the rod before it can force the line into the air and before the back cast is made.

The wrist now comes into play for the first time. The line is off the water. With a quick snap of the wrist, drive the rod tip up and backward with the rod leaning slightly to the right of vertical. The line will streak up and behind you. Stop applying power at about 11 o'clock but allow the rod to drift back free of line tension.

Here again, an important difference in the two systems of casting occurs. The rod and arm are allowed to drift back, with absolutely no power applied, until the rod is almost parallel with the ground. The elbow is now at about shoulder height and the rod and the elbow remain in this position until the line has straightened out behind you.

At the completion of your back cast, you should be able to look over your shoulder, through the guides and down your line.

The third and very important feature of the composite cast begins with the forward cast. The moment the line straightens behind you, the rod is carried forward with the elbow descending from slightly above shoulder height until the rod hand is about even with the shoulder. It is important to remember that from this moment until the cast is completed, the rod hand is carried parallel with the ground. After the hand has pulled the rod handle forward as far as possible, the wrist, at the last instant, is turned over and down, as though driving a nail with a hammer. Viewed from the front, the path the rod travels in the forward cast is with the tip pointing in a vertical position, then over and down, as described. At the completion of the cast, the rod is not pointing at the place where the fly is to land, but at eye level above that spot. If the cast is delivered at eye level and you've followed the previous directions, you'll discover the forward loop turns over perfectly and the fly will settle to the water cleanly. That's about all there is to the composite method of fly casting.

The article went on to talk in detail about double hauling and roll casting, but that passage is the crux of the piece. I wrote those words over forty years ago. In the meantime, I've written twenty-two books expounding on my theory and it's still deemed by many to be controversial. All I know is that if you ever went down to the South Pacific somewhere and put a fly rod in the hands of someone who'd never read a book on the topic and never seen a video, he would naturally implement something closer to my technique. That's because it's instinctive, it's natural, it's simple, it's easy, and it's effective. To this day, I am amazed at how many instructors and knowledgeable, experienced fisherman still use the 10-to-

2 method. Talk to any guide—one who works salt water, one who works the steelhead rivers out west or one who fishes for bass with larger flies and plugs—and every one of them will tell you that biggest hindrance to their clients' success is poor casting using the 10-to-2. But watch someone who has never been exposed to that method—say, native guides in the tropics—and they will be using full extension of the arm, back and front, for more efficient casting

I wrote another story that said short leaders and sinking lines would minimize a fly's proclivity for floating too high above the sinking line. Boy, I caught some heat for that one, too, but I kept going. I was contacted by Tom Schumacher from Wapsi Tackle Company, the largest supplier of tied flies in the world. He said, correctly, that I had always emphasized the importance of eyes on a fly. Then he said that he had designed some lead eyes that would make the flies go down deeper in the water. Well, he sent me some of these things and I tried them and I quickly realized that these lead eyes were going to revolutionize sinking-fly fishing. I wrote an article for *Fly Fisherman*. Well, John Randolph, the editor of the magazine, said you couldn't imagine how many letters they received complaining that a fly with lead eyes on it was not a fly at all, but a jig (of course, some of these people are the same people who today fly-fish the lead-eyed Clouser Minnow without a moment's hesitation).

Then there was a period in the 1950s when it became fashionable for anglers to use short fly rods, in the 5- to 6-foot range. I did a story for *Outdoor Life* that featured me on the cover of the magazine breaking a 6-foot fly rod over my leg. The article spelled out the advantages and disadvantages of the longer and shorter rods. I had researched the situation thoroughly. I found that in side-by-side comparisons long rods offered seventeen advantages and short rods offered only two. (The two: If you fish very, very small streams you don't have much room to cast and so a short rod will allow you a little more freedom to cast. However I've since learned that there is another way around the short rod even in small streams. The average rod is somewhere between 8½ and 9 feet long. If you stick 2 feet behind you, you automatically shorten the rod by 2 feet. The other benefit was that once you land a fish, short rods make it easier to get him in the boat and unhook him. But every other advantage lies with the longer rod.)

The magazine was inundated with letters (many of them said, "Hey, Lefty, instead of breaking the rod, how about giving it to me?"). People thought I was a radical. Today, I would say that fewer than 1 percent of all rods used today are under six feet long. The long rod is demonstrably superior.

All this controversy—unwanted and unsought on my part—led me to one of my core beliefs about the great sport of fly-fishing: There are way too many sacred cows in our sport. Unfortunately, the 10-to-2 technique is one of them. I now realize that if, after Joe Brooks' introduction to fly casting, I had only fly-fished for trout, I never would have become a decent fly caster. Casting for hours over longer distances for smallmouth bass forced me to develop a more efficient system. It's the one I teach today and I'm proud to say is used by thousands of fly fisherman all over the world. In 1972 I wrote a book called *Fly Casting With Lefty Kreh* that put some of my "radical" thinking into broader distribution. That book created a real furor. Among the old guard of the sport it was heresy to question the time-honored technique that fathers had been teaching their sons and that had been published time and again in every major magazine. Yet anyone who questions whether or not the technique works or whether clock-worn anglers are desperate for a better method need only look at the sales of that book. It sold more than ten thousand copies and was ultimately published in five languages. In fact, I always get a kick out the German title: *Flieger Fishing wit de Urflog*.

One more note about technique. I would advise anyone at any skill level to practice casting both lefty and righty. Your goal should be to cast confidently with either arm. I'll tell you why. Ev likes to turn the mattress every so often to air it out. So one day she decided it was flipping time and so I stood on one side of the bed to turn it over as I had many times, before. I reached out with my arm fully extended and flipped the mattress. Ev and I could both hear the muscle tear off the bone. It sounded like a sheet ripping on a nail. Where it ripped off the bone it felt like electric shocks. The muscle slammed up against my shoulder like an old window shade and the next morning this doctor buddy of mine at Johns Hopkins said, "Lefty, you tore your bicep." I asked him what he could do about it and he said, "If we act within a few days, we could open the arm up and put a bunch of screws in the elbow and take wires and attach them to the muscle and then pull the muscle back down and attach it to the screws and you have to leave the arm in a sling for three or four months. After that there are several months of therapy, meaning it would be maybe seven to nine months before you gained full use of your arm."

When I first started teaching casting I did it left-handed. I realized that if you are going to teach well you need to put your hand on the student's hand and help them feel the correct motion. I knew I needed to learn to cast right-handed. So as a young man I began to cast with both hands. Well, for the first two months after the injury I couldn't even lift a coffee mug off the table with my left hand. There was one shred of muscle that never left the bone and my therapy started with a one-pound weight. Now I can lift about forty pounds with the left arm, but if I cast left-handed for any length of time I get a serious charley horse, so nowadays I mostly cast right-handed. But if I'm on a trout stream and find myself in a situation where, because of trees or the fish's location, I can't make a right-handed cast, I'll cast lefty for a few casts. I can still cast well with the left hand, but not for too long.

My case is a little extreme, of course. Not many people tear their bicep flipping a mattress, but it goes to show the value of learning how to cast ambidextrously. By using both hands I was able to prolong my fishing career, but even if I'd never injured my arm, my ability to fish from both sides made me a better angler.

The Four Principles

I believe that like any sport, fly-fishing has physical principles that must be respected if you are going to have any success. All sports have them. Baseball and tennis require a player to keep his or her eye on the ball. Golf requires a static spine angle. Going back to my earliest days with a fly rod, I've developed four principles of casting. Because some people don't want to see the sport progress, these principles have not been universally accepted, but they are universally true and I think they play a key role in any fly-fishing and fly-casting success.

I have learned if you use the four principles you can make any cast—from a twenty-five-foot dry fly presentation to throwing a big striper fly across yards of water into the wind. Understanding these principles allows you to adapt to existing fishing conditions—something I believe is not possible with some casting methods.

For that reason, many years ago I began to teach the four basic principles of fly casting. I use the term "principle" advisedly. A principle is a rule of physics that cannot be violated. Regardless of how you cast, whether you're Steve Raejeff, Bruce Richards, Mel Kreiger, or me—we are all bound by these four principles. Indeed, the first guy who ever picked up a rod was chained to these principles. I am sure some instructors who have spent years developing their own styles will not want to join such an effort. But I believe that promoting and using these four principles will help all anglers. I certainly don't claim these principles as my own—they are principles of physics that have existed since the planet was created.

(1) YOU MUST FIRST MOVE THE FLY LINE END BEFORE YOU CAN MAKE A BACK OR FORWARD CAST. This causes the rod to bend or load, storing energy. It is also good fishing technique to lift all line from the surface before making a back cast.

(2) ONCE THE LINE IS MOVING, THE ONLY WAY TO LOAD THE ROD IS TO MOVE THE CASTING HAND AT AN EVER-INCREASING SPEED AND THEN BRING IT TO A SUDDEN STOP. The sudden stop is often called a power stroke. Applying power spoils the cast. It should be called a speed-up-and-stop stroke. The faster you accelerate the rod hand and the faster you speed up and stop the rod tip, the faster the line will travel. The size of the loop is determined by the distance the rod moves (or drops) in the final moment of the cast during the speed up and stop.

(3) THE LINE WILL GO IN THE DIRECTION THE ROD TIP SPEEDS UP AND STOPS. If on the back cast, the rod tip stops at any angle going up (or rising) the line will go straight in the direction the tip stopped. If the rod tip stops going down and back, then sag is produced in the line; this sag must be removed before a forward cast can be made. With almost all forward casts, the rod tip should stop in a direction either parallel to or slightly climbing above the surface.

(4) THE LONGER THE DISTANCE THE ROD TRAVELS ON THE BACK AND FORWARD CASTING STROKES, THE LESS EFFORT IS REQUIRED TO MAKE THE CAST. The shorter the rod moves through a casting stroke, the harder you must work to put the same load in the rod. When you need to cast farther, throw heavier flies, defeat the wind, or make a number of special casts (even when trout fishing) the rod must travel farther back and forward. Being able to take the rod well behind you on the back cast will allow you to make many different casts and produce more fish for you.

Let me give just two examples of how teaching the clock method confuses people. Principle Number One says you cannot make a back or forward cast until you move the end of the line.

Those who teach by the clock tell students to make the back cast at nine thirty or ten o'clock. Regardless of the rod position relative to the clock, you cannot make a cast until you move the line end.

One more example: Principle Three says the line will go in the direction the rod speeds up and stops. Clock people teach that you should stop the rod at eleven o'clock on the forward cast. Take a dart in your right hand and hold your left finger at the eleven o'clock position. Throw three darts, releasing each one at eleven o'clock. On the first stop, release the dart traveling toward the ground and the dart will go in the ground. Then release one going straight ahead—the dart will go straight ahead. Then stop at 11, but traveling upward, and the dart will rise. Others say that the line follows the tip—but halfway through a stroke if you stop the rod momentarily—the line will go in the direction of the stop—even if you dropped the rod tip to the ground.

Regardless of where you stop with a rod tip, a dart, a stone, a spear, or anything you project—it will go in the direction of the stop.

I think most instructors would agree that the second most screwed-up cast is the roll cast. Almost all instructors, books, and videos suggest that you raise the rod hand, bring the rod just beyond vertical and drive it toward the water. Some notable instructors say if you want the cast to go farther, accelerate faster. Look at the principle that says that the line is going to go in the direction of the stop. If you drive the rod tip toward the water—that's the direction the line will travel. It is why almost all casters make a poor roll cast.

Like any new thinking, my principles have been criticized and castigated, but I stand by them. I have a self-imposed responsibility to help anglers understand and enjoy the sport. Despite what a handful of paranoid traditionalists might say, I have no doubt that an understanding of and an appreciation for these four principles will add enormously to any fly fisherman's enjoyment of the sport.

Chapter 17
Fish I Have Known

FRESHWATER

People often ask me what about my favorite kind of fishing. Is it bass, trout, bonefish? The answer is that I really do like it all. It's sort of like children. Your children are all unique, with differing gifts and talents, but you love them all the same. That's how I feel about fishing. In fact, in the late 1970s I went fishing down in Homosassa, Florida. When I came home I called a friend of mine named Gus Janos, who lived near me in Maryland. He said, "Where you been?"

I said, "I just got back from Florida."

He said, "What'd ya catch?"

I said, "Six tarpon over a hundred pounds."

Well, he wanted to hear all about it. And I told him about the whole week. After about fifteen minutes talking about titanic tarpon, I said to Gus, "Hey, Gus, a few weeks ago you told me that this time of the year you knew where the biggest bluegill are . . ." Mind you, a big bluegill weighs three quarters of a pound. "Where was that again?"

Gus was floored. "Are you crazy?" he asked. "How can you fight hundred-pound tarpon one day and half-pound bluegill the next?"

I said "Gus, if you were a fisherman you wouldn't even ask that question."

I still love it all. In fact, as I write this I am planning a trip with my doctor. We are going down to Texas to fish this man-made bass lake that some guy built for $5 million. I'm taking two rods with me: I'm taking a 9-weight rod to catch big bass and a little 3-weight rod to catch big bluegill. And I'm going to enjoy catching both of them.

That said, I thought it might be fun to jot down a few thoughts about some of my very favorite species.

SMALLMOUTH BASS

If you talk to experienced anglers about their favorite type of fishing, they'll almost always gravitate to the kind of fishing they did when they were young. If as a kid you fished trout in small brooks in Pennsylvania, odds are that when you just want to have fun, you'll probably head out to the trout brooks of Pennsylvania.

I'm no different. Smallmouth bass was the first fish I ever went after on fly. That makes sense because they were the only game fish central Maryland really had at that time. And there were so many of them. I mean, we were catching dozens of them. One time as a young man I was fishing the Monocacy River with plug tackle from a canoe and we caught thirteen smallmouth bass over three pounds. I'll bet there's not a bass over three pounds in that whole river now. We used to float the Monocacy from the Pennsylvania state line down for thirty miles, two guys in a canoe. Today, because of overdevelopment, the water table has been lowered so drastically that you can walk across it. In many places it's not even up to your knees and there are very few pools that would go over your head. But while the environment may have changed, my passion hasn't. I just love the smallmouth.

I don't really care much for bass fishing in deep lakes, but river fishing with fly tackle I really like. I started my fly-fishing career back in 1947 on the wealth of rivers that were available to me—the Potomac, the Susquehanna, the Julianna, the Shenandoah. I really enjoy fishing for smallmouth in rivers. However, smallmouth fishing around here is not as good as it used to be. In fact, we're having a crisis in the mid-Atlantic area. We're losing a lot of our adult bass. Virginia seems concerned about it, but Pennsylvania and Maryland are just now becoming aware of the seriousness of the problem. They had a 25-mile kill on bass this year on the Shenandoah. That said, there still is some great smallmouth bass fly-fishing in Maine, particularly in northern Maine. The Penobscot River, up near Bangor, is a beautiful place to be and a terrific place to fly-fish for smallmouth. I wouldn't want to live there or any place where you can store meat outdoors four months a year, but in the summer the rivers are beautiful. They have that beautiful, crisp tea-colored water, and the smallmouth thrive in that pristine environment. You end up with really big smallmouth bass. I actually have a trip planned to the Androscoggin River in Maine, which is also supposed to be superb.

The smallmouth is an exciting fish. It fights much better than the largemouth bass. It does require a lot of casting, which is a downer for some people (you may make five hundred casts a day). You make long casts and strip flies back and there's a lot of technique to it as well. One of the best ways to catch smallmouth in rivers is with fly. Sure, you can throw a plastic lure in there that wobbles back and forth and has a couple of treble hooks hanging from it, but you'll probably have better luck with a fly that looks like a crawfish, or a minnow, or even using little popping bugs. A good fly fisherman usually does better than a good spinning fishermen when fishing a smallmouth river.

I have fished in hundreds of locations in dozens of smallmouth rivers over the years. In the late 1960s, there were a lot of them in the mid-Atlantic region. The problem is that the water in the Potomac region has become so clean that it's actually too clean. Is there such a thing as too clean? Well, yes, from an ecological or food-chain standpoint. When river water runs too clean, the prey species have difficulty hiding. So what happens in that the big fish can't get as much to eat and each year they spawn more and more predator species. As a general observation, when you have water that runs real clean, you'll see far fewer big bass in there. There are rare exceptions. Clean water coupled with the fact that the mid-Atlantic has been fished so much are two of the main reasons why we're losing fish.

Back in the 1960s it was common to catch 4-pound bass, but not to catch something over 5 pounds. In fact, in the first ten years I fly-fished for bass I only caught one over 5 pounds. I had a friend who had a jointed lure and he had hooked a bass that he believed was over 7 pounds. I laughed, but I went back and fished it. We called it "The Monster Hole." Well, I hooked a fish in there that jumped—and I am always conservative about estimating fish weights and sizes, because if you ever lie about one and you get caught you'll never be believed again—and I immediately knew he had to be between 28 and 30 inches. It was the biggest smallmouth I've ever seen anywhere in my life. He must have weighed between 7 and 8 pounds. It surely would have been a world record on fly—a river bass! After a few jumps he threw the fly and that was it. All about 25 feet from the boat. But we went back there every season for six seasons. I think he died of old age because as far as I know, nobody ever caught him.

The other thing I recall fondly about smallmouth fishing dates back to 1964. Joe Brooks called to tell me that I had gotten the job with the MET. I got the call in late August and had to be in Miami in late October. So I had the whole month of September. I quit the job at Fort Detrick mainly to get ready, but I also fished every day, mainly because I knew that with moving to Florida I wouldn't get a chance to fish in my native areas for a long time. During that month I caught nine smallmouth bass over 4 pounds on fly in the Potomac River. What makes that even more interesting is that I caught those nine fish in about eight separate places. I learned that there were several places in the river where big smallmouths would feed and what was important—vital really—was the angle at which you presented the fly. There was one, for example, where there was a rock ledge out in the middle that faced the current. The current ran around either end. After a long period of observation I realized that the big bass would hang on the left corner of the ledge, but not on the right corner. If you were on the right side and presented the fly to the left side you never got a strike. But if you were on the left and stayed above where the bass were and you presented the fly so that it swept down naturally with the current you could catch them.

Two more things about fishing smallmouth bass: First, they stay near rocks. Sure, they like logs and all that, but above all, they like rocks. Every rock you see in a river, especially if it has a current break behind or in front of it, is worth investigating. Suppose the current is coming from the north to the south. Suppose the rock slants to the north. There will be no fish in the north side of the rock, because the current is sweeping over the side of the rock. The fish will be back behind the rock in the quiet water watching the bait come by.

If the rock faces upward in any way at all it creates a slower buffer zone as the water hits the upslope. This is an ideal spot. The rock ledge gives a bass overhead protection from ospreys. Second, he is lying in virtually dead water expending little energy, and third, he can see every bit of bait that's coming toward the rock.

The second thing about smallmouth is that you really don't need many flies. If you have some Clouser Minnows, Popping Bugs, some Half-and-Halfs, and some crawfish flies, you'll catch bass. One of the deadliest ways to catch bass is to use a crawfish fly because the smallmouth bass really like to eat crawfish. Biologists have found that in many places, crawfish are bass' major food source even though there are other options available. The secret to fishing a crawfish fly is just the opposite of what most people expect. First, it should be slightly weighted most of the time, and it should never be retrieved. That's because crawfish don't swim in the current. They tumble in the current. And the closer you can get to the bottom the better, because the crawfish want to get to the bottom so they can hide. So the way to fish crawfish flies for smallmouth bass in rivers is to throw the flies upstream and then let them tumble down, almost like fishing a nymph for trout. Then just leave it in there until the fly has "tumbled" way past your target and then take it back.

That reminds me of a little-known fact about nymph fishing that might be interesting to some readers. Scientists have found that most of the trout taken on nymphs are within ten inches of the river bottom. There are two reasons for that. First, that is where the trout hide. Second, the currents on the bottom of a stream travel much more slowly than those at the top. So the closer you can get to the bottom of the current, the more advantages you have. That's where the food is, and because the food is there and the current runs more slowly, there'll be a lot of fish there.

That's why the bead-head nymph became so popular. They came into vogue about fifteen years ago. You put a little bead—tungsten or brass— at the head of your nymph. The bead doesn't so much attract the fish as it gets the nymph down to the bottom where the fish are.

LARGEMOUTH BASS

The largemouth is one of the most common and most popular fish in the United States. Its enormous impact on fishing has been mostly beneficial; however, in some ways, it's been decidedly detrimental.

Let's take the positives. For instance, the promotion of interest in and concern for the outdoors. If you and I discover a pristine trout stream and we don't tell anybody, we may have some great fishing. But when the area is considered for development only two voices will be fighting it. Deduction: The more people who are interested in a resource and care about a resource, the more they will protect that resource. The Bass Federation has created a tremendous amount of publicity and interest in America's bass fisheries. If someone starts messing with a bass fishery, that fishery will have a lot of friends, and, of course, politicians listen to groups more than individuals. From that standpoint, the popularity of bass fishing in America is an asset.

One liability, from my own point of view, is the "competitivization" of bass fishing that is now practiced and encouraged by some of the popular bass-fishing leagues, tournaments, and TV shows (more on this in a later chapter). This has reduced bass fishing into a money thing. It's denigrated the sport. Another negative is the obsession these guys have with winning. I have actually had guys run their boats up to mine and tell me, "Hey, you've got to get out of here. I'm in a tournament and I've got to fish this spot." That sort of selfish intensity doesn't help anyone.

Certainly, these leagues have improved their public relations. Early on, in order to sell the excitement and skill level of competitive fishing they'd put all the captured fish on a clothesline, take a picture, and put it in a newspaper. This really ticked off the locals—fishermen and nonfishermen alike—who felt these interlopers were coming in and killing all their bass. The organizers have since realized that releasing bass is a much more saleable message. I think they have become conservation-minded.

The largemouth lives in every state in the Union, with the exception of Alaska. The smallmouth bass can't tolerate the same high temperatures for long periods of time that the largemouth variety can. So in the southern states, pretty much from Kentucky south, all the bass are pretty much going to be largemouth. However, deeper lakes in the South will have cool enough water for smallmouth. Also, if you have a fishery in water that is coming through a dam, that's cool. The temperature of the water will determine the presence of the largemouth or the smallmouth.

Most of the bass tournaments you see or hear about pertain to the largemouth, but most anglers will agree that if caught in the same body of water, the smallmouth will offer a much better fight. One reason the bass is such good fishing is that, along with the grouper, the bass (smallmouth and largemouth) has a virtually perfect predator body. They have large mouths, which allow them greater margin for error when trying to capture prey. Furthermore, they have a relatively short but wide body, which allows them to make very short, very fast changes in direction. Contrast the bass' body with that of the barracuda. When fishing for the 'cuda you never use a big wobbling lure. That's because the long, thin body of the barracuda has a difficult time adjusting to the rapid changes in direction made by a wobbling lure. In fact, if you ever watch a barracuda pursue a school of baitfish, they rarely do it from within the school; they instead pursue baitfish from the periphery. Why? Each baitfish gives off reflected flashes of light. With all these hundreds or thousands of flashes going off at different intervals, the barracuda can't decide on which fish to target. Instead, the barracuda will swim on the edge of the school and wait for a baitfish to stray. As soon as this happens the barracuda can use its speed—its primary advantage—to track down the prey.

In World War II we used a similar theory to confuse German U-boat radar. We would throw Mylar chips into the water. The reflective nature of the Mylar would screw up the radar. What can we learn from this? When fishing for 'cuda, fish the edges of the bait school, not the center.

Knowing the predator skills of the bass make it easier to fish. With such a large mouth, it can inhale a huge amount of water and prey. As mentioned above, smallmouth prefer rock and the water breaks they create. Largemouth prefer logs and weed beds.

DIFFERENCES BETWEEN SMALLMOUTH AND LARGEMOUTH BASS

Size

The largemouth bass gets much bigger than the smallmouth. In a river system a 4-pound smallmouth is very large, although they do get up to 10 pounds and the world-record smallmouth is about 11 or 12 pounds. By comparison, the world record for a largemouth is 22 pounds, 4 ounces. The largemouth lives in slower moving water (which requires less energy than living in fast moving water) and lives in regions where there is a longer growing season. With food available in greater abundance, the largemouth spends less energy looking for food. Combine these factors and you end up with a significantly larger fish.

Mouth and Eyes

When the mouth of the fish is closed, a smallmouth's eye will be located in front of the mouth. The largemouth's eyes will be well behind the mouth.

Colorings

You can even tell the difference in the water. The smallmouth's coloring—splotchy bars—run vertically up and down the body. The largemouth's coloring—a large dark line—runs horizontally across the body.

As for flies or lures: Remember big fish such as largemouth don't like samples, they like groceries. If you want to catch bigger fish, you need to fish larger flies—say, 3 inches to 5 or 6 inches. People question that. They say, "Why would you cast such a large fly?" Well, I tell them, ask the guy in the other boat who's using a spinning outfit and who is casting a 5-inch Rapalla or an 8-inch worm to catch the same fish. If you really want to catch bigger bass, you should use larger lures. The exception to that rule is popping bugs. If the popping bug is kept in motion it creates so much disturbance around the bug that larger bass are convinced that these bugs are larger than they really are. As a result you can catch much larger bass on poppers than you can on smaller flies. The Half-and-Half (half Deceiver/half Clouser) is one of the best for largemouth. Another fly, the Seducer, which was designed back in the 1800s and has been renamed several times (it's also been called a hackle fly), is very effective. It's got red hackle right at the front and white hackle behind it and both are wound around the shaft. Then you have a tail on it of white hackle.

This is a good time to share an interesting note, something that I've learned over my years of trial and error. Whenever you have red and white on a fly, the red should always be in a small amount and always on the front end. I've found that if you reverse the order of the colors you catch nothing. I have a theory about this. I think that when a large fish approaches baitfish, it's usually from underneath and behind. From that view the predator always sees the red of the gill in the front and the long white belly behind it.

Another type of fly that I've used a lot for both large and smallmouth bass is a bend-back in which the fly is tied in reverse so that the hook rides up on the topside of the fly rather than the bottom. This style of fly allows you to fish through grass, over rocks and logs—precisely the kinds of locations that bass love—and it rarely gets snagged or hung up.

As far as lures go, the single best largemouth bass lure ever developed is the plastic worm. The precursor to the plastic worm was a lure called the Black Widow. It was a hunk of 7- or 8-inch-long pork rind with some of the meat left on. It came in a jar, they were dyed-black, and you'd pierce it with a hook. Its action was like an undulating snake and it was deadly effective. I don't know for a fact that this is true, but I would bet that the person who invented the plastic worm was inspired by the Black

Widow. The plastic worm gave you all the action and effectiveness of the widow, without the mess of black dye.

BLUEGILL

I don't think bluegill get the respect they deserve. I think they make for terrific fishing. Take a little 3-weight rod and go for ¾-pound bluegill; I guarantee you'll have a ball.

One of the places I used to fish for largemouth is Currituck Sound, located on the Outer Banks of the Carolinas. Back in the 1950s the Sound used to be loaded with all kinds of vegetation, which made it an ideal spot for bait to live and for bass and bluegills to feed. It used to be one of the great bass-fishing areas of the United States. Over the years the habitat there has diminished—there's not nearly as much vegetative cover for the baitfish as there once was—but we used to go there and catch a hundred largemouth bass a day on fly and *a lot* of those would have been over 4 pounds. I used to love to go after other local species as well. In the Carolinas they had (and probably still do have) this thing called a copperhead. Like the bluegill, it's a member of the sunfish or panfish family. It has a copper-ish head on it and it gets big; up to, say, half a pound or three-quarters of a pound. The other guys would be fishing largemouth bass and I'd pull out my 4-weight rod and have more fun catching these huge copperheads. For me, part of the trip was always devoted to the copperheads.

I enjoy all kinds of sunfish: stump knockers, green sunfish. In fact, few people realize that the bass is actually part of the sunfish family. There must be twenty species. Among the best known are the bluegill. The simplest way to identify a bluegill is to hold it up. A bluegill will have a faint dime-sized circle on the back of the top dorsal fin. If it's not there, it's not a bluegill.

Of all the sunfish, the bluegill is the most popular and it's the one that has been stocked most regularly in small ponds around the country. It's a lot of fun to fish for. People ask me why I enjoy the bluegill so much and the answer is simple: I never met a bluegill that wasn't hungry. Montana, California, Maine: they thrive in every state of the Union. One of the reasons they are so widespread is that federal government wanted it that way. Back in the 1950s and 1960s the U.S. government used to stock ponds on small farms across the country. The ideas was that if farmers kept ponds on their land they would be better equipped to fight a fire. This preparedness also got farmers a break on their insurance bills. As an incentive to pond building, the government offered to stock these ponds with fish for little or no cost. These ponds were often stocked with a mixture of largemouth bass and bluegill. Like their relatives in the sunfish and panfish families, bluegill are also prolific, spawning up to three times per year. This meant that farm ponds of the era became very efficient food chains: The bluegill would reproduce often enough that the largemouth had a reliable supply of food.

With such rapid reproduction, bluegill can overpopulate a fishery very quickly. For that reason it's advisable to take out as many as you catch. You don't catch and release sunfish or panfish. The good news there is that they make a very tasty fillet. I have a sneaking suspicion that that may be where the panfish name comes from. In fact, I've never seen this written before, but I think I know where the name sunfish come from as well. I've noticed over the years that sunfish really don't get active until the sun comes up. Likewise, when the sun goes down it's very difficult to catch them.

Years ago, when I was first getting into outdoor writing, I used to order all kinds of fishery management pamphlets from the government. The pamphlets said, as I mentioned above, that ponds can become overpopulated with sunfish to a point where there are no large ones at all. There are so many little ones looking for food that there's not enough food for any one of them to get very big. These pamphlets used to recommend occasionally poisoning the pond in such a manner that you would kill off the sunfish, but not the bass. Oddly enough, in its instructions for how to correctly poison the pond, the U.S. government inadvertently taught me how to catch bluegill. This one pamphlet said select a windy day and spread the poison (which worked by diminishing the water's oxygen content) close to the pond's banks. Furthermore, said the pamphlet, don't apply the poison until the sun gets high. If you applied the poison correctly, the wind would spread the poison throughout the water, diluting its impact, and the poison will likely not reach fish in deeper water—for instance, largemouth bass. The bass would feed along the edges only in low light or at night and the sunfish would feed there in the daytime. That told me how and when to fish for each of them. I started fishing for bass in deep water during the day and along the edges in late in the evening and early in the morning!

Using that kind of basic knowledge I used to clean up. In fact, I caught some of the largest bass in the state of Maryland for years. What I was doing was fishing at night using either popping bugs or a Jitterbug, which is a relatively noisy casting lure. I found that quite often the bass seemed to be biting at the sound of the lure, but missing the hooks. So I took a lure called a flatfish, which is shaped like a banana. On the inside curve there's a wire spring that sticks out from either side with a hook on the ends of it. I took off that big treble hook that was in the center of the Jitterbug and installed this wire outrigger-like design. If a bass kissed that lure, trust me, he owned it.

Note: Bluegill take all kinds of poppers and all kinds of wet flies. One of the things that works best is a wet sponge spider with a black sponge body with white legs wiggling on it.

CARP

I mentioned earlier that I used to like to fish carp using dough balls for bait. I still go once or twice every summer. I used to go by myself, but now I need somebody to help me put the boat in and out. I like to put the boat in, have my coffee and a sandwich, put on the dough balls, and reel in the carp, just as I did many years ago. Like smallmouth bass, I've fished for carp for most of my life.

I'm a terrible cook. I can't fry an egg. I mean, I have trouble making steam, but I can make coffee, and I can make carp dough. As a young man I loved to fish with fly for smallmouth bass and I loved to fish for carp with dough balls. A day fishing carp with dough balls brings me right back to my youth.

There are all kinds of ways to make bait for carp. You can soak Wheaties in water and mix it up and make it gummy and make balls of bait that way. You can use bread, corn, all kinds of stuff, but I haven't found anything that works better than old-fashioned carp dough. Here's my recipe:

You put a pint of water—no more, no less—in a pan. Into that pint you put one teaspoon of vanilla, one tablespoon of sugar, and half of a regular pack of strawberry Jell-O. Prior to all this you've mixed exactly two cups of cornmeal and exactly one cup of regular flour. I just pour them both into a Ziploc bag and shake it up thoroughly.

You bring the pan to a boil and stir it. Use very low heat. I cut a tiny hole in the bottom of the Ziploc bag and very slowly pour out the cornmeal-flour mix. The key is to make sure that you spread the mixture carefully throughout the pan so that the liquid and powder are evenly distributed. Keep some powder in the bag. As the new powder-and-liquid mixture cooks, the liquid will bubble up. As these bubbles arise, take a little powder from the bag and close the bubbles up. Continue to close the bubbles as they arise. Once you have run out of flour mix, stir the mixture in the pan for about a minute or two with a good heavy spoon and then lay the mixture on a bed of aluminum foil to let it cool. You know it's ready when you can take a piece, roll it into a ball the size of a golf ball, and bounce it a little bit off a kitchen table.

Make a large ball, about the size of a softball, and then pinch off small bait balls as you need them. The dough ball has to have enough tackiness to stick to the hook when you cast, but be soft enough that when the fish sucks in the bait and closes on the hook, the point will penetrate the dough and enter his mouth. That's a delicate balance. It's hard to get the consistency right, but Bugs Cross, who gave me this recipe, figured it out perfectly.

The Europeans use slingshots to throw carp food out in the river to chum carp. Carp fishing in Europe is a very big deal. They have big tournaments, all very sophisticated. There's a pouch on this little slingshot. You take whatever kind of bait you're using (Europeans actually use a lot of maggots) and broadcast it over the area you're going to fish. What I'll do is take a whole bunch of bean-sized pieces of dough ball and fling them onto the water. As the fish start enjoying the hors d'oeuvres, I put a bigger dough ball on a hook and serve them the main course. Aside from executing the recipe carefully, the key to good carp fishing with dough balls is to rig your outfit with an egg sinker. You cast out, and when the carp grabs the dough ball and runs off with it, the line pulls through the hole in the sinker and becomes tight. That's when you set the hook. I'm talking about carp that run anywhere from five to thirty pounds. They're by far the strongest freshwater fish we've got.

I'm also doing quite a bit of carp fishing now with fly rods. Precisely how you catch carp on fly depends on where you live. That's because you have to deftly mimic the food they're eating in a given area. For example, if you go out west on some of the trout rivers out there, they're primarily eating nymphs and insects, so you use a nymph-type imitation. Those fish don't get very big—about five to seven pounds—because nymphs aren't very big and the fish don't have a lot of other food options. If you go to the Great Lakes, they've got lots of carp there, all of which feed primarily on leeches and crayfish.

In Ohio they are big limestone quarries that are filled with water, some a half-mile long and a quarter-mile wide and very deep. In late May and June the mulberry trees that overhang the quarries drop their mulberries and the carp devour them. So the fly fisherman of the area have designed a fly for that region. You put a certain amount of weight on the hook and you tie this fly to make it look like a mulberry and it has to sink at the same rate as a mulberry. What the anglers do is they go to a mulberry tree and get a bunch of berries. Then they start throwing one berry at a time into the water and after a short while carp start flocking in from all over the place to eat them. I think they can discern the sound of a mulberry hitting the water. Once the carp get working on the mulberry "chum," you toss that mulberry fly in and you're in business.

What we do in the Baltimore-D.C. area on limestone rivers such as the Potomac and the Susquehanna is different. Here, the carp take rocks and turn them over and eat the crawfish that hide underneath. In fact, I once saw a carp, about a 20-pounder, that had a bunch of calluses and scars on his head from turning rocks over all his life. However, we don't use a crawfish pattern for these fish. That's because crawfish are quick. As they try to swim away from these Potomac and Susquehanna carp, they present a unique profile to the fish. The carp only see the crawfish from behind: the rounded body of the crawfish swimming away. So we need a fly that's round and has the same diameter and color as the crawfish. We use red fox tail on a hook with a little weight on it.

I think that no matter where or how you fish for them, carp are very spooky. Fly-fishing for them is a very delicate enterprise requiring lots of skill. We use 12- and 16-foot-long leaders for carp (Normally, if you're fishing salt water or for bass and stuff you use a 9-foot leader). You've got to make a very good presentation. But let me tell you: When you hook a 16- or 20-pound carp on a light bass fly rod you'll sound like a preacher at a revival meeting. It's exciting. Carp is one of the few freshwater fish that will run all your fly line off and a bunch of your backing as well.

NORTHERN PIKE

There are a number of things that make northern pike interesting. First, it is the fact that northern pike is not an exclusively "northern" species at all. While the name often conjures up images of the frigid northernmost reaches of our continent, it's important to know that you can find northern pike in Maryland and many other states in the southern United States where there is a body of particularly cool water. That said, the finest, most exciting and most rewarding northern pike fishing I've ever done is in northern Canada, particularly northern Saskatchewan, Manitoba, and the Northwest Territories. These areas are marked by extraordinary natural beauty and wildlife and are virtually undisturbed by development or even roads. There are some excellent lodges reachable only by plane and most of the top-notch northern pike fishing locations require fly-outs, where in the morning you get into a floatplane and fly anywhere from ten minutes to a half-hour to your fishing destination. If you look at a map of this region you'll see just how many lakes there are in northern Canada. You can find pike up there that run forty to fifty inches long. For fly fishermen, the key time to go is that last week in June through the first two weeks in July. The weather can be a little extreme that time of year. In fact I have been there that time of year when it snowed and two days later we were peeling off layers in the summer sun.

Pike spend most of their lives in deep, cold water, but in late June, when the shallower water off the main lakes and bays warms up to about 60 degrees, they head in there to spawn. That heating process takes place pretty quickly because the bottoms of these lakes and ponds are dark brown and absorb the sunlight. The pike have left 10 or 20 feet of water for 2 or 3 feet of warmer water. It's important to realize that the pike is the biggest, baddest predator in his environment. He's not afraid of anything. I mean it—these things aren't even afraid of outboard motors. You can catch pike 6 feet off the back end of a boat. In fact, I often send relatively new fly fishermen or people who can't cast particularly well on pike fishing trips because if they can cast thirty feet they are going to catch plenty of pike. Nothing has ever messed with a pike, so they have no reason to fear anything. Plus, when you head out to these pristine, untouched lakes, you are casting to fish that have never seen a lure or a fly. You go into these bays and see fish that are two, three, four feet long, lying in there like big barracudas and you have a great day of sight fishing in front of you.

Now a pike doesn't fight real hard—I use only 8- or 9-weight rods—but the grab, the take, is spectacular. They launch themselves at the fly like a torpedo and when they open that huge mouth it's just astonishing. Anybody who has spent a lot of time using light tackle and then sees a pike take his or her fly really gets a thrill out of it. Visually, it's very exciting. They put up a decent fight, though nothing like a saltwater fish. It's the grab that really gets you. Two years ago, I was with Dan Blanton, who is a good friend (and was kind enough to write the foreword for this book). He is one of the leading fishing writers in the country. We were fishing for pike on Lake Egmont at the North Seal River Lodge. I happened to be looking down when he threw a beautiful cast back under a fir tree. When it hit the water, a pike that had been back in this little pocket surged directly toward it. When this animal, about 50 feet away, opened his mouth, I could see red gills and the fly disappear into the mouth of this twenty-pound fish. As much fishing as I've done in my life, I still remember that spectacle and that's what pike fishing on fly is all about.

In most of those lakes in northern Canada there are a lot of leeches. These are a favorite snack for the pike. So I take a simple piece of black rabbit fur about ⅜-inch wide and 3 or 4 inches long and attach it to hook (I add a little epoxy to make it last longer). The pike go for this fly like you wouldn't believe. I've caught pike over 20 pounds on these little things that are no bigger than a golf pencil. You drop it out there in front of them on the bottom, sometimes 15 feet away, and tease it along the bottom. The pike will just jump on it.

The other thing that makes pike fishing so enjoyable is the setting. It is so different in so many ways. The climate has had its way with the landscape. Take the trees. All the pine trees are very large at the bottom, but taper as they go up to a very narrow triangle at the top of the tree. That's a survival strategy. If these trees had bigger branches they would break off under the weight of all the snow they typically get. When I've been up there pike fishing I've often heard loons call. I've seen a bald eagle fly overhead with a 15-inch pike in his talons. I've seen a mother moose standing with her baby as they snack on lily pads. I've seen wolves. I've seen the paths worn by centuries of caribou migration. This is remarkable. We've all seen the wide swaths of trees cut out of nature for overhead power lines. Well, throughout northern Canada you have the same well-defined treeless swaths, but they are not for power lines. They are paths cut over the centuries by traveling caribou. You see the Northern Lights at night. You feel frigid winds and the heat of summer in the same twenty-four hour time span. The shore lunches are delicious; small pike make very good eating. The gulls feel the same way. You might not see a gull for hours, but as soon as the lunchtime campfire starts up they come by the dozens. They'll fly in and wait 15 or 20 feet away from the fire knowing there will be some leftovers for them. It's all part of nature's choreography and that's why I love pike fishing.

I caught my first northern pike on Lake Baskatong, north of Montreal, in 1947. Now, Montreal is a big city with the usual suburban sprawl. Back then, as soon as you got north of the city center, it was all dirt roads. We caught pike, some on fly but mostly on plug tackle, and I just fell in love with the way these fish would take a plug-casting spoon. The fishing was like it is now in far northern Canada. My favorite places up there are Scott Lake in Saskatchewan and North Seal River Lodge in Manitoba. There are lots of good places up there to fish, but those are the two where I've had the most fun. Both lend themselves to fly-fishing, but if you go before late June or after mid-July, the pike are largely in the deep, cold water, so it's not sight fishing and it's not quite as easy as it is during prime time.

Many people who are in the novice stages of their fly-fishing careers want results. They want to see big fish and get the excitement of hooking big fish on fly. That adds volumes to their confidence, plus people want a sense of the exotic. Pike are just perfect on both counts. Since it's sight fishing, there's less mystery. Since these fish are big, it's exciting, and since the environment is so stunning you feel like you're in another world. I highly recommend a pike trip, whatever your skill level.

SALMON

Salmon fishing on fly is not for the faint of heart (or arm). Of all the species I've fished on fly, it's safe to say that salmon requires the most work for the least reward. In fact, they call the Atlantic salmon "the fish of a thousand casts." As you'll see, there's a good reason for that.

Atlantic salmon spend most of their time in the ocean. Once a year they come into very specific locales in rivers—the same spots each year. These spots are called lies. As they move up the river they stop at a certain lie to and then move on. There is still some debate about this, but most people believe that Atlantic salmon don't feed during this time in the freshwater. They do take flies, however. Why they would take a fly during a period when they're not feeding is still a mystery. Some people think they eat the flies simply because the lures irritate them. No one really knows.

The way you fish them is very well choreographed. A guide will take you to these lies. Five or six people will spread out. You make one or two casts across and let the fly and line swing downstream. Then each person moves one or two steps downstream until you have reached the end of the pool and then you go back up and repeat the procedure. Here's why they call it the fish of a thousand casts: Everybody in that pool might cast 150 times and it's possible that nobody will get a strike. In fact, on some salmon rivers if you catch two or three fish in week you've had a good trip.

As a result, salmon fishing has become very much a social activity. It's very expensive and time consuming, so you end up with many well-off people who go to fancy lodges to commune with the outdoors. It appeals to all levels of anglers—men, women, coordinated and uncoordinated— because the guides plan everything and it doesn't require much work. Think about it; the canoe is going due south. There's one person in the front, one in the back or middle, and a guide. The guide will have you throw at a very specific angle and to a very specific distance. For instance, he might tell one person in the boat to cast forty feet at 45 degrees to the southeast and the other to cast 45 degrees to the southwest. If you repeatedly do what he tells you, he'll then maneuver the canoe so that your cast passes over the lie of a salmon.

Most people who fish for Atlantic salmon don't know a lot about fishing. I've prepared guys for Atlantic salmon fishing who have been trying to pack up and I've had to write down, "Use this green reel with this brown rod." Of course, that's not true to all salmon fishermen, but it's true of a lot of them.

There are exciting and challenging forms of salmon fishing on fly. The greatest salmon river in the world is the Alta River. I had the opportunity to fish it several years ago. The Alta lies 140 miles north of the Arctic Circle in Norway. The largest salmon in the world are produced in the Alta. To give you some idea of what I'm talking about: The week I was there—it was 1987—there was a 52-pounder caught on the river during the day and I caught two 37.5-pounders on the same night, back-to-back. Most of the flies we used on the Alta ranged from 6/0 to 10/0. On a 10/0 hook, the shank alone is maybe 3½ to 4 inches long. In fact, we used these monster two-handed rods to cast them. For the sake of perspective, keep in mind that most rivers have never even given up a 30-pounder. By contrast, you'll hardly ever catch an Alta River salmon that weighs *under* 20 pounds.

The river is owned by a consortium of farmers, and because they keep painstaking track of the water conditions and the health, size, and population of the fish, you must, by law, keep every salmon you catch. In fact, I absentmindedly put my first one back and I was reprimanded for it. Beyond my first one, we kept fastidious records of everything we caught that week. And among eight of us in the party we caught 1,894 pounds of salmon in one week. That's 106 pounds short of a ton.

As thrilling as the Alta is to fish, there is one extreme drawback: It's virtually impossible to get on. Most of the dates are filled with European aristocrats and bluebloods whose families have been fishing the river since time immemorial. There are three beats on the river—an upper, a middle, and a lower. The week we were there, we were fishing the lower beat. That same week, the upper beat was being fished by the Duke of Windsor. There's actually a cute story there. I was having a heck of a week, and whenever the river keeper, Ole Massoon, would take his boat up to the Duke's section, the Duke would ask about the action downstream. Ole told him there was an American down there who was catching lots of fish. The Duke asked if, on Ole's next trip up the river, he could bring some of the flies that the American was using so successfully. I was using a little thing called a tube fly, which is a tube onto which you tie your fly and then you run your leader up through it and then you your hook on it. They're very simple to tie, so I tied the Duke about a dozen of them and had Ole bring them upriver. The Duke was so grateful that on Ole's next trip down, he sent me four flies. These were no ordinary flies. They came out of his grandfather's fly box. The Duke's grandfather used to go up to the Alta via steamship, and when he came home he'd have this huge box with all these flies in it and he would give it to a professional fly dresser in London who would replenish what they'd used.

These flies were exquisite, full of exotic colors and materials. One of them, a version of the General Practitioner, is designed to look like a shrimp and has lots of orange-colored feathers. But the feathers are not the only thing that's orange. Somehow the Duke's fly dresser also had the hook enameled into the same orange color as the feathers. In the nearly two decades that I've had these flies, I have asked a number of leading fly experts and fly tiers to identify the feathers. No one has been able to identify them yet.

Fishing the Alta now is a pretty closed affair. For the last hundred years or so, if you fished the river and wanted to return, you had to sign up on the spot. As a result, the same families that had access to the river a century ago are still filling all the slots. Back then they would cruise up there in steamships. Now they do it in private jets. The only way to get on the Alta is to be invited by a slot-holder or an owner. I was fortunate to be guest of Sir James Pearman.

That's a story in itself. Back in the 1960s when I was living in Florida, I was buzzing across Biscayne Bay with my son, Larry. My friend Bill Curtis was fishing nearby with another gentleman and flagged me down. He said, "Lefty, can you help this S-O-B? He can't cast worth a damn! He's screwed up on I don't know how many bonefish!"

Well, this very handsome, distinguished-looking gentleman—he was about sixty years old at the time—was standing up in the front of the boat with his head hanging down, so I tried to help. That night the gentleman called me and asked if I could come meet him on Key Biscayne the next day for a private lesson. I went over and we eventually became very good friends. A few times I went over to visit him at his home in Bermuda, where he had developed a reputation as a leading banker.

One day Sir James calls me and, in his distinctive upper crust tone asks, "I say, is there any chance you can join us on a trip to Scotland? We'll stay in the Ballanduloch Castle and fish the Spey River and then we'll fly on to Norway and fish the Alta. I'll fly you over the pond on the Concorde. Is there any chance you might be able to make it?"

I said, "Is Helen Reddy? Is a bullfrog waterproof? Of course, I'll go."

I started packing. You never know what you're going to need on these trips. I'd fished in England, but never in Scotland, and, of course, I'd never fished the Alta. Not knowing exactly what to pack, I ended up with about a hundred pounds of baggage. At the time the airlines only allowed about sixty pounds, but when I got the airport I was relieved to learn that the Concorde didn't charge for excess baggage. I guess you could expect that from an airline that had ice sculptures and caviar in the waiting area.

Atlantic salmon is great eating, but in my opinion Pacific salmon generally provides much better fishing. The Atlantic salmon fishery runs from Norway through Scotland and Britain. The salmon spend the summer off Greenland and then migrate over to the maritime provinces of northeastern Canada. They're considered the gentleman's salmon because they're fished by the upper crust of Europe and the United States.

There are five species of Pacific salmon, the largest of which is the king salmon, which can grow up to 80 or 90 pounds. Pacific salmon are fished everywhere from Northern California up to Alaska.

I've been lucky. I've done a lot of Pacific salmon fishing. I've been to Alaska seventeen times. The first time I went there was in 1966 with

Mead Johnson. His family, an offshoot of the Johnson & Johnson tribe, built The Mead Johnson Company into a huge business specializing in infant products such as Enfamil. Mead had just sold his company for a couple hundred million dollars and had asked me if would accompany him on a salmon fishing trip to Alaska. He was nice enough to arrange a first-class ticket for me on the old Northwest Orient Airlines. Well, when the airline went on strike I was out of luck, so I called Mead's secretary and told her things weren't looking too good. She said, "Oh dear, Mr. Johnson will be so upset if you can't make it."

Mead had offered me $300 a day to fish with him. In 1966 that was a lot of money. I thought to myself, "If you think Mr. Johnson's going to be upset, how do you think Mrs. Kreh is going to feel about it?"

Anyway, Mead called back. I was living in Miami at the time and he told me to be at Tamiami Airport the next morning and that there would be a plane waiting for me. I should have known that it wouldn't be a Piper Cub. My daughter was about 16 years old at the time. She drove me to the airport where there was only one plane there. It was a Learjet with a red carpet rolled out and three crewmembers standing at the bottom of the stairs. I had about $300 in my pocket and probably couldn't have paid to clean the rugs in that thing. Anyway, I walked up there like I knew what I was doing. Mead took another jet and met me in Ketchikan. Meanwhile, I had a breakfast aboard the jet like you'd have at the Ritz-Carlton. I had lunch in Wichita Falls, dinner in Seattle, and then on to Ketchikan to meet Mead. I flew home that way, too.

We took an hour-long flight from Ketchikan, to a place called Yes Bay Lodge, one of the oldest lodges in Alaska. Mead had brought along some of that Dom Pérignon, very expensive stuff. He was concerned that they might not have any in camp (I'm pretty sure he was right).

Mead was one of these type-A people. When we got to the lodge he asked the manager what the drill would be. The guy said, "Well, we'll take you out in the morning on a floatplane and fly you out to a remote fishing spot. The plane will leave. The guide will assist you and prepare your lunch. And then the seaplane will come back to pick you up."

Mead had a visceral reaction. "Suppose we want to go somewhere else?"

"Well," said the manager, "we only have one plane."

Mead turned to this young guy who had just flown us into the lodge. "What are you doing the next few days?"

You could tell this young pilot was pretty bright when he said, "Whatever you'd like me to do, Mr. Johnson."

He was on the team. We flew over the Northwest Territories one day and I saw this lake shaped like a banana and I asked the guide if there were any fish in it. He said he wasn't sure and I suggested that we give it a try. So we landed on the lake. There was a stream that trickled past an old cabin out in the bushes. We caught a lot of fish, and cooked up a couple Dolly Varden for lunch. Back in the early 1900s if you wanted to trap you had to get a license. Once you got one you'd split a log and then burn your license number into the wood and stake that by your cabin. These old log licenses have become collectible.

While we were fishing and eating our lunch, this young pilot went to see if he could find one of these old log licenses. He was gone about fifteen minutes and we heard him yelling. We figured he'd been attacked by a bear or something, so we grabbed our shotguns and ran toward him. He came out of the bushes holding a little green silk purse. He opened it and there were twenty-six silver dollars. They had been sitting in the purse inside this old cabin all these years.

I was there again in 1967 to write a magazine article on Alaskan fishing. It was a trip that would prove as memorable for the transportation as for the fishing.

Alaska is an enormous state. It's twice the size of Texas, but most of its land is virtually untouched. The only way to get around these vast stretches of nature is via seaplane. The most favored seaplane in the region is the deHavilland Beaver. It's a remarkably strong, reliable aircraft. It's got a huge rotary engine—about three feet across—and people rely on these throughout Alaska. They are not cheap and the fact that there hasn't been a new one built in thirty or forty years makes them even more expensive. In fact, in Alaska an industry has evolved around maintaining aging Beaver aircraft.

We were fishing Bristol Bay Lodge, which was just being constructed and is now considered among the finest lodges in all of Alaska. I went with John Gary, who operated the lodge with his wife Maggie.

John's son, Mogie, and I took John up on his mouthwatering invitation to fish "rivers that had never been fished." We flew along the Bering Sea and landed in the narrow end of an arrowhead-shaped bay. At this narrow end a river flowed into the bay. We taxied up to a gravel bar and put the anchor out on the bar. It was high tide. Then we went over to the river and we caught a huge number of rainbow trout, many in the 8- to 12-pound range. I was using a Muddler Minnow fly and I had to cut them off because these fish would chew up the end of the leader, forcing me to put a new fly on. My leader got shorter and shorter and shorter until on the last fish I caught, the leader was so short that I didn't have enough monofilament left to tie another fly.

We wrapped up our fishing for the day and walked back down to the plane. When we got there we were surprised to see that the plane was sitting on dry land a half-mile from the shore: the tide had gone out. Most of the Bay was empty. John said, "Lefty, how long do you figure until the tide comes back in?" I said usually about six hours.

Eight hours later the tide hadn't moved. It then occurred to me that we were dealing with a diurnal tide. There are some places in world where there are no real tides. Tallahassee is one. Fiji is another. They sit in between bodies of water that have opposing tides so they see virtually no change.

Imagine a seesaw. The ends go up and down, but the middle stays roughly the same. There are other parts of the world that have twelve-hour tides. That's what we were facing in Alaska, and that meant that after a full day of fishing and eight hours of waiting for high tide we had at least another four hours to go. The tide there was about 18 feet.

By now it was late in the evening. Down the beach we noticed a walrus carcass that had likely been poached for its tusks. The thing was huge. I would say it was about the size of a couch that could sit four or five people. The meat alone must have weighed 2000 pounds. It was undoubtedly going to attract a good degree of attention from the local Kodiak bear population. As the temperature began to fall, John told us about a traditional Eskimo survival technique. You dig a hole in the gravel deep enough to lie down in. One hole for each person. Then you get driftwood and build a fire. When the fire gets down to coals, put all the gravel back on top and lie down on top of that and lay your raincoat over you. It's like lying in a warm tent.

We did that. The only problem was that two hundred yards away from us two bears had begun to descend on the walrus carcass. In fact, they began to fight over it. All we had was John's .45 pistol.

By one a.m. we decided that it would be safer to wait in the cockpit of the airplane. At that time of night in the Alaskan summer it's not really dark. There's probably just enough light to read a newspaper. Suddenly, we hear the sound of rushing water, sort of like the sound of rushing rapids on a river. It was a wall of water about a foot high rushing back into the bay. The plane floated and we got out of there.

As we were closing in on the lodge, we were all exhausted and I noticed that John was reluctant to land. He just kept circling. I said, "John, what's the problem?"

He said, "I'm looking for ducks." Turns out that the lake was so calm that he couldn't tell where the surface was. He was looking for ducks to stir the surface and give him some perspective. He got us home safely and we all slept pretty well.

My real scare came on another trip to Alaska. We left out of Bristol Bay Lodge in a seaplane with a guy who was an experienced airborne game warden in Maine. He landed on a little lake and we all had to walk about a quarter-mile to the river. Mind you, walking on tundra is the hardest walking I've ever done. It's like walking on a double mattress. Your legs go almost knee-deep into it, which means that you've got to lift the other foot at least that high to make the next step. We trudged to the river and, fortunately, caught all kinds of salmon.

As soon as we were done for the day, we got back into the Beaver. I sat directly behind the pilot and I remember that on the back of his seat was a metal file for holding his charts and notes and things. He taxied to the other end of the lake and began his takeoff. But as we approached the far end of the lake, I realized we were still on the water. We only had about 150 yards left until the shore. The pilot was trying everything—rocking the plane and all. He finally got it off the water, but the pontoons hit the shoreline. We might as well have hit a cement embankment. The impact sheared all four bolts that held my seat to the floor. The plane bounced high into the air. I flew upside down and forward and my shoulder smashed into the metal chart box. The pilot tried desperately to keep it in the air, but he couldn't. It was about a quarter-mile of bouncing and jouncing before we finally came to a stop on the tundra

There were eighteen containers of gasoline stored in the floats. So we were all concerned about the possibility of a fire. The pilot was yelling, "Open the door and get out!" over and over again. I thought I'd broken my back because I tried to move and couldn't. That's when I realized I was still strapped into my seat. I was upside down and couldn't get out until I figured out how to get the seat belt off.

Finally we all got out, and while we had avoided any serious injury

I did separate my shoulder by smashing into the chart box. We couldn't get a radio signal out for emergency help and everybody else back at the lodge thought we were just out fishing, so it was another seven or eight hours before anyone even thought to come and look for us.

Finally, a man in this tiny plane came to help us. He could only fit two passengers at a time and he was very nervous. He went to the end of the pond and got ready to try his takeoff. I could barely lift my arm at this point. We go tearing down this little tiny pond and I looked out the window to see that we're—again—about 150 yards from the coming shoreline. I looked up and the arm that I supposedly couldn't move was up straight hanging on to the handle, pain free. We must have missed the shoreline by a foot. I was still pretty nervous because this guy flew so low to the ground for about the first mile. Seemed like he only flew about fifteen feet above the trees until we got out over the Bering Sea. I asked him about that later on and he said that he was seeking ground effect. I guess when you fly real low to the ground it compresses air under the airplane and gives you more lift. Needless to say we all survived to fish many more times, but these were some incredible moments.

For much of the year, the rivers of Alaska are relatively tame because the trout swim to different river sections or back to head-water lakes. This, of course, is true except for the period of time when the Pacific salmon are spawning. Whereas Atlantic salmon will spawn and return to the ocean, the Pacific species will spawn in the rivers and then, quite famously, die. The reason for this phenomenon is simple. There is so little protein in the rivers of the upper Northwest, that unless the parents die, thus furnishing protein for the offspring to live on, their progeny would never survive.

The king salmon are usually the first of the Pacific species to come in to spawn. That's usually sometime in mid-June to the first week of July. Then they're followed by the other species of salmon, the last being the Coho, or silver salmon, which usually spawns in late August. This species is the most popular among anglers.

If you look at a map, the Japanese current comes off the coast of Japan from Siberia, off the coast of Alaska, and hits the Alaskan chain. Then it's pushed back into the ocean. The point at which the Chain connects with the mainland creates a funnel of sorts. As a result, the Bristol Bay region is where the best Pacific salmon fishing occurs.

When the spawning season begins and those first king salmon move into the rivers, most of the rainbow trout clear out, heading up into nearby lakes. After the kings depart, the smaller species come in (the sockeye and so on). They come in by the thousands. In fact, I have photographs in which every square yard of a river has sockeye salmon in it. It's very easy pickings. Unlike their Atlantic brethren, which require enormous patience and effort, Pacific salmon are a breeze. It's incredible. Once I stood in one spot on the Tobiak River. I made twenty-seven casts and caught twenty-four Coho salmon. When I fish for spawning Pacific salmon, I often use a weedless fly because you end up running your fly over the backs of so many fish that you'll actually snag some, and you don't want to do that.

It's an incredible fishery. First of all, because there is so much action and the fish are so big, it's a great place for someone to learn how to hook fish and how to fight fish. Second, the authorities up there have done a magnificent job of managing the species. They have controlled both the commercial fishing of salmon in the ocean and the recreational fishing of salmon in the rivers so well that there are now as many, if not more, great salmon in the region than there were in the 1960s when I first fished them. But in my mind, the best thing about fishing in Alaska is the majesty of the surroundings. The vastness of the wilderness is incredible. You can fly for an hour and never see anything more than a bear trail—no roads.

If you go fly-fishing for Pacific salmon in Alaska at the right time of year and you don't catch anything, you need to take up golf or something, because you're never going to be a fly fisherman. But if you go with half a brain and a rod, you won't believe how many fish you'll catch. Truth be told, after you've done it a few times, it gets a little too easy. For an experienced fisherman, there's very little challenge. Then again, you always have the wonderful, pristine wilderness. It's one of those places that can truly remind a person of what a great country this is.

TROUT

Trout fishing is different. Nobody ever suffered a heart attack fighting a freshwater trout. It's more mental exercise than a physical one. The key to trout fishing is solving the problem. You see a fish feeding. First you want to identify what it's feeding on or at least something that resembles what it's feeding on. It doesn't have to be exact, which leads me to one of my pet peeves about fly-fishing for trout: There's more bull dingy in trout fishing than anything I've ever been involved in. You don't have to have a fly that has the underarm hair of an orangutan from South Africa mixed in with some other exotic animal. That said, there are a few factors that you have to consider.

The first consideration—before casting—should be: If I hook this fish, how can I land it? If you're standing in water that's waist deep and all the water around you is waist deep and you hook a trout, you're probably going to lose the fish. Why? Because you're fighting the fish in his environment. Look around and see if there is a sloping gravel bar nearby. That way, if you hook the fish, you can quickly get up on the gravel. Now, as the fish gets closer to you, he's in less and less water and you are more and more in command. So the first thing you do, after you figure out what the fish is eating, is figure out the blocking: Where you're going to start your approach, how you're going to cast to him (there are a myriad of casts you can use in trout fishing). It's got to be a drag-free cast so you don't spook the fish. You've got to have the right kind of fly, the right kind of leader, and—if you do everything right—the fish takes it. If you know anything about fighting fish, you'll probably land him.

Like most freshwater fishing, the key to successful trout fishing lies not so much in fighting and landing the fish as it does in solving those strategic issues. In this country, George Harvey was the best trout angler I've ever fished with. At 96, he passed away, but he and I fished together for about thirty years, off and on. In fact, the first time I ever fished with George, it was with Dr. Ralph Dougherty, a Pittsburgh surgeon, who was George's best friend. Ralph took me up to State College, Pennsylvania, to introduce me to George. George was a rough, gruff-speaking guy about 5-foot-7. We went to Spruce Creek Rod and Gun Club, which has been around for about a century. The creek it's named for—a beautiful limestone stream—winds through the property. George took Ralph and me way down to the end and as those two stood on the bank, George growled out, "Show us what you can do." I didn't know that I was going to be put on the spot like that, but I got in the water.

One of the things you have to do in a trout stream is wade very slowly and smoothly. Water carries vibrations very well. In fact, water transmits sound four times faster than air. Plus, if you make waves in a stream, those waves ripple through the water and are inevitably detected by the fish, warning them that something is up. So I was being very, very careful, wading very slowly. I got to casting and caught five trout out of this big pool I was working. I got out and George barked, "First outdoor writer I ever saw who could actually cast and fish."

It didn't sound like a compliment to me, but I took it as one. And as George started walking away Ralph came up to me and said, "That's the finest compliment I've ever heard him give anybody."

George wrote a book that had more information about catching trout on fly than any book I've ever read. It's entitled *Fly Tying and Trout Fishing* and it was published in 1976 by the Pennsylvania Fish Commission. It was really a leaflet, stapled together, maybe 64 pages, but it contained most of the vital information that people need to know to catch trout. I've seen books 6 inches thick that didn't have half as much information. It was George who made most people realize that you had to drift a fly "drag free" on the current rather than let the current pull against the line and pull the fly unnaturally across the water. There were some people who knew that before him, but he was the one who really made the public aware of that. As you would expect from George, there was not a lot of puffy prose. It was the basics, condensed into a readable, helpful form.

George, with whom I became quite close and fished with often, was also the angling professor at Penn State University. And over the course of his career there he taught a certified fly-fishing course for credit to over thirty thousand students. He taught them how to tie flies, how to build leaders, how to catch fish, and everything in between. He retired several years ago after something like twenty-five years on the job, but I think the class is still offered. George is one of the truly influential individuals in modern fly-fishing. I can only imagine how many additional people learned George's thoughts on fly-fishing through his former students. Stackpole Publishing has since published a larger, updated version of his book that still contains all the good stuff that George wrote. I highly recommend it.

Another tip that I've used over the years came from Europe, from a man named John Goddard. He's about 82 years old right now. He knows a great deal about entomology. He's also one of these people who are always wondering how and why things work. For a time he had a firm based in England that manufactured fishing apparel and tackle. He was an incredible observer and he began to really study trout fishing in the great chalk streams of England. One of the things he did was design a "slant tank." Basically this was an aquarium that let him observe things from a trout's-eye perspective. He began to look at flies not from the above-the-surface vantage point of the angler, but from the underwater perspective of the fish. Most flies at the time had hooks on the bottom where, he found out, the fish could see it. So he developed flies where the hook stayed above the surface and the fish never saw it. He was one of the first people to create a fly that looked like an emerger on the surface of the water. He used a little piece of fabric from a woman's stocking to create the appearance of the cocoon in which these creatures rise to the surface before spreading their wings.

He was a very ingenious guy, a great river fisherman, but he was a tremendous fisherman on reservoirs and lakes as well. We are about one hundred years behind the Brits on that. They use very long light rods, about 12 to 15 feet long. They use very light leaders so that they can suspend the fly and tickle it across the surface. They use two sea anchors on the boat to control the drift of the boat. They've got that stuff wired. We've got some trout fisherman in the United States who are as good as John on streams, but we don't have anybody that knows as much as about reservoir and lake fishing as he does. All around, he's the best trout fisherman I ever fished with.

I got to know John when I went to the U.K. to give some seminars outside London. John was kind enough to let me stay at his house and after my talks were over, he and I spent a week fishing. John was very well known throughout Europe and he had access to some of the best private streams of the area. Over there the best rivers are privately owned and even if you can get on them you have to pay a real stiff price, something like $100 a day, just to wet your line. Well, he had access everywhere, the Kennett and all these other famous trout rivers. We'd get up, have breakfast, and go to all these famous places. Well, the first day I went with him to the Kennett, which I think is the best trout stream of them all. It was private, but John got us on. It was beautiful, just as you'd imagine the pristine countryside of England: lush trees lining the river, green fields. I appeared in my usual old fly-fishing vest which was khaki colored. John said, "Don't you have another jacket?"

"What's wrong with this one?" I asked.

"Well, it's the wrong color," he said in that great English accent. "It conflicts with the background."

Well, I fished with that jacket for that day and I caught a bunch of trout, but the next day he loaned me a dark green jacket that blended with the background and I caught significantly more trout. He taught me that if you want to fish trout, you need to blend with the surroundings.

SALTWATER

PEACOCK BASS

The peacock bass comes in several subspecies. There's speckled and butterfly, but the one I like best is the royal povon. It's the biggest of the peacocks and the biggest I ever caught was 19 pounds, 13 ounces, weighed on an accurate scale. The best place I ever fished for them was in the northern Amazon Basin. People don't realize how big the Amazon is. One-fifth of all the fresh water in the world flows down the Amazon River. Three of its tributaries are each about the size of the Mississippi.

Big as the basin is, you want to fish in areas where they fish out of small tent camps. You can go on these great big air-conditioned boats down there. They anchor up and the tenders go out for a day of fishing, but these charter groups are hitting the same water over and over and over. I like to fly in with floatplanes about one hundred miles or so below the Venezuela border. They set up pup tents and you fish there for two or three days and then you move on. In other words, you're fishing new water all the time. They have these canoe barges that are about 22 feet long and 5 or 6 feet wide, and they tie a number of them together and they have a tow boat upfront that tows this snakelike procession behind it. Each boat has a function. Behind the tug is the mess boat; the others are for sleeping and so on. They can snake into all kinds of little pools and rivulets. The group I have always gone with is Frontiers International, which may be the best outfitter in the hunting and fishing business. The best time to go is December, January, and February. There are scores of lagoons connecting to the river that serve as catch basins for the last of the summer rainwater.

Some guys go down there and throw lures out, then rip them across the surface. They catch a lot of peacock, but with all the commotion, they alert every remaining peacock in the area. You go in not long after some of these guides have been there and all you see are white foam strips; it's like throwing grenades.

You can get in there with large streamer flies and fish all day long. The only thing you're disturbing are the fish. Every time I have ever gone for peacock bass we caught more and bigger bass on big flies than did the people who used plug or spinning tackle. We generally use a 9-weight rod because the flies are either large Clouser Minnows or Half-and-Halfs (half Lefty's Deceiver and half Clouser Minnow). The back has a big tail like a Deceiver and the front end is like a Clouser with lead eyes. The other one we use is a Deceiver. We use these at lengths of about 6 to 8 inches. They're very light and you can cast them on a fairly light rod. We never use more than 20-pound test leaders on them. We use a short length on the front, maybe 10 inches of 40-pound test, because while the peacock does not have teeth, he does have serrations throughout the mouth.

There are several species of peacock bass. In terms of overall shape, they're very much like our bass in North America. The mouth of the peacock, however, is much larger. A 15-pound peacock bass could probably fit a soccer ball in his mouth. When they take a lure on the surface it's the loudest noise I've ever heard from a fish. Snook make similar sounds, but they're amateurs compared to these things. Peacock are much stronger and much bigger than our bass, but they have beautiful colors on them, a lot of oranges and olives. The big ones, the povons, have orange-ish colors with vertical stripes in them. The speckled peacock only grows to about 8 or 10 pounds and they have little specks or dots all over their bodies. The butterfly species doesn't get as big as the povon, either, but they have round spots that have multiple colors within the spot.

STRIPED BASS

I have a love affair with the striped bass because it was the first saltwater fish I ever caught on fly. It was on the Chesapeake Bay back in the mid 1950s. I had just been introduced to Bob Pond. Bob created a lure called the Atom Popper. You threw it out on the water and if you retrieved it rapidly it spluttered and made a lot of noise. Just about everybody who fished for striped bass in the Chesapeake at that time swore by bait, but Bob proved that you could catch stripers on artificial lures. I thought, *Well, if you can use an artificial lure to catch these things, you ought to be able to catch these things on popping bugs with a fly rod.*

So I started using popping bugs and doing pretty well (I would later learn that stripers have been taken on fly since the 1800s). Then I started using underwater flies, and in late 1950s I developed Lefty's Deceiver precisely for fishing striped bass. So, for the first few years the most of my saltwater fly-fishing was centered on the striped bass in the Maryland portion of the Chesapeake Bay. Then it occurred to me that there were striped bass in Delaware Bay and off the New Jersey coast, and then I fished in New England for them. In fact, most of the stripers that populate the East Coast spawn in Chesapeake Bay. They do so in the spring and then head up the East Coast. There are some fish that spawn in the Hudson River, but that population is minimal compared to the numbers produced in Chesapeake Bay. The stripers follow the baitfish up the coast throughout the summer and when the bait retreat south in the fall, they follow the bait south and spend the winter in deep water. In the spring they spawn again.

From a purely biological viewpoint, the striper is a fascinating fish. First, the largest of the species are almost always female. While some males do reach 25 or 30 pounds, it's very rare. The vast majority of males weigh less than 10 pounds. By and large, it's the females who migrate up the coast. Often the males will stay in the Chesapeake all summer.

Second is their spawning technique. As much time as striped bass spend in salt water, they do not spawn in salt water. They actually spawn in rivers and are very precise about the composition of the water. Before they lay their eggs the water needs to be a certain proportion of salt water to freshwater. The female will then suspend her eggs into the water and the male will cast his sperm over them. The eggs float for several days and then hatch.

The striped bass really takes a fly well. They put up a decent fight, though nothing like bluefish or a lot of other saltwater fish. However, they lend themselves to fly-fishing so well. You can catch them on the surface, you can catch them deep, you can catch them right on shore or offshore. I now do most of my striped bass fishing in New England between June and October. In June there's usually a nice run of squid close by the shore and the bass know where the food is. I enjoy fishing with Captain Jim White (White Ghost Charters, Coventry, Rhode Island) for stripers in Narragansett Bay off Rhode Island. They have great striper activity there in late May into early June and it's pretty lightly fished. Another place I like to fish for striper is the Chatham area on Cape Cod. Captain Dan Marini is one of the best guides up there. Even if he is already booked, he'll put you in touch with someone who is reliable. The place that I *really* like to fish in New England, though it's almost impossible to get accommodations there, is Nantucket. If you don't know someone who has a house where you can stay, you're pretty much out of luck.

There are a handful of ways to fly-fish for stripers. Some people like to go out at night. Stripers are basically nocturnal animals, anyway. You can put some waders on and cast for them. I have done that, but I don't really enjoy it because fly-fishing is a very visual sport. I not only like to see what I'm casting at, but I love to take in the surroundings. Another way is to get in a boat and go to where fish are breaking on the surface and chasing bait, or where your guide simply knows that they congregate. Another way, and this is without a doubt the most exciting method of all—it requires a guide with great expertise—involves bringing the boat close to the large rocks near the shore. The guide will ride the top of a wave until he gets you within casting distance of the rock, about seventy to ninety feet. The moment you cast the line, he backs up the boat to keep it off the rocks. You cast the line to an opening between two rocks. The fish know that when the water gets compressed between those rocks it will create funnel of rushing water that will likely contain bait, so they are waiting there. It's very exciting. It's not for everyone—you can get rope burn saying your rosary so fast—but it's really something.

The Cape is also famous for the stripers that get up on these shallow white sand flats. They look like baby tarpon. They cruise around these flats looking for bait, and it's almost like bonefishing for stripers. The best place for this type of fishing is in Nantucket.

In the summer of 2005 I went up to Cape Cod the first week in July. In Chatham, the beach swarms with sand eels up to 10 or 12 inches long that time of year, and right in the surf you can catch 25- to 35-pound striped bass. It's almost automatic in the first two weeks of July. However, within two weeks, by the end of July, those same eels will leave the Cape and keep heading south.

As mentioned earlier, I developed the Lefty's Deceiver specifically for stripers. I still use it, predominantly in shallow water, because it doesn't sink very fast. I also use Half-and-Halfs. Regardless of the fly I'm using, the important thing is to key the size of the fly to the size of the baitfish the stripers are pursuing. For instance, when the stripers are off the coast of New Jersey in late October en route back to the Chesapeake, they chase a baitfish called the rainfish, also known as the bay anchovy. These things are about the size of your little finger. In that location I might use a Surf Candy fly that imitates the look and approximates the size. We also use small Deceivers or Clousers. Often with striped bass it's not the color of the fly as much as the size that makes all the difference.

BILLFISHING

Billfishing has been around a long time, but billfishing on fly was really given its start in the 1960s in Key West, Florida by a couple named Helen and Dr. Web Robinson. Dr. Robinson was an avid fisherman. He had retired early due to back problems and he used to walk the shallow-water flats hours at a time to strengthen his back. Helen was also a very good angler. She held several world records during her life. The Robinsons had a captain named Lefty Regan. Earlier in the book I mentioned the technique that Web and Lefty developed for teasing billfish toward a boat by allowing them to hit a decapitated, gutted bonita carcass that was trolled behind the boat on a long 100-pound test trace. Then they'd pull the bonita away from the billfish until it got madder and madder and closer and closer to the boat. Lefty then learned that if he allowed the billfish to taste the bonita as well and then pulled it away, that really pissed these fish off. Finally, they'd get the fish right up behind the boat. Lefty'd kill the motor, they'd pull the bonita out of the water, and then Web would throw out the fly—it was a cork popper in the beginning—and the fish would go for it.

These were the crude beginnings of billfishing on fly. The method has since been refined, but it is essentially the method we still use today. I mentioned earlier that this technique, which came about while I was running the MET tournament, spurred several other innovations. We found that the chugger lures that make a lot of noise could be used to tease cobia and amberjack up to a boat. The teasing technique, developed by Web and Lefty Regan, became an internationally recognized technique for tempting not only billfish but also other fish.

If you're going to fish on fly for marlin, the top end is roughly 200 to 300 pounds. There's a place in the Great Barrier Reef off Australia where you can find these smaller marlin, so a lot of people will go there to catch a black marlin. There have only been a few blue marlins ever caught on fly and there's a reason for that: most of them are 15 to 20 feet long and weigh over 1,000 pounds. It's hard to find blue or blacks that are small enough to be captured on fly.

Now the Pacific sailfish, which averages from 60 to 100 pounds and has been caught up to 130 pounds, are more receptive to teaser baits. It's not unusual for one boat off the west coast of Costa Rica or Panama to go out and catch four to ten sails in a day.

The hardest billfish to tease is the white marlin. You can get them all teased up and ready to go, but for some reason, they can lose interest in the snap of finger.

I've caught six sailfish on fly. The trick is this: Once the fish is close by, the teaser bait has been removed, and the boat is thrown out of gear, you cast the fly across and slightly behind the fish's mouth. The reason for that lies in the anatomy of the sailfish's mouth. The whole upper mouth is solid bone, impenetrable to just about any hook. With that being the case the only way you can reliably hook a sail is in the softer tissues on the side of the mouth or on the tongue. So, if you have a fish swimming due north, you throw the fly southeast or southwest of the fish's head. He'll turn around and head for the fly and as he takes it in, the fly is automatically dragged to the corner of the mouth, where it sets firmly. That's the main trick to catching sailfish on fly.

I used to do a lot of offshore fishing. I don't do much anymore. Like a lot of older guys, I just don't enjoy it that much. For one thing, it's hours of boredom interrupted by minutes of pandemonium. You're out there and the sea's flat and all of a sudden there are fish all over. You rush over, throw your flies out, get hooked up, and everybody's frantic for five or ten minutes, then things go dead calm again. The other thing is that out on the sea you're bounced all over the place and when you come home you've got bruises all over the place. Furthermore, most of the stuff you hook out there requires a real time commitment just to bring it in.

I remember the first time I went to Bermuda. I was about forty years old. We were offshore and I had a reel that held almost 500 yards of line. I hooked a huge yellow-fin tuna off of Challenger Bank. It went down about 450 yards. If you sat in your room and wound 450 yards of line onto your reel, you'd get pretty tired. Now put a disagreeable tuna on the other end and that's a lot of work. I just don't enjoy offshore fishing anymore. Billfishing and tuna and the like—that is a young man's game.

BLUEFISH

Blues are one of the more interesting fish in the ocean. Although they are fished in the United States as far south as Florida (they get smaller the farther south you go), they are most typically associated with the Northeast, from the Carolinas up through New England. That's because in the fall of the year the water up there turns cold and all the baitfish off the Maine coast start heading south to warmer waters. September and October, that's the red-hot season to fish for blues off Cape Cod or in Long Island Sound or off Montauk on Long Island. It's not really because the blues are "running" per se, it's really because the baitfish are "running" on their way to warmer waters and the blues are following: The groceries are on sale.

Blues are an excellent fighting fish and they are very aggressive predators. I've seen bluefish bite other bluefish. In chum lines I've seen them gobble up chum and spit it out only so they could gobble up more chum. From the mid-Atlantic north, they are certainly among the strongest fish you'll catch in inshore saltwater fishing, no question about that. Small tunas with their sickle-shaped tails will swim faster and harder, but the bluefish will fight much longer (although they don't make long runs).

Blues also have extremely sharp teeth. So when it comes to proper tackle, you have to use wire. Fortunately, blues are not what I would call leader-shy; that is, they are not easily spooked by leaders. So I recommend at least 4 to 6 inches of wire between the fly and your monofilament leader. Some people will use monofilament, say 60- or 80-pound test, but I've lost enough 12-pound bluefish on monofilament that I've stopped using monofilament altogether. I just use wire, usually a No. 3 to No. 4 solid wire or a 30-pound test braided wire (standard plastic-coated braided wire works fine). If you do use braided plastic-coated wire—the old-style stuff—the plastic coating will often begin to shred after a few fish. These threads of plastic will eventually scare off fish, so you'll need to change that out. There's some new material out there called nickel titanium or multistrand wire, which is made up of quite a few strands of very fine stainless wire. This stuff is very thin. I would say that 50-pound test multistrand wire would be about the same thickness as 20-pound test monofilament. It's very flexible, so you can get a lot more action out of your fly. Of course, it's more expensive, too, but then again you're not using that much. Manufacturers say you can use it the same way you use monofilament in knots, but my experience has been that it doesn't work very well with monofilament knots. The one knot, however, which seems to work very well with this new multistrand is the nonslip mono loop. It gives the fly action. Even in Australia, where they catch some very large fish, like dogtooth tuna, that knot has held up very well.

There are three basic approaches to fly-fishing for blues. Bluefish feed a couple of different ways. Quite famously, they chase baitfish to the surface. When they are in this mode any fly you can throw into the water that makes some noise, like a popping bug, will work. The problem is that you'll get two or three bluefish attracted to your popping bug and pretty quickly your bug is destroyed. A lot of people will use a streamer-type flies such as a Surf Candy, made up with synthetic hair rather than regular hair (this makes it a little tougher), and after you make the fly you cover the straight part of the shank with epoxy. That makes for a very durable fly that can stand up to quite a few fish. When they're chasing bait up on the surface, you can almost guarantee an instant strike.

What about when they're not on the surface? Well, blues are known to have a preference for oily prey such as alewives and bunker and menhaden. If you (or your captain or guide) know what you're doing, you can sometimes spot oil slicks on the surface of the water. This indicates an underwater picnic. Not only is the slick apparent to the naked eye but also the oil will often deaden the wave formation in the immediate area. If you see these two phenomena, and you use a sinking line and fish deep, you'll catch some fish. For this technique I would recommend a fly with lead eyes on it. A minnow imitation works very well in these cases. You should try to lend a little action here, imitating the baitfish below. When doing this kind of fishing (and really any kind of fishing using sinking lures or flies), I often use the countdown method. I cast line out and count 1,001 to 1,008. If there are no strikes I go deeper on the next cast, maybe 1,001 to 1,015. If no strikes, I'll go deeper still. This way, when I do get a strike, I'll know precisely at what depth the fish are. It's a simple process, but it works remarkably well.

The most popular approach for blues is to chum them. Fresh baitfish work best for this. In fact, buying directly from commercial fishermen who are on the water is the best option, but frozen bait works, too. What they do in a lot of places is they'll have a professional-grade sausage grinder mounted to the sideboard of the boat. The captain anchors the boat in an area frequented by blues. They put the baitfish in the grinder, grind 'em up, and then ladle the chum out every thirty to fifty seconds. It's amazing how quickly bluefish will home in on that chum line. I mentioned earlier in the book that I created a chum fly, which I made with maribou, but which some people now make with rabbit hair. Basically it's a 1/0 or 2/0 hook. You tie the material on, make it look like a piece of chewed-up chum, and you throw the fly right in amid the chum. You should have these flies tied so that they are only about 1¾ or 2 inches long. The idea is to make them look like shredded meat. It's a dark red color.

You should have chum flies made up in varying weights; some unweighted, some lightly weighted, and some heavily weighted. The reason for that is that you are trying to imitate dead fish meat in the sea. Such meat sinks at different rates depending on the tide and currents. An unweighted fly would work best when the tide or current is strong and a fish would expect more lateral movement than downward movement. When currents and tide ease off, you may want a lightly weighted fly and when the water is still, of course, you stop chumming, but you may want to use the heavier fly to match the more rapid descent of the meat. In each of these three scenarios remember this: You do not want action on chum flies. Chewed-up fish meat doesn't move. People make the mistake of trying to give it action, but if you do that you're going to screw it up.

This chum-flying can be very effective. Years ago, in the 1980s, the heyday of fly-fishing in the Chesapeake, people were catching so many bluefish. We would catch 100 to 150 bluefish ranging anywhere from eight to fifteen pounds in a day. I remember people bringing them onto the dock by the wheelbarrow-full. Blues are not particularly good eating and so, tragically, I think a lot of those massive hauls were wasted. That said, bluefish are a lot of fun. It seems as though they never stop eating. I often joke that I've never seen a bluefish or a jack crevalle that wasn't hungry. In the salt waters of the northeastern United States, the striped bass is still the headliner, but the bluefish is a much more aggressive fish. In comparable sizes, a striper can't fight a third as hard as a blue (of course you're much more likely to catch a 30-pound striper than you are a 30-pound blue). When the season peaks in New England in October the bluefish population in well into the billions. They will literally jump out of the water as they pursue their feeding frenzy all the way to the sandy shore. It's not unusual to have baitfish leaping out of the surf and onto the beach in an effort to avoid being eaten by perpetually famished blues. In fact, sometimes when these rapidly swimming schools condense, some of the fish get pushed to the surface by the school and they simply die of suffocation.

Time your trip right and the fishing can be phenomenal. In 2005, in two-and-a-half days of fishing off Cape Cod with Captain Jim White and my friend and fellow outdoor writer Dan Blanton, we caught 192 bluefish, plus forty stripers, one of which was 42 inches long. It was the only time I'd ever seen Dan when he'd actually caught enough fish.

BONEFISH

The first bonefish I ever caught was in Cuba, back in 1959. One day, during that incredible trip, Castro's people put us on a sailboat, a beautiful 50-footer (probably confiscated from some plantation owner). They gave us a crew and they sailed us along the north coast of Cuba to a place called Cayo Galinda, where we anchored. There were these huge flats there and, of course, all I had was my Medalist freshwater fly reel and a fiberglass rod that Joe Brooks had picked out for me.

Although I had often heard about bonefishing from Joe and other friends, I had zero experience. I knew nothing. So when I saw my first bonefish, I really didn't know if it was big or little because I had no point of reference. I threw the fly where the guide told me and I stripped it the way he told me, and this bonefish bit. He ran. And ran. And ran. He was so far out that he nearly used up all my line. In fact, I had a very hard time believing that the fish I was watching so far off in the distance was actually attached to my line.

Still, I could see him flopping around and all I heard the guide saying was, "*Mucho grande, mucho grande.*" As you know, I didn't speak a lick of Spanish, so I didn't know what he meant. I do now. We started walking forward and I got most of the line back and then the fish did it all over again. I couldn't believe that a 10-pound fish (I've since learned that that's a pretty big bonefish) could run so far against a drag like that. That was the first big bonefish I ever caught, and I fell in love with the species right there.

I've caught a lot of tarpon, big tarpon. And when you first catch tarpon it's the most exciting thing in fly-fishing. That's because you're standing there with a little tiny rod and a little fly and suddenly something six feet long with a mouth as big as water bucket shows up and he takes the fly, and before you know it he's out of the water, splashing and jumping around like crazy. Same with sailfish. The first time you catch one of those things it is the most exhilarating experience you can imagine. After a while, however, you realize that tarpon are not the smartest fish in the ocean. The ones in the Keys are getting a little wary because they're fished so heavily, but they're really not an intelligent species. The fact of the matter is that you can do a lot of things *wrong* and still catch a tarpon. With bonefish, there's just no margin for error. They spook as easily as cats in a dog pound.

There are countless ways to spook bonefish: The fly hits too close; the line hits too close; the line is too high in the air and they see it flash; you rock the boat; you clunk the pole against the hull; you strip line incorrectly. I mean you could write a book about spooking bonefish. The point is that with bonefish you've got to do everything right and you've got to do it NOW, because in three seconds he'll be on a whole new course.

Among the other reasons I like bonefishing: First, you're in the flats, which, regardless of what you might be fishing, are always beautiful. Second, you're either wading or you're moving across the flats on a boat, so the environment is changing all the time. You see rays come by and all kinds of other fish and birds and mangroves. It's almost like you're in a movie where the plot is about to thicken. Third, I like the fact that bonefishing only requires very light tackle; most people use 7- or 8-weight rods (I prefer an 8-weight most of the time), and you're throwing very small flies—a size 4 is pretty much standard for bonefish in most places. Combine light tackle and little flies with one of nature's most beautiful backdrops, add to that a fish that won't swim more than twenty feet in one direction, and you have the makings of a great day.

The biggest difference between freshwater trout fishing and fishing on the saltwater flats is time. If you see a trout rising on a stream, you can simply go downstream and put a little net in the water to see what they're eating, come back, change flies and catch fish. When you see bonefish (or tarpon or permit) moving across the surface, you have about ten seconds to make a cast. If the cast is not accurate and the fly is not well presented, that fish is gone, probably forever. In freshwater you can cast a dry fly thirty times to one trout and still catch him, but in the flats if you make any mistakes, you lose. I've seen this time and time again when I've taken experienced trout fishermen on their first flat-fishing trip. They get frustrated. The main problem, of course, is that they don't know how to cast. They use the old 10-to-2 technique, which can work when you're throwing tiny dry flies to trout because if you don't make a good cast to the trout, you can always make another one. Not with bonefish. Make one bad cast and they're gone.

Additionally, with bonefish there's just about always a wind to contend with. If the fish is directly ahead of the boat you have to wait until the poler moves the boat sideways so that he won't get hooked on your back cast. You have to anticipate the tide, the currents, and the wind, whereas on a trout stream all you really have to do is put the fly up so that you get a drag-free drift.

Another mistake trout fishermen make on the flats is that after they make a poor cast they tend to fish it out. Let's say you have a streamer fly on a woolly booger and you throw it to a trout and he doesn't take it. A trout fisherman will just fish out the fly, pick it up, and make another cast. That's easy to do in freshwater because the fish is usually moving very little and the water is moving a lot. In salt water it's precisely the opposite. The fish is moving a lot and the water is fairly still. If you make the wrong cast in freshwater you can let the fly get swept away by the current and then you can make another cast. In salt water, the fish is moving—it has to keep moving because everything in the ocean is always under threat of getting eaten up by something bigger than it, which is the fundamental reason why saltwater fish are so much stronger. In trout fishing, nothing is chasing the trout. He can stay there all day. They are two totally different worlds.

I've always believed that if you can become a good saltwater fly fisherman it's easy to then become a freshwater fly fisherman. You'll already know how to cast long distances, under tougher conditions, with heavier flies. You'll be accurate as well as fast. Trout fisherman do not have to cast heavy flies and they typically don't have to cast long distances. A long dry-fly cast is 35 feet with a weightless or near-weightless fly. You can make several poor casts and the trout will still take the fly. If you're a beginner and you really want to learn how to be a very good fly caster, go to a saltwater fly-fishing school. If you can pass muster there you can fly cast anywhere. For those who rely on the old 10-to-2 motion that too many trout fishermen still swear by, you'll really be limited to fishing in windless places where you throw small flies short distances.

By the way, here's a little-known secret: In freshwater fly-fishing school when you hook a big fish, they'll tell you to keep the tip of the rod up. Well, here's an interesting experiment. Pull off 10 feet of fly line through the guides. Wrap that fly line around your hand and then have another person wrap the end of the line around the rod. Then have them pull away from you bending only the butt end of the rod. With a 6-weight rod they'll apply close to 6 pounds of pressure on the hand. As they raise the rod, and the bend moves up the rod and you approach vertical position, the pressure on your hand is only about 3 ounces. I do this with students all the time. A lot of people fish albacore along the East Coast and they are constantly breaking their rods. That's because they are fishing albacore the same way they fish a trout. Instead of bending the butt of the rod, they bend the tip of the rod, especially when the fish comes close to the boat and they're trying to lift it out. With a big fish that rod'll blow up. We call it high-sticking. In saltwater fly-fishing school you learn so many things that you just don't learn—and don't have to learn—for trout fishing. It's like skipping high school and going right to college.

Back to bonefishing. There are plenty of fantastic bonefishing areas to choose from. Belize is a great one. Bob Stearns is a friend of mine who lived across the canal from me in Florida. He was a good fisherman and he dearly wanted to get into outdoor writing. I took him to Belize on his first trip there. This was 1967 or 1968 and we went out to the Tourneff Islands, which are about 30 miles offshore. The outside edge of the Tourneffs is a reef. It drops off into very deep water, but there are huge coral flats there and water comes rushing in and hits these flats almost like coming in against a building and rushing up the side to the roof. We motored out there and as we got out of the boat I remember saying, "My God, would you look at the bonefish?" He didn't know what I was talking about. I said, "Bob, see all those waves that are rolling across the flats?" The wave was about a quarter mile long and coming toward us. "That's all bonefish."

Well, Bob jumped out of the boat right away, cast a fly and hooked one, then he grabbed a spinning rod and hooked another one. Now he's got an active rod in either hand and he starts passing a rod to me and says, "Here, take this."

I said "Hell, no. You got into this, I want to see you get out of it." He ended up losing both fish, but there were plenty more where they'd come from.

The supply of bonefish back then, nearly forty years ago, seemed limitless. Then the local government began to allow the netting of bonefish. They caught these things by the thousands and sold them for a dollar each in the local market. The netting cut so deeply into the supply that we'll never see that kind of bonefishing there again. There is still good bonefishing in Belize now, but nothing like it was.

The place in the United States that's most closely associated with bonefishing is the Florida Keys. But things have changed there as well. Used to be that if you were a good bonefisherman you could catch six to ten bonefish a day in the Keys. Now the bonefish have been fished so hard and for so long that a *very* good fisherman might catch three in a day and most fisherman will catch none or maybe one. They're very difficult.

The good news is that bonefish live all over the world, wherever there is warm water. Some of the most exciting bonefishing I've ever done is in the Christmas Islands, which are about 1,200 miles south of Honolulu. That's where they used to do the testing for the atomic bomb. Military officials picked it because it's so remote that the nuclear fallout could drift for thousand of miles across the ocean before impacting civilization. There were only about nine hundred natives on the atoll, about 60 miles around. It's shaped like a wedding band with a break in it and named Christmas Island, because Captain Cook discovered it on Christmas Day. The whole interior of the "ring" is bonefish flats. Well, after the flash of the nuclear explosion it turned out that thousands of the islands' birds were left blind. So the natives passed a law that said that if you do anything to injure a bird you pay a $500 fine and go to jail. Trust me, the $500 is nothing: You haven't seen their jail.

Anyway, as a result of this legislation, the birds of Christmas Islands are uniquely comfortable with humans. You can walk right up to Man-O'-War birds and touch them. I remember there's a thing called a longtail tropic bird, which is about as big as a pheasant and has one or two feathers that stick out way longer than the tail. I went to this one island where they were nesting. And I wanted to photograph them. I got down low with my camera and the bird was sitting down on a nest. I photographed it from about three feet away. Then I wanted to get a shot of the eggs, so I carefully got up, picked the mother bird up off the nest, photographed the eggs while the mother watched me, then I put the mother back on the nest. No problem. They have no fear of people. You can walk right past any bird on that island and they won't move.

Throughout the whole interior there is nothing but bonefish. I remember having forty- and fifty-bonefish days when I was there in the 1960s and 1970s. On one of my first trips down there, the natives were still taking care of things like cooking and cleaning for visitors. The only problem was, as much as they may have known about cooking, they didn't seem to know much about eating, at least not the kind of eating I like to do. As you probably know by now, I don't like spicy foods. That can be a problem when you go to, say, South America, where it seems they'll put onions in the Jell-O if you don't watch 'em. So now, whenever I go to a real out-of-the-way place like the Christmas Islands, I always bring some old reliable staples with me. I'll take some corned beef or maybe some peanut butter. It can come in very handy.

On one trip, for instance, I was flying from Honolulu to the Christmas Islands for some bonefishing with a guy named John Smale and his wife. John began to tease me for the fact that I had packed two huge jars of peanut butter. Well, we got to Christmas Island and on our first morning there we had some great bacon and eggs for breakfast. Then what they do is they pack you a lunch and drive you out to various flats all around the atoll. You eat your lunch out there and then come back for dinner. When lunchtime came, I opened up my peanut butter sandwich and started eating it. John and Phyllis opened their brown bags. The native cook had put green mint jelly on bread, which didn't look too good. Then he put some strips of curried octopus on there. Looked like dead night crawlers to me. John and Phyllis pulled the octopus strips out and tossed them—not even the birds went after it—and munched on mint jelly sandwiches with a hint of octopus.

The same thing happened the next day. Again, there I was digging into my thick peanut butter sandwich. So the second evening, John came over with a hangdog look on his face and apologized for teasing me about my peanut butter stash. Then he very nicely asked, "Could you please fix Phyllis a peanut butter sandwich?"

I said, "Of course I would. Would she like two?"

And he said, "Yes, we would."

When he said "we," I climbed all over him.

Well, of course I ended up giving peanut butter sandwiches to everybody in the troop that week, and when I got home there was this real heavy box waiting for me. I could barely get it inside the house. When I got it opened there were six half-gallon jars of Jif Peanut Butter in there and a business card that read, John Smale, Chairman and CEO, Procter

& Gamble. On it he had written "To Lefty: Just repaying the favor." I had no idea he was such a big shot. I've met him a few times since and we've always laughed about the peanut butter (which I ended up donating to an orphanage).

Anyway, in the Christmas Islands you'll see waves and waves of bonefish. With an increase in the number of lodges and fishermen making pilgrimages, the fish population has certainly diminished over the last thirty years. They're not quite as big as the ones we used to find, but little bonefish act just like big bonefish. They're all fantastic.

Where else would I go today if I was looking for great bonefishing? In my opinion, the best bonefishing is where you can catch both big *and* little bonefish and catch a good many. And the best bonefishing in this hemisphere is probably in Las Rocas, which is about eighty miles off the northeast coast of Venezuela. Las Rocas means "the rocks" and there are lots of them there that jut up out of the ocean, but between these rock outcroppings are incredible flats. Part of it is a marine preserve, which you're not allowed to fish. In the other part they only allow a limited number of fisherman at any one time. So compared to, say, the Florida Keys, you have fewer people pounding on the fish. It isn't the easiest place in the world to get to—you've got to go to Caracas, and then fly to Las Rocas in a smaller plane—but it has huge numbers of small bonefish and good numbers of big bonefish. If you tell your guide you want to go for the big ones, he'll know where to go. The best way to go there now, especially with the political problems our countries are having, is to fly to Miami or New Orleans and then the next morning fly to the Caracas airport, get on another plane, and fly directly to Las Rocas. That way you avoid the city and lots of potential problems. Las Rocas really is the best bonefishing that I know of.

PERMIT

This is good fishing. It's among my favorite saltwater species. Permit are easily spooked, so you have to be good to catch them, especially on fly. Additionally, they're very strong and they're great fighters. In fact, any fish with that sickle-shaped tail—wahoo, tuna, jack, billfish—they are high-speed swimmers and true fighters. You get a sickle-fin fish on the line and you've got your hands full.

Permit are now prized by fly fisherman, but as late as the 1960s most people actually believed that permit were simply uncatchable on fly. One day I was fishing in the Marquesas Islands, which are about twenty-five miles west of Key West. I was with Mark Sosin, a longtime friend of mine with whom I have collaborated on a couple of books and who has become a well-known outdoor TV personality. We were fishing for bonefish and I had a bonefish fly on my line. Mark was slowly poling the boat about 10 to 20 feet from shore and I saw eight or nine small permit, each weighing about 4 or 5 pounds. I thought, oh, what the hell, and threw my fly to them. Damn if one of the permit didn't take it. It was the first permit I had ever caught on fly. Mark actually took a picture of me kissing it.

I would classify that as an accidental catch. Not long after that, a guy named Dick Coe, who was a dentist in Miami and belonged the Tropical Anglers, caught one on a back cast. He was fishing for bonefish, threw the fly backward, and when the fly nipped the water at the bottom of the back cast, some permit reached up and grabbed it. Intriguing as these incidents were, they were still pretty anecdotal and accidental. Then a guy named Nat Ragland, a captain who was good friend of mine from down around the Marathon, Florida, area, came up with a fly called Puff the Magic Dragon. It was a crazy name for a fly, but Nat always had crazy names for his flies. This thing had a fast-sinking head, and his clients caught a few permit on it.

It had long been known that you could catch permit quite easily using live crabs as bait. My friend Paul Crum from Frederick once caught a 42-pounder on live crab. It wasn't until the 1980s that we learned that if you could create a fly that resembled a crab, you could routinely catch permit on fly. Dell Brown, who passed away in 2005, proved the point more powerfully than anyone else. Dell was one of the greatest permit fishermen of all time. In his lifetime he caught over five hundred permit on crab flies. Dell was also a very good friend of mine. We fished together in Alaska, South America, New Zealand, all over the place. He was a character. He was married to a very wealthy woman from a California winemaking family. Dell was just an old shoe and I used to tell him that if Doris ever put her glasses on she'd get rid of him in a hurry. That said, she adored him and he adored her.

Dell designed a crab fly that today remains *the* fly for permit fishing. It was fashioned out of acrylic yarn, feathers, and rubber bands. He called it the Merkin, which is a long story. In the Greek and Roman days men would go off to war for years and outfit their wives in chastity belts until they returned. Over time these belts would chafe away at the hairs of the ladies' privates and so eventually the women would buy wigs for their nether regions. These wigs were called merkins. In 1987 I was doing a revision of my book on saltwater fly-fishing. By this time people were beginning to catch permit on Dell's fly and so it had to be featured in the revised book. He called and said, "Lefty, you've got to help me."

I said, "What is it, Dell?"

He said, "Doris just found out what a merkin is." I got to laughing.

"This isn't funny," he said.

Then I really started laughing. I said, "What do you want me to do?"

"Just don't refer to it as a Merkin in the revised edition."

Well, in that book I did refer to it as the Dell Brown Crab Fly, but it'll always be the Merkin to fly fishermen.

From the 1980s on, we've learned a lot about catching permit on fly.

One thing is pretty intuitive: crab flies that really imitate crabs, that is, flies with some lifelike action, are very effective. We've also learned that you need different colored crab flies for different locations. One time I was fishing with John Aplanaph and Gordie Hill over in the Bahamas. I hooked an 8-pound bonefish that ran off and got tangled in a sea fan. Well, before we could release it from the plant a little bonnet shark came by and chewed the bonefish's tail off. Given that the fish was crippled, our guide asked if he could keep it to eat later on. We said sure and we cleaned and gutted it. When we opened its stomach we saw that it had nine crabs in there; no two were the same color. There were dark ones and green ones and light ones. The lesson for us was that if you're fishing in water that has a snow-white, sandy surface at the bottom, you might need a cream-colored crab fly. If you're fishing in an area that has a lot of turtle grass, then a darker brown or green or tan crab fly will work best.

We also know that we need crab flies of different weights, some that sink fast, and some that even float. But the most important thing we found out about fly-fishing for permit is that you don't strip for them, that is, you don't retrieve them. What you want to do is drop the fly almost on their nose, no more than three feet in front of them. (Used to be we didn't want to do that because permit are so easily spooked.) Then you try to keep the line taut and let the fly sink to the bottom. You will probably scare off half the permit in the area as soon as the fly hits the water, but trust me: the permit that stick around will be interested. If the crab goes to the bottom and the permit circles it, but doesn't take it, then you just barely jiggle the fly, just enough to impart motion. Remember, no crab is going to sit on the bottom and dance around while a hungry permit is staring at him. The idea is to move the fly just enough to convince the permit that the crab is alive.

The other valuable thing we've learned about fly-fishing for permit is that they can be extremely stealthy. It's very common for permit to take crab flies that have been presented to them and for the fishermen to be completely unaware of it. It has to do with the anatomy of the permit. The interiors of their mouths have crushers. They inhale a live crab and quickly crush it. You can sometimes see pieces of shell exit the gills—and it's all over in eight or ten seconds. If you are unaware that they have it, you will probably miss the strike. What we've learned over time is that there are certain signals a permit sends out before he inhales a crab. If you pay attention to these signals, you'll never miss the strike. If a permit comes over the crab and wiggles its body or its tail, that's the moment of truth. That is the moment when he is sucking in the fly. Immediately move to hook the fish.

One of the things improving fly fishermen's odds with permit is the mantis shrimp. These are large shrimp with a powerful "knuckle" that they can use to fend off attackers. They are a favorite food of permit. In the Keys, most of these shrimp are greenish. In other places, such as the Yucatán or Belize, I have seen them in sort of a khaki color. Mantis shrimp flies no longer than your ring finger can be swum in the water column rather than letting them lie on the bottom, where you don't know for sure whether the permit grabbed it or not. If your mantis shrimp fly is swimming in the water column your line is taut, and when the permit takes the fly, you've got a hookup. In the future, I think we'll see more and more mantis shrimp flies taking permit.

Permit fishing has become almost the Holy Grail of fly-fishing, at least in the United States. It seems more and more people want to do it. It's hard to do, and I wouldn't recommend it for a novice fisherman—it's pretty tough to put a fly no more than three feet from a permit's nose without spooking him; add in wind and you've got real headaches. But it's a lot of fun if you get a good guide. The best place in the United States for permit right now is the southern part of the Florida Keys, particularly around Key West. But if you're looking for sheer volume, go to Mexico and the Yucatán and Belize; that's where the numbers are. The biggest permit, however, still swim in the Keys. A 20-pounder in Belize is a very large permit. In the Keys you find them in excess of 30 pounds.

REDFISH

The most popular form of redfishing is in the flats. There are a couple of reasons for this: One, there are lots of them in the flats. Two, it's mostly sight-fishing.

Most people fish for redfish the same way they do for bonefish, that is, they pole a boat or drift over the shallow flats. The name redfish, however, can be a bit of a misnomer. They aren't really red, they're reddish toned, but they can be different colors in different places. If the water in a given area is a little murky, the fish take on a more silvery hue. If the water is clear and has that sort of dark ginger-ale-ish color to it, the fish become a deep orangey-red. Curiously enough, one of the best ways to spot a redfish is not by looking for the red. Some of the best fishermen I know are aware that since redfish tend to take on the color of their surroundings, the best way to identify them in the water is to look for the bluish tint on the tail. That blue shows up more distinctly than the red, regardless of the color of the water.

Reds have what we call an inferior mouth; that is, like that of a bonefish, the redfish's mouth is low on his body. This means they will feed primarily on the bottom: shrimp and crab are their favorite foods (although they will chase and eat minnows, too). The average redfish weighs anywhere from about 3 to about 8 pounds. Some people make the mistake of using too large a fly for them. Typically you'll never need a fly any longer than your pinky finger for successful redfishing. They love grass (especially turtle grass) and they love to root around in it looking for food. You need bend-back flies that can be fished through all sorts of grass. I also use a lot of Clouser-type minnows for reds, but almost always with a weed guard. Often these are lightly or moderately weighted depending on how deep the fish are. A lot of times, particularly in South Carolina, redfish feed on oyster bars, and if you don't have a weedless fly or a bend-back you'd just be hung up on oyster shell all day.

Redfishing has changed over the years. I used to write that if you wanted to learn how to catch bonefish, go fishing for redfish because they're dumber than bonefish. That used to be true. I remember one time back in the 1960s my son Larry and I went out of Flamingo in the Everglades and caught 66 redfish in one day (most of his were on light spinning tackle; all of mine were on fly). This was when they were everywhere and they were not very heavily fished. That's changed. They are so pressured now that in Texas and Florida redfish are every bit as skittish and wary as bonefish. That's due to a couple of factors. First, more and more people are fishing—fly or not—and the redfish's ubiquity has made them very popular. Second, there have been drastic changes in the design of flats boats. Back in the 1960s, a flats boat that weighed 2,000 pounds required at least a foot or so of water. Today's modern poling boats, such as the 600-pound Hell's Bay boat, can operate in as little as 4 inches of water. This means that we are now able to pursue redfish (and other species) into the shallowest hideouts. Redfish in particular are adept at feeding in shallow waters. In fact, I have seen them feed in water so shallow that almost half of their bodies are above the surface. Tragically, these new boats have allowed anglers to fish in what used to be sanctuaries. Even when you can get up close to them now, they feel the boat and they move on. The upshot of all this is that the fish are very wary. It used to be that a 25-foot cast was plenty good enough to catch reds. Now, even though we are getting closer to their sanctuaries, they are getting wiser. Today you often need to be able to cast 50 or 60 feet to a redfish.

This has led some to suggest that we are running out of redfish. I don't think so. Here's my theory: The redfish population is robust. That is, I think we have just as many redfish as we always did, but by encroaching so aggressively on their sanctuaries, we have fundamentally changed their feeding habits. We have chased them out of their hideouts and I believe that redfish are now doing most of their feeding in deeper water. There's no shortage of reds. I think they're still out there, they're just not in the same places they used to be.

The one place that is still very good for redfish, even in very, very shallow water, is Louisiana. There have not been that many guides working the area and so the species is not very heavily pressured. You can still catch some very large redfish—I'm talking up to 25 or 30 pounds—in state's shallow waters. Two years ago, I spooked one that I honestly believe would have been over 30 pounds. Second, there is a huge number of estuaries there. Eventually, what's happened to the reds in Texas and Florida will happen to the reds in Louisiana, but not for some time.

The biggest red I've ever caught weighed 30 pounds. I caught it in Mosquito Lagoon off Cape Canaveral, Florida (with a blue-and-white Deceiver on a 2/0 hook). The lagoon is very shallow, but in the center of it they do have some water that goes down to about 10 feet. It used to be that larger redfish would occasionally gather in this deep water and swim in schools. The whole area would turn a coppery-red color. I was with John Kaminsky and his young son, Max, and we drifted down on a big school of these reds. Little Max, had a spinner outfit and he caught one about 18 pounds. The trouble now is that those fish get pounced on so badly.

Few people realize that the biggest redfish are actually found in North Carolina and Virginia. In those parts of the country they are not, however, referred to as redfish. Locals there call them "channel bass" or if they are on the small side, they'll call them "puppy drums." These puppy drums are the same redfish that are so popular in Texas, Louisiana, and Florida flats.

TARPON

I've been fishing tarpon for about forty years and to this day it still amazes me that even a tiny fly can still catch the attention of a giant tarpon. It's hard to believe that such a big fish would even be interested in such a small thing. Fortunately they are interested, and it makes for some of the most exciting fly-fishing you'll find.

Ninety percent of the time, the moment you hook a tarpon he'll come out of the water. You set the hook, and up comes this silver monster out of the water throwing water like a leaky fire hose. You just stand there thunderstruck and he pops the leader and he's gone. You've hooked your first tarpon and lost your first tarpon all in about five seconds. The secret is after that initial awe, once you hook the fish, wait until he jumps. Then, as he jumps, you've got to bow toward him to create slack. That way, he can't tear the line because all he's got is a fly on a loose line rocking back and forth. As soon as he goes back into the water you can apply pressure again.

Tarpon fishing is extremely exciting, but after you catch a lot of tarpon, something changes. Most of the people I know who are really experienced saltwater fly anglers eventually get to the point that they'd rather fish for bonefish or permit than tarpon. There are a variety of reasons for that. First of all, a tarpon is going to take you twenty or thirty minutes to land. It should rarely take more than thirty or forty minutes (people who take two or three hours to fight a tarpon don't know how to fight a tarpon). Second, you use relatively heavy tackle and have a relatively long fight, whereas bonefish or permit fishing requires relatively light tackle. You're poling across the flats. You're seeing things going on and I think that, particularly in the Keys, it's more difficult to deceive bonefish with a fly than it is to deceive a tarpon. There are so many guides fishing tarpon in the Keys now that most of the tarpon have become almost bulletproof. They don't even get spooked by flies anymore. They slip by and you can almost see them thinking, *"I know what that thing is . . ."*

If you are lucky enough to find a fresh push of tarpon that has not been around a while, they'll take the flies. Consider the tarpon that swims the distance from say, Key West to Key Largo, a distance of about one hundred miles. In that stretch he's probably seen five hundred flies, so it becomes very difficult to catch him. Nowadays most of the better guides and fishermen are no longer using the standard Keys-type flies; they're using the Toad.

One of the top guides down there, Dustin Huff, has developed a crab-based fly. It's so realistic and so effective and it remains shrouded in secrecy. He cuts them off his line before he arrives back at the dock. They've had to develop new flies and new techniques, which is very difficult.

What's really good fishing—and you can't really do this in Florida, but you find it Cuba and the Yucatán and some places in the Bahamas—is fishing for 5- to 40-pound tarpon that live in the mangroves. In fact, that best cast I ever made in my life was on a tarpon that weighed about 15 or 20 pounds.

I like fishing that forces you to make quick decisions. Some of the most fun and exciting tarpon fishing I've ever done is down in the Garden of the Queen in Cuba. These fish range from about 5 to 20 pounds. You use an 8-weight bonefish rod and a tarpon fly. The guide takes you out on these little channels and anchors you. Then the guide jumps overboard and starts doggy-paddling behind these tiny mangrove islands. It's like a dog flushing out quail. Suddenly, out come all these tarpon that have been back in there—dozens of them—and you just know one of them is going to take it. I promise you that, for an experienced tarpon fisherman, it's more fun than catching a 100-pounder.

TUNA

I've only done a small amount of fly-fishing for tuna because I learned very quickly that it's just not something I wanted to do a lot of. This is hard fishing. First off, tuna have a sickle-shaped tail. That's always a bad sign, at least for an old guy. It usually indicates a fish of enormous strength, speed, and stamina. Not surprisingly, pound for pound, tuna are among the strongest fish in the sea. They're tough. Real tough.

Second, tuna tend to live in deep water and as anyone who has ever fished for them on deep-sea tackle or fly tackle knows, they dive. And dive. And dive. Of course, you look at all the world records for tuna on fly and all those fish are caught in 60 to 80 feet of water. That's because the shallow water keeps the fish from diving to the kind of depths that truly test the average man's patience and stamina. But it's not unusual for a tuna to dive 500 yards. When that happens, all you can do is lift, and that gets old. I hooked my first yellowfin in the late 1960s off Bermuda. After it ran about 500 yards of backing off the reel I told the guys I was fishing with that if the fish did that again I was cutting the line. Whether you're sitting in your backyard or aboard a boat, going through five hundred yards of line is tedious. Doing so with an unhappy tuna on the other end of the line is a tough job. Tuna fishing, regardless of the tackle, is a young man's game. It's a muscle game. A few years ago, one of my best friends, Mark Lamos, called to tell me that he had set the North Carolina state record for tuna on fly. Now, a 50-pound tuna on fly is quite an accomplishment. I asked him how much it weighed and he said something like 60 or 70 pounds. Rather than say congratulations, my response was, "Are you nuts?"

He said, "Yes, I am."

Tuna, as you can imagine, require very heavy tackle, much heavier, for instance, than you would use for giant tarpon. Tarpon are a large fish, why the difference in tackle? Because tarpon are caught in very shallow water. They can jump, they can run around, but they can't go down deep. Tuna are caught in deeper water. There are several kinds of tuna and they run the size gamut from say 10 or 12 pounds for a blackfin to over 1,000 pounds for a giant bluefin. Of course, no one catches 1,000-pounders on fly. Typically bluefin caught on fly weigh less than 50 pounds. To put things in perspective, a 50-pound tuna on a fly rod is quite an accomplishment. That tells you what a powerful fish they are.

For large tuna you need large, specialized tackle. The best tuna rods, fly or not, have collapsible tips. The theory is that if I gave you a ruler and had you hold onto the bottom end while I tried to manipulate the top end, you would do a pretty good job. But if I gave you a yardstick and we did the same thing, you would have less leverage and a harder time controlling the stick. That theory has been put into practice in fishing rod design. A tuna fly rod may need a flexible graphite tip for presenting the fly, but once the fish is hooked, power transcends accuracy, so the tip of the rod collapses, putting the weight of the fish on the stronger central and lower section of the rod. The bottom third of these rods often is made of fiberglass, which will withstand four times more flexing than graphite. Many people think that rods break when the material on the outside of the bend is stretched too far. That's usually not the case. It's actually the inside that loses its integrity first. The outside has enormous flexibility, but it's the inside of the curve (the bottom of the rod) that succumbs to the pressure and begins to crumble and fall apart. Then the whole rod loses its integrity and snaps. Fiberglass is much better at resisting this crush than graphite. In fact, some of the best rods for fly-fishing tuna are all fiberglass. This stuff is well designed and strong. Unfortunately, it's also pretty expensive because there is a lot of material and workmanship in each rod and there are not enough crazy people who fly-fish for tuna and so they can't mass-produce them.

Once you have the tackle, you need a captain who knows where to go. It's important because tuna are always on the move. They are not only seasonal, moving to different areas of the sea at different times of the year but also must swim constantly or die (other sea creatures, such as sharks, can actually sleep).

One of the greatest places in the world to fish for yellowfin tuna (also known as Allison tuna) is off Bermuda, in the month of June. There are two huge mesas that rise up thousands of feet from the ocean floor there, making the depth only about 150 feet. One of these plateaus is called Challenger Bank and the other is called Argus Bank. Anchor your boat on this mesa and you can use either small dead baitfish, such as minnows or what are known as hogmouth fry in Bermuda, or chunks of fish. Throw this stuff in the water and in a few minutes you've got tuna all around your boat. If you're using dead minnows and you've got a minnow imitation fly, you can throw it out there, but don't move it, because the minnows are dead and so your imitation better look dead as well. If you're using chunks, then you have a range of options. I've seen people tie a big bunch of fuzzy-looking stuff on a hook—rabbit fur or synthetic materials that are colored to approximate the look of dead meat. They're about the size of a golf ball.

Unlike much of fly-fishing, in which the timing of the strike is so important, you don't really have to strike tuna. They swerve in so fast that they pretty much hook themselves. I caught my first world-record blackfin off Key West in the late 1960s. Blackfin are smaller tuna. Their backs are cobalt blue. A really nice one will weigh somewhere over 22 pounds. The one I'd caught was actually the first blackfin ever recorded on fly. It weighed 19 pounds, 4 ounces. Unfortunately, before the records were published someone came in with a larger one.

Tuna have a tendency to break the surface of water, or porpoise, especially when they're chasing bait. They rise up and come down right on the baitfish. I'd go out with Captain Lefty Regan, probably the greatest offshore captain ever to work the Keys (you'll recall he was a key player in the development of teasing techniques in the 1960s). He'd run ahead to where the school of tuna was going and cut the motor. When they got close by, maybe thirty feet away, I threw a Deceiver fly in there. This blackfin rocketed out of the water and he was flipping his tail back and forth like he was trying to manipulate himself in the air. He hit the water with the fly in his mouth. I have been convinced since then that tuna and other species do see the fly when they are in the air. Think about how tuna pursue flying fish. As the flying fish are being chased, they generate a lot of speed and then catapult themselves just above the surface of the water for about twenty or thirty feet. It's hard not to watch the remarkable flight of the flying fish, but if you look carefully into the water right below the flying fish you'll see the predator swimming there, eyeballing them from below the surface. I think these predators see both flies and flying fish above the surface.

I love to catch albacore, also called little tunni. They can get up to 26 pounds, but a good-sized albacore is 20 to 22 pounds. One of the best places in the world for albacore fishing is the southern part of the Outer Banks down to around Morehead City, North Carolina. In the fall they appear there in huge schools. I've caught as many as twenty albacore a day.

Bluefin tuna, I don't fish for. These things can weigh up to 1,000 pounds and have been fished for in every sea of the world. The Japanese love these things. If you catch a 700+ pound bluefin, it can be worth several thousand dollars. The tuna is bought and air-freighted to Japan for seafood, a trade that has decimated the population. However, there has been a lot of regulation intended to save the tuna. Last year off Rhode Island and down to Montauk, New York, there was a big bluefin run of 20- to 35-pounders. Surely, that's a good sign.

SHARK

There are two kinds of shark fishing. One of them I enjoy a great deal, and the other I'm not that crazy about. There's shark fishing on flats, in which you pole a boat across the flats just as you would for say, tarpon. That's very exciting. The other kind of fishing for sharks is deepwater fishing. That's where you anchor or drift in an area known to have sharks in it, kill a barracuda (barracuda work best because, along with the northern pike, they are the most pungent fish in the world), hang it over the bow of the boat, and sharks will come from all over the area. Then you throw the fly and it's an hour or two to land the fish. I'm not very interested in this type of fishing. First of all, an hour or two fighting with a fish that can weigh a few hundred pounds isn't my idea of a day spent fishing. Second, it's pretty dangerous. You get a couple guys in an eighteen-foot boat with a thin fiberglass hull and mix in an angry shark, not many good things can happen. The heaviest fish ever caught on fly was a lemon shark that weighed over 400 pounds and it was taken by a friend of mine, who only weighed about 150 pounds himself. In that case, the shark actually attacked his boat. Fortunately he was aboard a sturdy 28-footer that could handle it.

Poling for sharks in the flats, however, can be really fun. Sharks undulate very slowly, back and forth. They may look like they're not moving very fast, but it's an illusion based on size. They are inevitably moving faster than you can pole a boat. They not only move quickly but also present some interesting problems to the angler. If you look at a shark in profile you'll notice that his mouth is actually set well in back of his nose. So if you try to use surface lures or popping bugs on a fly rod it's very difficult. The problem is that as the shark rises to the fly, his nose inevitably pushes it out of the way. Therefore, a fly that sinks below the surface is most effective. The best presentation is dictated by the shark's own natural body movements. If you ever watch a shark take bait on film or video, you will see that they violently thrash their head sideways when they take a bite. So you need to get your fly alongside the eye of the shark, not in front of his nose. It's actually a little more technical than that if you want to be good at it.

Let's say a shark is approaching from the north and you are on the southeast side of the fish. If you throw the fly to the west side of the fish and he takes it there is a good chance that the fly line and/or the leader would cross over the back of the shark. That gives his sandpaper-like skin a very good chance of cutting the line. To catch sharks on fly or any tackle, the best strategy is to remain on the same side of the shark that you hooked him on. The skin is really like sandpaper. In fact, in the old days woodworkers used to dry out sharkskin and use it for sandpaper.

As far as tackle is concerned, it depends on the size of the shark. Contrary to the myths propagated by movies such as *Jaws*, some of these sharks in shallow seas such as the Caribbean and the Bahamas are only 12 to 18 inches long. The lemon shark and the blacktip can be aggressive, but they are fairly small. These small sharks can usually be handled on a bonefish rod. For any shark over 5 feet I think you want to have at least a 10-weight, because these things are aggressive and strong. When one takes off in the shallows, it's like a runaway snowplow, throwing mud and all into the air.

As for flies, I have found that orange and red tend to be the most productive colors for catching shark on fly. Another good color combination is white and chartreuse or orange and yellow. Those are the three that seem to work the best. Any one of those combined with a little Flashabou, thin little strips of Mylar that flutter and give off flash, is likely to work very well. Note: Sharks don't have very keen eyesight. Most experts agree that sharks rely much more heavily on vibration. For instance, most swimmers know that the vibrations sent through the water by a swimmer can be interpreted by a shark as a fish in distress. Sensing vulnerable prey and an easy meal, the shark will approach and attack. Anyone who has ever fished for other species in water occupied by sharks has seen this same phenomenon occur when you hook a small fish. It starts fighting and moments later it's chomped off the hook by a shark. This can be used to your advantage. When I fish sharks on the flats and it looks as though a shark may be swimming away from me, I will slip my rod tip into the water and swish it around, and you would be amazed at how often the shark will come right back at you. That kind of shark fishing can really be demanding and exciting. But just baiting them in deep water with a dead fish and then hooking up and hanging on—to me that's not really exciting.

When I think back on my years angling for shark, the first memory that comes to mind is that it was while shark fishing that my son Larry learned to pole a boat. It was 1964 and he was about 13 or 14. I had decided to do a story for *Field and Stream* about fly-fishing for shark, something very few people were even aware you could do at that time. I would pole to the fish because Larry didn't know how, and then I would hand him the pole, run across the boat, and pick up the fly rod and by the time I got the fly rod ready the fish was going one way and the boat was going another. Finally, I decided that this had to stop and that was the day Larry learned to pole.

I have not had any really exciting or dangerous run-ins with sharks, but I know plenty of people who have. I have a word of caution for anyone who's thinking about fishing for shark on fly or any other tackle. Sharks, as you may know, have no bones. Their equivalent of a skeleton is made of flexible cartilage, much like we have in our lower noses. This gives sharks incredible flexibility and the unexpected ability to virtually fold over on themselves. Early in my years with the MET, I went to Islamorada to weigh a very large lemon shark that was leading a shark division at the time. It had been hanging, head down, for several hours. People had been walking by it and touching it and having their pictures taken with it, when all of a sudden it lashed out and bit the pole from which it was hanging. I have known of a lot of people who've caught sharks from eighteen inches to a few feet long. They hold them up by the tail or tie them up on a rope and stand by them for a photo. As unlikely as it may seem, these things can curl up like a yo-yo and bite. It happened to a great guide and a good friend of mine named Captain John Donnell. His client had caught a pretty good size blacktip shark and brought it to the side of the boat. Captain John was leaning over to take the fly out when the shark curled up and dug in real bad. He had something like eighty to a hundred tooth marks on the side of his arm. There was blood all over the boat and they had to airlift him to the hospital. From that lesson and others I have determined that boats are no place for sharks. With the big sharks I prefer hanging them by a noose around the tail. Another way to secure a shark, especially if you are in a tournament and want the catch to retain its blood for weighing purposes, is to gaff the shark in the softish tissue underneath its pectoral fin. These don't bleed, and a typical gaff hook won't tear through them. I just don't think you should be putting any shark in any boat unless you really know what you're doing. I am also happy to report that most sharks caught by anglers today are released.

CHAPTER 18
THE TOUGHEST FISH I EVER FACED

"HEY, LEFTY, WHAT'S THE STRONGEST fish you've ever caught?" I hear that question a lot, and you might think that with all the fishing I've done all over the world in the last sixty or seventy years that that'd be a difficult question to answer. The very fact that the answer is a complete no-brainer tells you just how strong this darn fish was.

The answer to the question starts with the location. The strongest fish I ever caught was hooked in the single best fishing destination I've ever been to: New Guinea. Most places that offer really good fishing are sort of isolated. Take Manitoba, which is way up in Canada, up near the Arctic Circle. You can catch northern pike up there well over 20 pounds on a fly, but if you fish 500 miles south of there, you'd be lucky to get one that weighed 10 or 11 pounds. The presence of human civilization and the environmental pressures that come with it really do affect fish.

That's why New Guinea was such an anglers' paradise. Located just north of Australia, the island of New Guinea is surrounded by the Pacific Ocean to the east and the Indian Ocean to the west. In 1992 I was asked to come to Australia to tape a fishing show. The plan was to spend several weeks in the remote outback of Australia, close to Western Australia on the Drysdale River.

We did a bunch of filming for the show in Australia and then moved over to our second destination, New Guinea. Oddly enough, New Guinean men don't fish. The males in New Guinea actually believe it is beneath their dignity to fish. They consider themselves hunters, and so while they hunt on land they send the women out on the ocean to fish. These people are truly living as they lived two thousand years ago. For instance, on a previous trip to New Guinea we came upon a guy who had a bunch of watermelons. We asked him if he would give us two of the watermelons. He said he would, but only if we promised to bring the seeds back.

There are no roads, no electricity, no stores, no radios. One day at lunch we were high up on a hill relaxing in the shade of a jungle. We looked across the river below us, which was about 150 yards wide. On the other side there were about a hundred rusa deer—they look like our whitetails, but they've got bigger antlers and smaller bodies. Nearby a similar number of kangaroos were sharing a grassy meal with the deer. We watched them for a while until down the river came two natives in a dugout canoe. They were carrying on a tradition that had been a part of life here for thousands of years. They had nothing on but a pair of shorts, but each had a bow and arrow and a spear.

They snuck down along the bank in the dugout, pulled it up on the grass, and then crept up as close as they could to the deer and kangaroos without alarming them. If you've ever been to the zoo you know how kangaroos stands on their back legs. Sometimes the kangaroos will thump their feet in the ground. So the natives, still hiding, started thumping their forearms down on the ground, aping the sound of the kangaroo. A couple of kangaroos looked up and looked around. No flag or bait was used, only the thumping of their forearms on the ground. A couple of the kangaroos hopped closer and closer. In ten minutes or so, they were down pretty close to these two natives The bows must have had a pull of about 90 pounds. They're handmade and they don't use string. They nick a certain kind of tree and peel the bark off and use that as the string. It's probably a half-inch wide. You can shoot an arrow out of sight with this thing.

They shot this kangaroo in the chest at very close quarters. Of course, the injured kangaroo and all the other deer and kangaroos took off. When our lunch break was over, we put our stuff back in the coolers and put the coolers back in the boat and we got down there on the river and starting casting around some of these big sunken trees. Twenty minutes later one of the guys says, "Here comes that kangaroo." It was in bad shape. The two natives cornered it against the river, killed it, dressed it out, put it in the dugout, and took it to the village.

Later on, I asked Terry, our guide, if we might be able to stop at the village. There are something like 240 languages spoken in New Guinea. All the tribes, even those that are only ten miles apart, speak different languages. Terry could speak the local dialects well, so he said he'd take me into the village. I was amazed to see what had become of the kangaroo. We take our refrigerators for granted, but these natives have no way of keeping anything, so when a hunter brings a kill back into the village he lets his wife get the best cut of meat and then anybody in the village can have a whack at it. Terry, with his wry sense of humor, said to me, "You know Lefty, the best-looking woman in any village is married to the best hunter."

I said, "You know, I've met a lot of millionaires in my life, and they're all married to gorgeous women. Nothing's changed in two thousand years."

During our time on the Drysdale and all the way to New Guinea, the Aussies in our group kept talking about this fish called the Niugini black bass. It lives in the lower reaches of rivers that flow into saltwater and thrives in brackish water. They said over and over again that this was the biggest, baddest, meanest fish in the world. In fact, when they took to calling it the "River Rambo" I was all but certain that they were setting me up for a practical joke.

We flew to Port Moresby, then from there to a place called Hoskins on New Britain Island. It's one of the finest diving resorts in the world. You can see the bottom of the ocean in 60 feet of water. To this day it's the clearest ocean water I've ever seen. The next day they picked us up in the helicopter and took us to the Kulu River. Our guide had hacked a hole in the jungle and built for us a fragile shack of reeds and twigs and palm fronds. Walking around the shack, it actually shook.

Anyway, all the way over to New Guinea my good friend Rod Harrison, who is the preeminent fishing writer in Australia, was telling me how tough and mean this Niugini black bass was. He got into the River Rambo bit and all the rest, but I played it cool. I refused to rise to the bait.

Well, we get to our destination and Rod said, "Would you help me load some line on some reels?" He took out these great big reels that are really like small trolling reels, and he had one big box full of 40-pound and another big box full of 50-pound test line. So I helped him wind this line on there, all the while completely convinced that he, the tribe, the guides, and everybody else were setting me up for a 4-ounce sunny.

Next—and even to a lover of practical jokes this seemed a little over the top—Rod gets out some big Rebel plugs, uses pliers to rip all the all the hooks off, and tosses the hooks in the garbage. I said, "What's wrong with them?"

Rod said, "They ain't strong enough."

Well, now I really thought he was putting me on, but I didn't say a thing. I fixed up my 12-weight outfit with a 2-pound test tippet and shock leader. Between you and me, I thought I was loaded for bear. I mean, here we were on this nice quiet little river and I was sporting tackle on which I'd caught sailfish and all kinds of big gamefish.

After a night at camp, we got in the boat and headed downriver. Beautiful indigenous birds, I think they call them Eclectus parrots, were everywhere. All the females were a vivid green and all the males were cardinal red. You'd have maybe two hundred of these things flying by at a time, a passing cloud of bright green and red. We had a great, scenic ride down to our appointed spot.

The first thing I learned is that when fishing for the Niugini black bass, you look for trees that have fallen into the river. I was told that these fish like to lie underneath the branches: they dart out, grab their prey, and go back. They are actually in the *Lutjanus* family, which is the same family as the cubera snapper, a very fierce saltwater fish. We pulled up to where this one tree had fallen in and Rod, whom they call the "Gentle Giant"—his arms are as big as my thighs—said, "Okay, Lefty, you have a go."

I looked at his gear. He still had this 50-pound outfit in his hands and it suddenly occurred to me that this might not be a joke.

I said, "No, you have a go first, Rod."

"No, no," he said. "You have a go."

I was uncertain. I said, "I ain't going 'til you go. I want to see what's going on here."

So Rod got up. He had his big plug, it must have been 10 or 11 inches long on the end of his 50-pound test line. He took his pliers out and locked the reel's star drag so it wouldn't give an inch. Dean Butler, who is now a very famous fishing writer down there—he was just a kid in those days—was handling our boat, a 22-footer with a 40-horse Yamaha outboard. Dean eased the bow within casting distance of the sunken tree and put the motor in neutral. Rod stepped up and threw this big green plug into the water near the tree. Then he started reeling. Like a scene from a cheap horror film this great big green thing jumped out from behind the tree and *just smashed* the lure. Rod set the hook and yelled, "Hit it, Dean!" Dean put the motor in reverse trying to drag this fish out of his lair. After a few seconds the line went "Pow!" The sound of the snapping line was still echoing through the jungle, as I switched out my 20-pound test line and went straight for the 40-pound. I was a believer!

I was still rigging my tackle when we got to the next tree. Rod still had his 50-pound outfit on. He throws back in. Again this river monster came out and chomped, and Rod yelled for Dean to hit it. This time the fish managed to get himself well into the tree. We tried to break the fifty-pound test, but you just can't break that stuff. We had to actually cut it. The fish owned the lure.

We started heading to the next tree. Now they had the cameras rolling for the TV show. I'm armed to the gills. I've got a 12-weight rod on which I'd caught sailfish, billfish and tuna. Now I've got 40-pound test right from the fly line to the fly. And I got this great big 5/0 hook on there with a big hairy fly on it and I'm ready. So, we get to the next tree and from the bow of the boat I cast this big thing out there and let it sit down in the tree. I made about three unsuccessful casts, but on the fourth this demonic Niugini black bass came out and inhaled my fly. I grabbed the line and set it like I would on a tuna or a tarpon and yelled, "Hit it, Dean!" Dean put the motor in reverse and this fish put so much tension into the line that it burned a groove right across my hand. I couldn't hold the line. This was years ago, and I was pretty strong, but my first Niugini black bass had gotten away.

When we came to the next tree, I was all rigged again. One came out and grabbed the fly. This time I wrapped the line three times around the reel and called on Dean to use the boat to drag the fish into open water. The odd thing about these fish is that, as tough as they are, they only fight for about two minutes—but it's the damnedest two minutes anybody ever had on a fly rod. Of course, two minutes gives them time to get back into a tree, in which case they're virtually home free. Most of the time they come out and get the fly and before you can get set the hook and recover, they're back under the tree. But if you wrap that line right around the reel—and the Niugini black bass is the only fish I've ever caught where you had to do this—you've got a chance. These fish are unreal. They make tarpon look like sissies. I'm told, and I believe it, that only ten or twelve people have ever landed Niugini black bass on fly rod.

When we finally got this fish in it weighed only 18 pounds. It is incredible how strong that fish was. Once, on another trip, I had one about 15 pounds on the line and another black bass came out, looked like it weighed close to a 100 pounds, and swallowed the 15-pounder whole! Bob Marriott was with me. Bob owns the largest fly shop in the country, in Fullerton, California. He hooked a fish that looked like it weighed about 7 or 8 pounds and almost had it to the edge of the boat, when all of a sudden another fish, about 60 pounds, came out, swallowed the first fish, and started running. Bob wrapped the line around the reel again and it pulled him right over against the side of the boat. This is a 200-plus-pound man and he was hanging on for dear life. I had to grab him by the belt to keep him in the damn boat. All of a sudden, the line went loose and we figured it broke the leader. Actually, the one that swallowed the smaller fish pulled so hard on his prey that he straightened out a 5/0 stainless steel hook and broke free. A few years later somebody said to me, "Well how big do these Niugini black bass get?"

I said, "I don't know, we never caught no big ones."

That fish is without a doubt the baddest fish I've ever caught in my life. It's no exaggeration—and I think it's scientifically accurate—to say that the Niugini black bass is the strongest fish to ever swim. For many years, researchers were certain that it only grew to a maximum length of about 12 to 14 inches. Highly respected Australian ichthyologists had spent decades studying skeletal samples and never found one longer than 14 inches. I'm here to tell you that they get a lot larger than that. Nothing compared to it. The fight is worth it, too; they're delicious eating.

Sadly, few American fishermen will ever know the thrill of fighting the Niugini black bass. Things have changed dramatically since I was last there. The Japanese came in and promised the people of New Guinea that they would build schools and hospitals and things like that in return for allowing the Japanese lumbering access to New Guinea's spectacular forests. The Japanese would start the lumbering and they would start to build the schools, but when the trees were all gone, the Japanese just left. Half the schools never got built and because they clear-cut all those trees, the landscape began to wash off into the rivers. It ruined their waterways. Then the Indonesians came in looking for gold. I don't know if you've ever seen the big water hoses they flush into riverbanks to flush gold out of the bank, but for several years now the Indonesians have been flushing New Guinea's riverbanks in search of gold. In the process they've further damaged the ecosystem. Between the Japanese and the Indonesians, they've defiled the place so badly that much of New Guinea has again become hostile to visitors.

I'll never forget those days fishing for Niugini black bass. To my knowledge, the biggest one ever landed was caught on 50-pound-test plug tackle. I think it weighed around 45 pounds. That's really remarkable. They have another fish farther up river called the spottail bass. It's in the same family as the Niugini black bass, but it has a perfectly round 4- or 5-inch spot on either side. They're a little lighter in color, and I don't think they get quite as big—I've never caught one over 12 pounds—but they're nearly as mean as their downstream cousins.

A NOTE ABOUT FIGHTING FISH

Most people don't know how to fight fish. If you elevate a rod when you're fighting a fish, the part of the rod that's bent is really what you're fighting the fish with.

If you know how to use a 9-weight rod properly, I don't think there's a bass in the world that you couldn't land with it. Now most of the plug tackle and spinning tackle guys aren't very well informed on how to fight big fish. They'll use 40-, 50-, 60-, 70-, 80-, and even 90-pound lines, but if they only knew how to use the rod they could easily get by on 20- to 30-pound test.

CHAPTER 19
SELLING SALT

GETTING PEOPLE TO RETHINK FLY-CASTING technique was tough, so you can imagine just how hard it was to get dyed-in-the-wool freshwater fly fisherman to think about fly-fishing in . . . *salt water*. Even as recently as the 1970s a lot of people thought the idea of casting flies to tarpon and other major saltwater fish was laughable, utterly ridiculous. It was not unlike the early 1960s when I was trying to convince people that they could actually catch Chesapeake Bay striped bass on flies. They just weren't buying it.

As early as ten years before that time, guys in and around Florida had been catching a few tarpon on fly, but the overall idea of saltwater fly-fishing was little-known and often frowned upon. In the mid-1960s the sport was truly in its infancy. In fact, the Salt Water Fly Rodders of America was formed in 1965 primarily to get people to believe in the concept.

That organization was not alone. In 1965 three organizations formed that would change American fly-fishing forever. Prior to 1965 trout fishing was shrouded in secrecy. Most people who fished trout wouldn't tell anyone what they caught or where they caught it or what they caught it with. Up in Michigan they started a group called Trout Unlimited.

The basic mission of Trout Unlimited was to save the cold-water trout streams. In order to fulfill that mission they had to organize the trout fishermen, and in order to do that they formed chapters or local clubs. Now you had whole bunches of guys getting together and, for the first time, sharing information. At the same time, in Eugene, Oregon, the Federation of Fly Fishermen, now called the Federation of Fly Fishers, was created. It was formed with a similar mission in mind—that anglers ought to get together to share information on conservation and other issues. At the same time, in Forked River, New Jersey, a guy nobody had ever heard of named Fred Schrier and a few of his buddies started a group called the Saltwater Fly Rodders of America. They invited Frank Woolner, who was then the editor of *Saltwater Sportsman* magazine; the legendary Joe Brooks; Charlie Waterman, who was an extraordinarily well-known fly-fishing writer; Jim Green from California, who was the guy who designed the modern ferrule for fly rods; Stu Apte; Harold Gibbs, who was a legendary striper fisherman from New England; me; and one or two other people to help out.

They started a magazine called *The Double Haul*. Joe and Charlie and Frank and I started to give the Schrier group a lot of publicity. I was an early senior advisor to all three organizations. We really began to spread the word. They each had annual meetings where Charlie and Joe and I would help out with clinics on how to build leaders and how to catch this and that. These organizations, their publications, and their annual gatherings brought together the American fly-fishing industry for the first time. Tackle companies got involved and started contributing money and equipment.

We decided we needed to have rules regarding records. Mark Sosin wrote the rules using the MET tournament rules as a guide. We decided that it would be best for the organization if we did not change the rules for two years. The thinking was that if a new organization changed its rules too soon or too often, it would risk its credibility. We set a standard, determined to use it for two years, then modify as needed.

They were getting more and more publicity and Schrier and his buddies increasingly wanted to control everything. What they lacked was a national scope. They didn't see the American fishing landscape as broadly as Charlie and Joe and Stu and I, and frankly, a lot of the other members did. So, two years after the group was formed we got this letter. It started:

"Before the coming fishing season we need to modify the rules . . ."

Before the coming fishing season? This was a national group, and Stu and I, who were living in Florida, had been catching tarpon and bonefish all winter long. My first reaction was that there ain't no *coming* fishing season in Florida, or in a lot of states. Stu and I sat down and wrote a letter suggesting to them that they bring in some other geographically diverse directors. The mind-set of these guys was *I've got mine and you ain't getting none of it.* In response, I got a 15-page diatribe from Schrier accusing me and Stu of trying to hijack their organization. Of course, we had so much to do that even serving on the board was hard for us. Even if we'd wanted to, we didn't have time to hijack anybody. We just felt strongly about the Rodders' original mission.

From that point on, the Rodders went downhill and eventually disintegrated. Oddly enough, a few years later they did try to expand their board's geographic diversity, but it was too late. They had lost their momentum. About ten years later I met Fred Schrier at a fishing show and he told me, "Lefty, I realize now that you and Stu were right. We ruined a great organization." He actually cried.

In 1974 I wrote a book called *Saltwater Fly Fishing*. I wrote that book because at that time, saltwater fly-fishing was so new, so misunderstood, that we were getting dozens of questions about it. As I mentioned earlier, of all the books I've written, that book is the only one I didn't write for money. I wrote it to answer the rapidly mounting questions that newcomers to the sport were asking. I never thought about making money or even making a name for myself. I just figured if they had a book they'd have the answers.

There was another book written at about the same time by a fellow named George X. Sands. In fact, his book came out a few months before mine, but George didn't really know his subject, so his book fizzled pretty badly. Mine sold like crazy. In fact, some thirty years later, it's in its third edition and has sold about 70,000 copies. That may not sound like much, but in the fly-fishing world any book that sells ten thousand or twelve thousand copies is considered a real success.

It was the first time anyone had written down basic technique and knowledge and made people aware that there were a lot of saltwater species they could catch on fly. There have been some people who've generously said the book gave rise to the popularity of saltwater fly-fishing. In fact, I've heard it referred to as the "Koran of saltwater fly-fishing." Yes, it's been very well received. It may have helped inch along a movement that was already forming, and it's helped my career a lot, too, but *Koran*, I'm not so sure. It came along at the perfect time and established me as someone who knew something about this niche sport.

More books followed. By the 1970s and 1980s an entrepreneur named Les Adams, who made a lot of money selling bound-leather volumes to doctors and lawyers, got bored and came to me to propose the idea of a twenty-five-book library on all aspects of fishing. It would be called Lefty's Little Library. He put together a beautiful prospectus and at the bottom he had the estimated cost for getting this idea up and running: $750,000. I asked Les, "Where in the world are you going to get that kind of money?"

He said, "You do the writing and I'll worry about the money." In two and a half weeks he had $1.5 million lined up.

Our research showed that about 56 million people fish at least a couple times a year and buy tackle and that sort of thing. In order to reach those people, we decided to acquire fishing-oriented mailing lists. We went to L.L. Bean, but they would only sell us the overall mailing list. That didn't work for us because we were interested only in fishermen, particularly in fly fishermen. Because I had a long-standing relationship with L.L. Bean, Leon Gorham, who runs the company and whose family controls the company, eventually sold us the fly-fishing list. Bob Marriott owns the largest fly-fishing store in the world in Fullerton, California, and he had never sold his list, yet he sold it to us. After merging those lists with others and purging bad addresses and such, we came up with what was undoubtedly the greatest list of serious fly fisherman in the country. The 56-million-name list of fisherman that we started with was reduced to fewer than 900,000 serious fly fisherman.

After the book came out we still heard from a lot of avid fly fisherman who wanted to know where they could get the book. So, let's say that in contacting our 900,000 we only reached half of the potential audience out there. That would put a generous estimate of the U.S. fly-fishing population at 1.8 million to maybe 2 million people. It's an affluent group—most of the people in the sport are well educated and make good money—but it's not a large group. Small as it is, this group is very literate. And fly fishermen are the only anglers who habitually buy books. In fact, I believe that there are more books about fly-fishing than any other outdoor topic. England, France, Spain—every one of those countries has at least one major magazine on the topic.

It's not a very large group and when you're dealing with outfits like ESPN you better have a large audience to offer. I've had many people come to me with pilot episodes for fly-fishing programs, and several of them were very well done, but they could never get on them on TV. One issue is sponsors. Network TV and the big cable channels are fueled

by advertising dollars that flow from huge corporations like General
Motors, Pfizer, and Anheuser-Busch. Those huge sponsors are attracted
by the numbers of viewers the TV shows draw. People who want to put
fly-fishing on TV say, "Even if the big marketers aren't interested I'll
get a bunch of rod, reel, and line companies to sponsor the show." The
truth about the fly-fishing industry is that there are virtually no large
companies in the sport. If you broaden the base and talk fishing in general
you've got companies such as Shimano and Daiwa, then you are talking
about millions and millions of dollars. But most of the companies in the
fly-fishing business are small, conservative companies with miniscule ad
budgets. The sponsor base is just not there. Well, people will say, even
if a fly-fishing channel won't work, what about a fishing channel? They
cite the Golf Channel as the rationale. Surely there are more fishermen
in the United States than there are golfers, but golfers tend to have high
incomes and are attractive to advertisers. Many of the avid fisherman in
this country have very little money.

The bind in which our sport finds itself is worrisome to me because
in an age when media is increasingly important, our sport is losing out.
The fishing industry is struggling to fund deserving growth initiatives
such as TakeMeFishing.org, which encourages adults to take kids fishing.
I worry that fishing will ultimately go the way of hunting. That sport, I'm
sad to say, is fading away. Why? Not liability issues, not even media issues,
but societal issues. When I was a young man, the star of a quail-hunting
trip was the guy who could bag a triple on one covey. He was the hero.
Today, that guy is branded a killer. The liberal elements of our society are
winning the battle for the conscience of the American people. Hunters
have been cast as mindless and heartless demons. We know that's not the
case, but children will not emulate the behavior of a person, even a parent,
if that person is looked down on by popular media, by neighbors, and by
friends. I have seen many groups (most of them laughably unsuccessful)

try to demean the humanity of fishing and fishermen, and if we don't get in front of these criticisms, our sport's image and future could become seriously damaged.

Chapter 20
Go Fish

Why do people go fly-fishing? Better yet, why should they?

1. The Environment
2. The Art
3. The Visuals
4. The Camaraderie
5. The Flies

This makes sense. It wouldn't be much fun to fish in a dirty river with trash on its banks, to cast poorly and see ugly fish, to hang around with annoying people and use poorly made flies.

The environment is one of the key reasons that anyone fishes. A lady once asked me why she would want to take up fishing. I said there were two major reasons. One, you get to go to lots of pretty places. Two, rich men fly-fish. She nodded her head and signed up.

Casting and presenting the fly is an art, and it's something you can enjoy without even leaving your house. You can have fun on your front lawn practicing by yourself. I often refer to it as shooting a bow and arrow without having to pick up your arrows. Then there is the visual of seeing the line unroll. When you throw a lure all you really see is a splash.

Then there's the camaraderie. Let's say you're out bass fishing near a group of people who are catching a ton of bass, but you're having a tough day. Many people won't tell you what they're doing. But if you're fly-fishing on a stream and you're not catching anything and the guy downstream is catching fish, there's a good chance that person, a perfect stranger, will walk up to you and say. "Look, I'm using such and such a fly and such and such technique." Fly fishermen are not competitive. You can fish all day and catch fifteen fish. You could come back to the lodge and some beginner, maybe a lady, will come in all excited that she caught a fish. In other kinds of fishing she might be looked down on, but fly fishermen will want to hear all about her one fish. She'll never know that the guys at the bar caught ten times more fish than she did, because it's not a competition, it's a shared spirit.

Competition, while fun, can be counterproductive in fishing. Did you ever wonder why bass clubs have a hard time retaining members? These clubs are formed around competition. They have three-month, six-month, or twelve-month competitions to see who catches the largest or the most bass. If you have sixty members, over three or four years you can easily identify the four or so guys who are going to have any chance at the title. They're the best fishermen. What you end up with is a club full of losers. After a while the people who lose all the time grow tired of it and go to a club where they can be a winner or they drop out. Fly-fishing is just the opposite. The best flytier in the club will hold classes to teach others how to tie flies. The best casters will do the same. They share locations. That's one of the reasons so many women are entering fly-fishing, because it's not competitive. Another reason is that it doesn't require muscle. I'm 81 years old and I can still throw 85 feet of line with one thumb and one finger. If you do it correctly it does not require power. Another reason is that you don't kill your fish. Most women don't want to kill anything, with the exception of their husbands.

Finally, there is the fly itself. If you're a bass fisherman you'll go to

Bass Pro and you'll buy some lures and you'll catch fish on them. If you're a fly fisherman you sit down at a fly-tying table and create the flies that you are going to catch the fish on. It makes a big difference. It is the most relaxing thing I've ever done. You can get lost in it. Second, you're creating something. How many people today get to do that? I think any fly fisherman who doesn't tie flies is missing out on half the enjoyment of fly-fishing. An example: In Chesapeake Bay they grind up fish and throw this chum out on the water and it attracts bluefish like crazy. So they come and they eat this bloody mess, little chunks that are floating away. When I first started, people would use regular flies, like a Deceiver or something like that, in the chum line and the fish would hit one now and then, but not very often. This was many years ago and I said to myself, you know, *if I made a fly that looked like the bloody meat it would work.* So I tied up this fly out of brown maribou and I went. Well, I didn't weight the fly and it floated near the surface. When the tide was running fast the meat would not sink. Instead, it was quickly carried away by the current. It worked well, but as the tide slowed down the chum would descend toward the bottom. My fly, even though it resembled the bloody meat, was way above the chum line. I observed this, came back, added a little bit of weight to the hook on one model, and a good bit of weight to another. Now I had three different kinds of bloody meat chum flies: one that would sink fast if the meat was falling down in slack tide and two more with increasing amounts of weight. With all three, I caught fish after fish after fish. I made an observation, came home and created something that worked beautifully based on simple observation. That's another part of the fascination I have with fly tying.

There's a skill ratio involved in it. People who have never fly-fished or have done so only a handful of times might find this hard to believe, but most times a fly that looks exactly like what you're trying to imitate will not work as well as a fly that looks slightly different from what it's trying to imitate. That's because when you try too hard you end up with stiffer, less natural materials. The most effective nymphs are ones that don't look exactly like the ones being fed on in the water. The best ones looks something like the bait, but they have a lot of soft materials or fuzzy stuff in there that traps air. Also most real nymphs will tumble and drift in the current so if you make a nymph with two bellies on it rather than a back and a belly, a lot of times it will outfish other flies because the fish are used to seeing it both upside down and right side up. It's a learning process. I've been fly-fishing since 1947 and I learned a couple of things just this weekend. You have to approach every day of fly-fishing with an open mind. I don't care how good you are. Even experienced fishermen and instructors will know that something works, but if they're honest they'll tell you they're not always sure why something works. I'm friendly with the guy who invented the mouse we use on our computers. I asked him one time if he would he come over and spend a few hours with me. I knew that when a cast is in progress and you are not shooting line, the bottom of the fly line is not moving. The top of the fly line is unrolling like crazy, but even though I knew that to be the case I couldn't really explain it. So I asked George to explain it.

He started talking about negative forces and positive forces and all this. He showed me how a tire on a car starts out with positive forces, but when a point in a tire reaches the top, it now takes on negative force and starts slowing down. When that point gets down to the bottom it's not moving. If it were moving, there would be sudden lurch in the vehicle with every rotation. So a tire is actually sitting still for split second when it completes the circle.

I was still a little baffled, so I said, "George, give me something I can explain to myself and to my friends."

He said, "Okay. Take an army tank. The treads on the bottom of an army tank are not moving, but the front end is moving like crazy."

I realized that that is the best way to explain the action of a fly line coming off a reel. The bottom part is not moving at all, but the top part is moving like crazy. He got back into the negative and positive forces and lost me again, but I had the mental image and that's all I really needed.

If you go into fly-fishing with an open mind you can learn an enormous amount. Take someone you know to be a very good saltwater flats fisherman. I doubt very much if that same guy is a very good trout fisherman. If a trout is feeding on nymphs, how can you tell that he took the fly? Here's one way. The nymphs are drifting the current. The fish just open their mouths and let the fly come to them and then they swallow. If you know what you're looking for, you'll see a tiny white flash when they open their mouths. If you see that flash you set the hook, but you don't set the hook by sweeping the rod up—you set the hook by snapping the rod down. This is another one of those things that I know happens but can't explain why (I should probably visit George again). Sometime, just hold a fly rod horizontal to the water and the snap it down. When you do, the tip goes up first and then it comes down. The advantage to this technique is that you're striking faster, but the real advantage is less obvious. You fish nymphs pretty close to you. If you try to set the hook in a upward motion and the hook doesn't set, you are going to remove the fly from the water. You'll have to recast and since you're close to the fish you may very well frighten them. On the other hand, if you snap down and still fail to set the hook, the fly continues to move with the current and drifts more naturally.

I have long told students of mine that if something doesn't work, try it backward. It's true. Very often the solution to a problem is the exact opposite of what you might think. For instance, suppose you're throwing a dry fly onto fast water upstream and it's drifting fast on the water. You need to remove the slack, and we generally do that by taking it out by hand, but sometimes we resort to raising the rod to keep the slack out. There's a slight sag in the line as you're doing this. If at that moment a fish takes the fly, you are pulling on the slack as you pull away from the fish. However, if your line is vertical or near vertical, and you cast toward the fish, forward, the snap forward actually pulls the fly line toward you for a second before the slack catches up and throws the fly farther out. It's counterintuitive. People tend to do things in the most logical way. Very often, if they do exactly the opposite they'll have more success.

I worry from time to time about the future of fly-fishing. Not only have we made it harder for people to cast successfully, the sport has very little visibility. Look at ESPN. They've obviously decided that since bass fishing is available in all fifty states, more people are interested in bass fishing than are interested in light-tackle offshore fishing or fly-fishing or anything else. So they've killed off all these other programs and now on Saturday mornings on ESPN all you've got are shows about bass and walleye fishing. They're playing to the numbers and the big bucks. In fact, some of the very best fishing programs, such as *Walker's Cay*, which is produced by my longtime friend Flip Pallot, are now on at five a.m. or seven a.m. Eastern time. Any fisherman who's up that early on a Saturday is already in his boat. And those poor guys out on the West Coast are still in bed. Nobody's watching. What sponsor is going to pay to put his product on a show that no one's watching, no matter how good it is? To be honest, unless you are the most observant bass fisherman on the planet, each of those bass shows looks just like the last one! In each episode they show up the same way, they fish the same way, they weigh the fish the same way. The only thing that changes from week to week is the winner, and even that is a small number of guys.

The sad truth about fly-fishing is that as much as the sport has grown over the last thirty years, it's still too small to attract big money. However, there is a big crossover between fishing spinning/plug style and on fly. In fact, most fly fisherman also use spinning and plug tackle from time to time. People who fish for trout do so in a lot of places. Then they realize that there is an ocean out there. Something like 75 percent of all Americans live within 150 miles of the coast. These oceans don't have a whole lot of stocked fish. Second, saltwater species are generally bigger, badder, and meaner than their freshwater cousins. That's because everything in the ocean is getting eaten up by something bigger and badder and meaner than *itself*. The only way you can survive it is to get away fast and if you can't do that, you ain't gonna be around too long. What's happened over the years is that a lot of those avid trout fishermen still trout fish, but they also have taken to saltwater fly-fishing. The crossover is something I enjoy tremendously and I think a lot of other anglers do as well.

Partly as a result of that crossover, fly-fishing has grown in recent decades, and not only among men. There is an organization called Reel Women, formed for the sake of female fly-fishers. I've given several clinics and seminars for women, several of which actually barred men. I went to Birmingham, Alabama, and did a clinic. I could tell by the jewelry that these ladies had a lot of money. Anyway, their husbands drove them out to this magnificent lake—about the size of a football field—with another smaller lake beside it. The lawns surrounding them were beautifully mowed. I imagine that whoever cut that grass never stopped; by the time he got done it was probably time to cut again. Anyway, they got out of some fancy cars and I started talking to the women. The guys—CEOs and banker types— were sort of hanging around, watching from behind trees and stuff. Well, this one gal, said, "Hold on a second, Lefty," and she ran over there and ran the guys off like they were a bunch of little boys. She came back and said, "Sorry." I gave her a hug and said this was the funniest thing I'd seen in a long time.

I strongly believe you can teach any woman you're dating or married to how to fly cast. In fact, I think they listen better and learn quicker. Casting does not require muscle, just some basic skills. Women listen and they don't emphasize power so they cast better right away. Women also tie flies better than men do.

As a result, women are really getting into the sport. There are a few reasons for that. Outside of sex there aren't really too many things that men and women really like to do together. But fly-fishing is something that a husband, a wife, and even their family can really enjoy together. The other thing is that fly-fishing usually takes place in pretty settings. That appeals to everyone. Also, it's noncompetitive, although there's an insidious influence coming from TV in the form of these big-money fly-fishing tournaments. Most real fly fisherman are resisting this influence. Most of us do not believe that fly-fishing is an activity in which you try to beat someone. It's something that you share; it's an experience, not a contest.

Some companies have actually designed equipment lines for women, but the women have largely resisted, wanting to stay on equal footing with the guys. They do like their own clothing and we can all understand that, but other than those things, this is a unified sport. There are some up-and-coming women in the sport of fly-fishing who are really making names for themselves, too.

Cathy Beck is a good friend of mine and may very well be the best all-around female fly fisher in the world today. There's a woman named Cindy Garrison who was recently on the cover of *Hooked on Fishing Magazine*. There's another woman named Amanda Switzer who is a very well-respected guide up around Montauk, New York. There's a woman who I brought into the sport named Sarah Gardner. She's now a captain down in the Outer Banks of North Carolina. She has clients who wouldn't think of going out with anyone else. I think these trends bode very well for our sport. If we get the women involved we'll eventually get the families involved and that's great all the way around.

While women are joining our ranks, and we hope to welcome many more, there are a few anglers who give fly-fishing a bad name. The elitists.

And I have nothing against trout fishermen, but the only elitists I've ever met in fly-fishing are dry-fly trout fisherman. Certainly not all of them are—in fact, most are great guys—but there are a few who think that the only things special in this world are themselves, their expensive equipment, and the exclusive locales they fish. To be honest, most of them couldn't catch fish in an aquarium if they had a bucket full of bait and the fish hadn't been fed for a week. You know them, they're the ones who read all the fancy prose on the sport and have all the most expensive equipment, and they tend to look down their noses at the rest of us. I try not to focus on them.

To help the sport, we really need to help people cast better. This is so obvious that it sounds like I'm joking, but the biggest hindrance to the growth of fly-fishing is the fact that a lot of people can't fly cast very well. I often say, "If you can't shoot, don't hunt." Well, it's true for fly-fishing as well. If you can't cast a fly line you're going to have a problem with fly-fishing. As we mentioned earlier in the book, most of the people in this county who promote fly-fishing at the grassroots level, shops, and fly-fishing schools are focused on freshwater trout. That kind of fishing requires very short casts, over small bodies of water with very small flies and very lightweight lines. The old-fashioned 10-to-2 technique is adequate for that limited type of fishing. As I have argued in this book and throughout my adult life, that technique does not work well when you are fishing for larger fish with larger flies on heavier lines over larger, windier bodies of water. As a result, most people who learn traditional casting technique while fishing for freshwater trout can't perform in other conditions. They get turned off. That limits the growth of our sport. If we could only encourage and teach techniques that allowed more people to learn the sport more easily and enabled them to transition more easily between stream fishing and saltwater casting, fly-fishing would be in a much healthier position. We don't all need to be perfect, we just need to taste success.

Earlier in the book I wrote about shooting pool as a young man. When I cleared 129 straight balls, there was a whole bunch of people standing around watching. I'd hit a lot of difficult shots during the streak, but the 130th ball was actually a very simple shot and I just plain blew it. A voice in the back of the hall goes, "That's the same son-of-a-bitch that just made 129." The crowd just roared, and I laughed right along with them.

That's life. That's fishing. I've loved them both.